'To Maltsia e madhe I first turned my steps – not to see the mountains, but to see life, history, the world, and the great unknown, as it looks to the mountain man.'

Edith Durham, *High Albania*, 1909

Author's note

In order to protect their identity, the names of some people have been changed.

Place names in the Caucasus can be a fraught affair. I have tended to use those that are employed by the majority of current inhabitants: for example, Sukhum rather than Sukhumi. This is not meant to endorse the position of one or another nation in conflicts over territory or origin.

The trek into Abkhazia
The main North Caucasus walk
The minibus and APC ride to the warzone

RUSSIAN FEDERATION

•Stavropol

•Nevinnomyssk

KRASNODAR REGION

ADYGEA

•Maykop

4

3 Guzeripl

Kislovodsk•

KARACHAY-CHERKESSIA

KABARDINO-BALKARIA

Nalchik•

•Sochi

GREATER Arkhyz

MOUNT ELBRUS

Gagra

1

2 Tsebelda

C A U C A S U S

Black Sea

Sukhum ABKHAZIA

SOUTH OSSETIA

•Poti

GEORGIA

THE AUTHOR'S JOURNEY
1. Father Feofan's monastery
2. Partisan encounter
3. Wild boar
4. Wolves
5. School Number One, Beslan
6. Roki Tunnel
7. The defile where the author took fright
8. Gadzhi-Isa's road

•Batumi

0   10   20   30   40   50   60 miles
0   20   40   60   80   100 kilometres

TURKEY

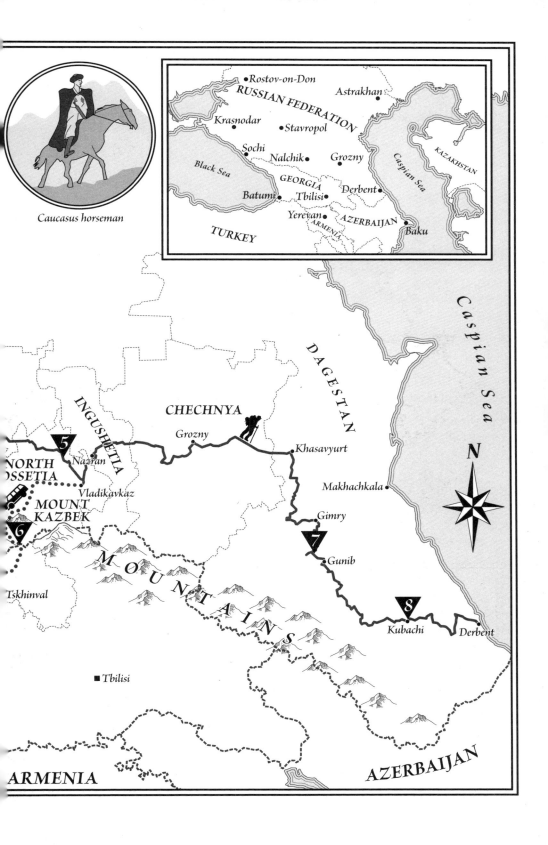

Caucasus horseman

RUSSIAN FEDERATION

Rostov-on-Don
Astrakhan
Krasnodar
Stavropol
Sochi
Nalchik
Grozny
Black Sea
KAZAKHSTAN
Caspian Sea
GEORGIA
Batumi
Tbilisi
Derbent
Yerevan
ARMENIA
AZERBAIJAN
Baku
TURKEY

CHECHNYA
Grozny
DAGESTAN
Khasavyurt
INGUSHETTIA
5
NORTH
OSSETIA
Nazran
Makhachkala
Vladikavkaz
MOUNT
KAZBEK
Gimry
6
Gunib
7
M O U N T A I N S
Tskhinval
8
Kubachi
Derbent

Caspian Sea

N

Tbilisi

ARMENIA
AZERBAIJAN

Contents

EAST

BEGINNINGS

1

School Number One

In the hills of southern Kyrgyzstan, my horse places its feet carefully among the autumn leaves.

The air is filled with the damp, acrid smell of walnuts. Akmal is ahead of me, perfectly at ease on his stallion, their bodies swaying in harmony. All morning we climb through the forest.

At midday, the trees give way to a clearing and we stop to eat. Akmal reaches into a saddle bag and pulls out a packet of cold lamb chops edged with grease, a disc of bread and a jar of relish. Turning towards the sun coming through the trees, I feel its feeble warmth on my cheeks.

A farmer who occasionally works as a trekking guide, Akmal is a stocky man with a high brow and carbon-black hair. We were introduced a couple of days ago. Once we were alone, I told him why I had come here, and he looked straight at me and nodded and said: 'I noticed your eye.'

I said: 'Yes, it's a spasm. I hope it will go away.'

Every morning, we set out from the village not long after dawn, when frost crunches under the horses' hooves and the peaks above the forest flash with snow. Today's ride is circular. There is no mountain to scale, no deadline to meet. It is late September, and here and there are groups of women harvesting walnuts, picking them up from the ground or shaking them down from the trees. No other figures move in the landscape. Most of the time, we occupy a silence broken only by the snap of twigs or the shriek of a bird.

At the foot of a gully, our path crosses a stream and the horses yank our arms as they lower their heads to drink. Later, in the failing light of afternoon, we descend towards the village.

'You will soon feel better, Tom,' says Akmal, shifting his hips on the horse to turn my way. 'This nature can cure anyone.'

I stay with a family who have let me a room in their house. In the evening, cool mountain air comes through gaps in the window frame. Some days as I climb into bed, I feel flooded with calm. Others, there is a tension in the base of my skull and I know the nightmare will come.

When it does, the woman in Beslan is falling, always falling.

She wears a dark headscarf, as if to foreshadow her life of mourning to come. I see her in profile and slightly from the back, so that her face is hidden by a lock of hair.

Her left hand grasps at the air.

She is groaning like a wounded animal.

She has just learned that her child was killed in the school.

The grief has entered her body fast and deep, and she is crumpling to the ground. Two men are reaching to brace her fall. One is a policeman. One, perhaps, is her husband.

The woman is a single figure in a scene of bedlam. Hundreds of desperate people surge around her. They are searching for loved ones who were inside the gymnasium; inside, before the explosives detonated and the shooting began. They grapple at anyone who might have news.

Children who survived move through the crowd, blank-eyed and spectral. Many are in underwear, their skin streaked with

4

soot. An immense, broad-shouldered figure in a helmet is clambering from the back of a van by the hospital steps: an injured commando.

I see only the woman.

I look on, transfixed, just as I did on that terrible day, 3 September 2004. Each detail of the scene is just as it was, with one exception. In reality, everything unfolded with frightening speed. But in my nightmare, the woman falls to the ground in slow motion; floundering, plunging before my helpless sight. Three seconds torn from a reel of terror and decelerated into endless purgatory.

*   *   *

It started with a phone call on my day off. 'Some gunmen have stormed a school in southern Russia,' said an editor in London. 'It's on the wires. Chechens, I guess. They've got hundreds of hostages. Kids, teachers. Sorry, but you'd better get down there. Place is called Beslan.'

Oh God, I thought. Not again.

I was sitting in the kitchen of my flat on the thirteenth floor of a Stalinist high-rise overlooking the Moscow river. The lime trees shone in the yard below, the kettle had just boiled, and a fresh copy of Private Eye, brought from London by a friend, lay on the table.

And now this. A sense of dread; a tinge of nausea in the mouth. I went to the bedroom, pulled a holdall off the wardrobe, stuffed it with clothes, a notebook and a phone charger, and rushed to the airport for a two-hour flight to the republic of North Ossetia.

By evening, I was in the Ossetian capital, Vladikavkaz, where second-hand trams bought from Germany squeaked up and down a boulevard shaded by plane trees. Next morning, the summits of the Caucasus mountains punctured a blue sky to the south, and the steppe beneath them shimmered in the late summer sun. On the edge of Beslan, a patrol car was parked across the road, door open, with an exhausted policeman sleeping in the driver's seat, one foot resting on the asphalt. As my taxi driver nosed past, I could feel the tension growing in my shoulders.

Other correspondents had already made it. One group had rented a van and parked it with the engine running in a street close to School Number One. They had a satellite internet terminal and a generator, and were sitting inside behind curtains to keep out the sun, tapping out reports on their laptops.

Known for its vodka factory, Beslan was a small, dust-glazed town of about 35,000 people. The militants, said my colleagues, had seized their hostages the day before, on 1 September, at School Number One, the main school of the town, with pupils aged from seven to seventeen. It was the first day of the school year, a joyous occasion across Russia. Children, accompanied by their parents, had arrived for class carrying new satchels and bunches of flowers for their teachers. The boys wore dark trousers and white shirts, and the girls wore dark skirts and the gauzy white ribbons known as bantiki in their hair, one cluster on each side of the head. Some parents brought infants and toddlers along to School Number One, where their older children were taking part in the celebrations. Music was playing and hundreds of happy relatives crowded into the schoolyard as the pupils formed groups according to age. One of the first-graders, seven-year-old Dzera Kudzayeva, had been chosen for the 'first bell' ritual, in which a new girl is hoisted on the shoulders of one of the oldest boys and rings a handbell.

When they came, the militants leapt from the back of a flat-bed truck, firing automatic rifles in the air and shouting: 'Allahu

Akbar!' There were dozens of them – they had arrived across the railway tracks that ran behind the school. 'First bell' had been just about to start. It was 9.10 a.m.; the ceremony had been moved forward an hour because of the unusual heat that week. Some of the children could not understand what was happening. They thought it was a military training exercise. In the chaos, small groups of people managed to flee the schoolyard; perhaps a tenth of the hundreds there. The terrorists shot two security guards and herded everyone else into the school's gymnasium: pupils, relatives, teachers. Balloons let go by panicking children floated into the sky. Later in the day, the hostage-takers murdered a group of the strongest men and forced hostages to dump their bodies through a first-floor window in another part of the building. The reporters who arrived before me said the corpses were lying contorted in a heap in the schoolyard. This was not visible to us, because Russian police and security forces had set up a perimeter.

In a daze, I paced streets around the cordon where pink-cheeked army conscripts sprawled on verges. The soldiers looked frightened. Officers from the *spetsnaz*, Russia's equivalent of the SAS, were rumoured to be nearby, preparing for a possible assault on the gym. At the cordon, locals were talking animatedly about a report on state television. 'They say there are only three hundred and fifty-four hostages,' said a man in a pancake-like flat cap, his voice cracking. 'There are at least a thousand people in there! The bastards want to cover it up.' (The exact number of hostages would later be confirmed as 1,128.)

I was struggling to comprehend the enormity of what was happening. At a community centre where red-eyed Beslan men were gathering, there were vigilantes clasping assault rifles and speaking of their desire to act: to kill the terrorists, to exterminate them and free the children.

BEGINNINGS

No officials had appeared to speak to the relatives of the hostages. There was talk of the security forces establishing an emergency headquarters somewhere in the town. 'No one knows where it is,' said one of the men.

My colleague Julius had also flown in and come to Beslan with Yulia, our fixer. I was reassured by their presence. Julius, with his shock of wild hair and his laconic manner, was a veteran war reporter. 'This thing could go on for weeks,' he said. We made a plan to work in shifts.

The majority-Christian republic of North Ossetia lies at the centre of the North Caucasus, a mostly Muslim region of fantastic cultural variety and richness that occupies a swath of southern Russia on the country's mountainous border with former Soviet Georgia and Azerbaijan.

The Muslim nations in this region – Chechens, Avars and so on – were conquered by Russia in the Caucasian War (1817–64), but some defiance persisted. After the Soviet collapse in 1991, separatists in Chechnya launched two bids for independence. Out of those attempts had grown an insurgency that spread across the North Caucasus. Islamist militants began to target Russian civilians with terror attacks, hitting Moscow and other cities and calling for an end to 'occupation'. That the Christian Ossetians were historically the allies of Russia made them a soft target.

I had moved to Moscow in 2002 at the age of twenty-nine, after studying Russian politics and language at the School of Slavonic and East European Studies in London.

Not long after arriving, I went to a party in a building over-looking the Lenin statue on Kaluzhskaya Square, where I met

School Number One

Mike, a Canadian with a clipped beard who had also just shown up in the city, having given up a job at the *Prague Post*. Mike and I became friends and found a place to rent in a scarred apartment block in Prazhskaya, a district at the southern end of the great concrete sneeze of suburbs that sprays out from Moscow's city centre. The stairwell reeked of rissoles and cat's urine, and the lift didn't work, but our third-floor flat was warm and cost us $175 each per month. Soon, we were freelancing for papers in our home countries. Broke, for the first year or two we shared one ancient laptop that Mike had lugged from Prague. Thick as an encyclopaedia and too heavy to carry anywhere, it lived on the desk in our box room, beside a window into Mike's bedroom, which he covered with a blanket when he needed privacy. In the evenings, we went to smoky bars or drank vodka and ate pickles in the nook in the kitchen.

It was just over a decade since the Soviet break-up. Millions of people had lost jobs and savings, turning to whatever they could to stay alive. Traces of that desperation remained. Walking to the metro across a car park one evening, I saw a line of cars, the one at the front shining its headlamps on a semicircle of young women in short skirts. The men in the driving seats were clients choosing prostitutes; the waiting cars a ghastly twilight parody of the McDonald's drive-through. In the metro, where half the passengers had their heads buried in books, Afghan War veterans with no legs paddled themselves from carriage to carriage on little wooden trolleys, begging, while outside at the entrance, *babushkas* sold socks and flowers, or a single item outstretched in a quivering hand – an egg or a twist of sunflower seeds.

Only a couple of years earlier, I had been working as a newspaper reporter in rural Norfolk, writing about snowdrop competitions and chimney fires. Now, a theme darker than anything

9

I had seen so far in Russia was about to emerge. One Wednesday in October 2002, during Act II of a treacly new musical called Nord-Ost, a team of Chechen militants stormed a large theatre in southeast Moscow. Firing assault rifles in the air, they harried the actors off the stage and into the auditorium to join 850 audience members, before setting up explosive charges. For three days, the hostages would cower in the aisles, only moving to relieve themselves in the orchestra pit.

In the finale, Russian commandos released a gas into the auditorium which put most of the hostage-takers and their captives to sleep. Then they stormed the theatre. More than 120 hostages were killed by the gas, which the security services refused to identify to doctors. Many choked to death on their own vomit or by swallowing their tongues as they lay on a forecourt outside the theatre, or in the buses that lumbered to hospitals filled with the injured, the victims' heads lolling with blank, staring eyes over the backs of the seats. Their lives had been deemed expendable in the cause of exterminating the terrorists.

I did not witness the raid, having been relieved by a colleague outside the theatre the night before. Instead, I saw the aftermath on television the next morning, along with the rest of the nation. The camera lingered over the body of the terrorists' leader on a blood-dribbled floor, a half-full bottle of cognac placed upright next to his outflung hand in a crude attempt to portray the pious Muslim as a degenerate. Worse were the pictures of the unconscious hostages slumped in those buses, unattended, their mouths gaping, their final breaths steaming the glass. It was those images that came to mind two years later as I rushed out of my flat to fly to North Ossetia.

*

School Number One

On the day I arrived in Beslan, a former army general named Ruslan Aushev volunteered to enter School Number One to discuss the militants' demands.

Aushev had been president of Ingushetia, the Muslim republic that borders North Ossetia to the east. A popular figure with a moustache like a yard brush, he might have some leverage with the hostage-takers, who were likely to include Ingush and Chechen fighters. Only later did I see footage of him that day as he strode alone towards the school in a grey sports jacket. Inside the building, the video showed that Aushev was calm as he met the militants' leader, nicknamed The Colonel, who handed him a demand addressed to President Putin for all Russian forces to leave Chechnya. Aushev agreed to pass it on, and persuaded The Colonel to release twenty-six breastfeeding women and their infants.

The women filed out together with their sons and daughters in their arms, and were taken to hospital, while Aushev carried out a baby whose mother chose to stay behind with her older child.

Some of my Russian colleagues managed to speak to the released mothers. The hostages, the mothers told them, were jammed against each other in the stifling gym without food or water. Boys and girls had stripped to their underwear because of the heat; some had soiled themselves because they were not allowed to go to the toilets. The captives were terrified and racked by thirst. Children were sucking their own urine from their clothes. The militants stood by switches, ready to detonate explosives which they had strung in the basketball nets and along the floor, said the mothers.

Everybody inside was convinced they were going to die.

*

BEGINNINGS

Vladimir Putin, by this time, had been president for four years.

His promise to 'waste' Chechen separatists 'in the outhouse' had grown threadbare. Since he had assumed the leadership, hundreds of civilians had been killed in bombings and hostage-takings attributed to Islamic radicals from the North Caucasus. In one of the most damning incidents, a week before the school was stormed in Beslan, police at Moscow's Domodedovo airport had arrested two suspicious women who flew in from Dagestan, the republic to the east of Chechnya. The women were released without being searched. Shortly afterwards, they paid a bribe of two thousand roubles (forty pounds sterling) to buy tickets on planes leaving in the next hour to Volgograd and Sochi. The women, it turned out, were Black Widows: female suicide bombers said to have been driven to the edge of madness after losing husbands and children in the fight with Russian federal forces. Just before 11 p.m., each used a concealed explosive to blow up the plane on which she was flying south. A total of ninety people on board the two aircraft were killed.

In Beslan, the day wore on and the hostages prepared for their second night. The gunmen were nervous. They fired rocket-propelled grenades at two cars that got too close to the school.

I patrolled the cordon, speaking to relatives of the hostages. Men gathered on an apron of grass outside the town's cultural centre, where they squatted on their haunches, talking in clusters, as if at some grim picnic. Another group leaned against a car, listening to the news from the radio: negotiations over possible deliveries of food and water to the captives had failed.

The world's media were now here in force, tripping the locals with television cables. Many of us newspaper correspondents had no internet access. To file our reports, we drove to an internet café in a basement in Vladikavkaz. Nerves frayed, we sat typing in the gloom as teenagers either side of us played Counter-Strike, yelling, 'Behind the wall! Waste him! WASTE HIM!'

At about 1 p.m. on the third day, a colleague and I were on the edge of Beslan, looking for the home of a woman who had been released, when we heard two explosions about twenty seconds apart and the dry clatter of gunfire.

I pulled out my mobile and phoned Julius, who had stayed on watch near the school. 'It's begun, get over here,' he said, and hung up. We had hired a man with a derelict van to take us around. Now we implored him to hurry as he crunched through the gears and the van lurched with agonizing slowness back to the school. 'We're going to fucking miss it,' cried my colleague, beating the dashboard in frustration.

Near the cultural centre, long bursts of firing cut the air from the school. Beslan residents, some armed and some not, were trying to advance towards the gym, running hunched towards the corners of buildings. Some of the army conscripts still lay on the verges, their rifles resting on little piles of broken asphalt, aiming towards the school. They looked confused as we cantered past. I ended up alone by a crossroads next to a newspaper kiosk. Smoke was rising from the direction of the school, still hidden by apartment blocks. There was the faint sound of screams. Only later did I understand: the two blasts we'd heard had torn through the gym and its roof had caught fire, collapsing onto the surviving hostages as a gunfight broke out between the militants and the commandos and vigilantes outside. Some of the captive children and adults had managed to clamber out of smashed windows; others were dragged out by rescuers as the gunmen retreated from the gym.

BEGINNINGS

Up a lane towards the school, unarmed Beslan men charged towards the bullets, heads down, carrying stretchers. Others were already coming back the other way, loaded with victims. A large woman lay motionless and caked in debris, a gash stretching the length of her thigh. In a man's arms, a girl of nine or so had blood trickling from the corner of her mouth.

The firing intensified and the sound of a heavy machine gun broke out. Afraid to go on, I retreated to the crossroads, where an activist I knew was sobbing and clutching her face. 'I can't believe this is happening,' she said. The corpses of four children lay covered by sheets, and a man in shredded clothes was curled in a ball on the ground, gibbering in terror. I suppose that scene will be with me always.

There were no ambulances. At the mouth of the lane, the men of Beslan bundled the injured and the dying into the backs of cars, which swerved wildly as they sped away. I hung back, numb with shock.

Later, failing to find a safe route closer to the school, I went to the town hospital. Outside, there were hundreds of people crowding the approach to the entrance and a great clamour of voices. Doctors stood on the steps, performing a hasty triage as victim after victim was brought forward: a boy who lay quiet and gaunt like a wounded bird; a man in camouflage with his fists raised in blood-soaked rags. 'Second floor!' one doctor told the stretcher-bearers.

In stippled sunlight beneath trees, a handful of boys who had escaped serious injury lolled on stretchers, stripped to the waist, drinking water and comparing their scratches and bruises. Some giggled. A boy of five or so, in nothing but grubby under-pants, stood surrounded by female relatives who constantly stooped to caress him, as if unable to believe he was alive without the evidence provided by this touching. 'Alan, Alan, everything is OK,' they repeated, stroking his head and shoulders.

It was here, among the crowd at the hospital, that I saw the woman collapse as she learned of her child's death, a moment that would visit me for years in my nightmares. Her cry of anguish was utterly visceral and shocking, as if it might tear her soul from her body.

That evening, after we had filed our last reports to London, a group of us journalists sat in semi-darkness at the single, rickety metal table outside a hole-in-the-wall café, drinking beer and eating traditional Ossetian pies stuffed with beetroot leaves and cheese.

It was warm and the atmosphere oddly buoyant. A sugary nervousness ran through my body. We were still wired on adrenaline, I think, and not yet aware of the scale of the carnage. At that point, it appeared that many of the hostages had escaped. But overnight and in the coming days, the death toll would rise above three hundred.

We discussed the moment it had all started. 'I may not be an expert in Russian politics, but I know what to do when the shooting starts,' said Julius. 'Head for the frontline.' As I had hesitated, he had edged forward to the corner of a building right by the school, where a huddle of *spetsnaz* officers in helmets and armed local men squeezed against a wall, leaping out to fire their weapons at the terrorists as they retreated from the gym, further into the building. Children, smeared in blood and dirt, had scrambled out of the ruins, and bullets smashed into masonry. One hit a wall four metres from Julius; another opened a large wound in the top of a soldier's leg. A small boy in underpants emerged, clutching a half-eaten packet of biscuits. He looked lost until a huge man swept him up and carried him to safety across the road. As he was lowered to the ground, the boy turned and said politely: 'Thank you very much.'

As night fell, we turned to tales of other assignments, as reporters do, and we laughed too loudly at a story Julius told about a bacchanalian party in Kabul. The owner of the café, a woman of my mother's age, appeared in the doorway, a silhouette in a rectangle of orange light. What are we doing? I thought, and hurried over to say sorry.

'Is everything OK with your family?' I mumbled as I pulled notes from my wallet to pay for the pies.

'Everything is fine, thank God,' she said. 'There's no need to apologize.' The others got up from the table and we walked guiltily into the night, hating ourselves a little more for being alive.

In the morning, we turned on the television and found that Putin had been to Beslan unannounced in the early hours, speaking briefly to some of the survivors at the hospital.

Already back in Moscow, he was said to be receiving condolence calls from world leaders. He addressed the nation from the Kremlin. 'We showed ourselves to be weak,' he said. 'And the weak get beaten.' The hostage-taking, he suggested, had been orchestrated from abroad. The country, he said, was facing 'a total, cruel and full-scale war'.

After the siege, the funerals. Day after day, fresh graves were dug in a field outside Beslan. A stream of processions turned the ground to mud, and a motley brass band moved among the mounds of earth, parping mournfully as the dead were laid to rest.

In the town, the sound of weeping came from windows and doorways.

School Number One

We were staying in the apartment of a man whom we had met in the street. With the only hotel in Beslan full, we had resorted to asking the first passer-by, a young man in an untucked, ironed shirt buttoned to his neck, for help. He immediately invited us to use his place and went to stay with a friend, refusing payment and making occasional visits to check we were all right. Julius and I took turns to sleep on a brown polyester sofa in the living room, with the other sleeping on the floor, while Yulia occupied a bedroom. It was a typical post-Soviet apartment with a carpet on the wall, a dripping tap and a hallway lined with slippers.

I asked our host to help me meet some of the bereaved. One morning, his neighbour took me down a path to a tiny, single-storey cottage beyond the railway tracks, where we were beckoned inside by a man at the door. In the living room, Natasha Rudenok lay in an open coffin that rested on two chairs. Her partly crushed face was covered in heavy make-up. By Natasha's body, with several other women, sat her mother, Olga, cradling her daughter's head in her hands. Natasha, explained Olga, as we were shown to chairs, was twenty-nine, a technical drawing teacher at School Number One. She had still been alive when rescuers found her in the rubble of the gym but died later from blood loss. She would be buried later that day.

'She was such a beautiful girl,' said Olga. 'Just look at the photographs.'

Two pictures lay with a handful of carnations on Natasha's body, which was wrapped in white cloth embroidered with silver thread. One of the photographs showed a slender young woman sitting next to a basketball court bisected by sunlight.

The mourners took turns to address the body. 'Oh, my poor Natasha! You promised me this year you would get married,' cried one. 'But now I've been called to a funeral, not a wedding.'

BEGINNINGS

Natasha's coffin lid and a wooden cross were propped by the door outside. Her male relatives chainsmoked in silence under an awning.

In the centre of the town, a group of haggard men were scouring new lists of the injured and their conditions in hospital. The lists were taped inside the windows of the cultural centre. With an unsteady hand, I wrote down entries in my notebook: 'Tsgoyev, VG. Age 3. Mortar explosion wound. Lower-leg amputation. Third-degree shock.' 'Digorov, VV. Age 42. Abdominal gunshot exit wound. Collapse of the left ureter.' 'Albegov, V. Age unknown. Open skull fracture, brain swelling.'

Everywhere, on walls and lamp posts, were flyers with pictures pleading for news of missing children. One asked for details about Madina Pukhayeva, aged twelve, with silky black hair: 'At the moment of the explosion she was sitting next to the safe in the sports hall. 153 cm. Longish face, green eyes. With a ring on her middle finger in the form of a snake with a white eye.'

The wreck of the school opened for visits and I went to look. In torrential rain, people were piling flowers on the windowsills and in the centre of the gutted gym. Down a corridor, classrooms had been turned to rubble, and three young women teetered past in high heels and make-up, perhaps come from a wake. A chunk of flesh still lay on a windowsill.

One night, a taxi that was carrying me and two colleagues as we raced back to Beslan from Vladikavkaz lost a wheel on an unlit country road and spun into a ditch, narrowly missing an oncoming car. In our frazzled state, this latest challenge to sanity seemed almost funny. Unhurt and cackling with relief, we flagged down another car and continued our journey.

School Number One

I stayed on for a few days to report on the aftermath of the siege, and then told the newspaper I could not bear any more. I felt raw and jittery. A tic caused by stress had returned to my left eye, firing in bursts like a camera shutter. To try to calm it down, I had to tip back my head and cover the eye with the palm of my hand.

I flew back to Moscow.

2

Stealer of Hearts

Beslan was a turning point for me. Almost twenty years later, I still think about it every few days. For a long period after the siege, I was in a kind of wilderness. Nothing I did seemed to have the same significance or intensity of emotion. I wanted to write about what I had seen and experienced in the North Caucasus, and the journey that resulted – not as a reporter but as a human being, as someone moved and horrified and confused and intoxicated. But I couldn't find a way to get across all that I felt. Only recently did I realize that if I didn't put fingers to the keyboard soon, my story would slip away forever.

You might ask if that would that matter. I believe that it would; that I have something to tell in the light of current events. Last winter, President Putin invaded Ukraine. Russia's euphemistically named 'special operation' against its Slavic neighbour has fundamental differences with the war on the breakaway Muslim republic of Chechnya in the 1990s and 2000s. When Russian federal forces invaded Chechnya in 1994, they were at least responding to a threat of sorts – General Dudayev's declaration of independence and the chaos that followed. By contrast, at the moment of Russia's attack on Ukraine in February 2022, that country had been a sovereign state for more than thirty years.

Stealer of Hearts

What unites the two conflicts is Moscow's nauseating readiness to resort to civilian slaughter, and to wilfully distort the truth, framing Ukrainians as fascists and North Caucasians as primitives in need of taming.

The idea that a North Caucasian is simultaneously ignorant, cruel and double-dealing persists in Russia today. What I discovered in Chechnya and the neighbouring republics made me think just the opposite. Yes, there were locals with blood on their hands; no doubt about that. But it was a merciless, blundering state that had caused much of the mayhem. There was no innate tendency to evil. On the contrary, I found, time and again, that people in the Caucasus behaved with a dignity that transcended their circumstances; a dignity that I doubted I could match if I had suffered a similar fate.

In May 2022, I was forced to leave Russia, two decades after I arrived. My newspaper decided it wasn't safe to stay in the atmosphere of hatred swirling around the war on Ukraine. It was a nasty blow for me and my family. My wife is Russian and so is our son, and we didn't want to give up our lives in Moscow, despite the appalling things the government was doing.

I'm so sad about what became of my adopted country. One aim of this book is to explore what gave rise to the siege at Beslan, how the North Caucasus became synonymous with violence, and how personal and national traumas take their paths. It may cast some light on why Moscow has behaved the way it has in Ukraine. Most of all, I hope it is a testament to how things can and will be better: to the wellsprings of goodness that, nurtured through years of darkness, will – I am sure – one day give rise to a new, invigorated Russia.

*

BEGINNINGS

After Beslan, I had tried to concentrate on a few redeeming moments.

The morning after the siege ended, I spoke to four cousins from one family who had all survived the fifty-two hours in the gym. A downpour had brought some relief from the heat, and another journalist and I picked our way to the family's front door past pools of water on a dirt street lined with plum trees. Squeezing tightly together on a couch, the cousins – two boys and two girls, aged twelve to fifteen – talked with nonchalant calm about how they had scrambled away from the school, feeling bullets rush past their heads.

There were other miracles. The day I had arrived in Beslan, a colleague managed to speak by phone with one of the women released with their infants. The mother's name was Zalina Dzandarova. Zalina had faced an appalling dilemma. She was in the school with her two-year-old son, Alan, and her six-year-old daughter, Alana. Yet when the militants had agreed to free the mothers with the smallest children, they refused to allow Zalina to take Alana as well. 'You'll go now with your son or you'll stay here with both of them,' a gunman told her. With a few seconds to decide, Zalina had chosen to save at least one life and go out with Alan. Now, she was choked with remorse. 'I pressed my son to my chest and walked towards the exit,' she told my colleague. 'Behind me I could hear Alana crying, "Mama, Mama!" I thought my heart would burst . . . She will die there, she will die there without me!' At the other end of the line, my colleague heard Zalina say quietly, 'Forgive me, I can't speak anymore,' before putting down the receiver, sobbing.

Zalina's story was published on the third day of the siege, 3 September 2004, and caught worldwide attention. Within a few hours, the two explosions detonated in the gym, cutting through the hostages slumped against each other on the floor, wilting with the heat. It was only later that my colleague found out what had happened to Zalina in those moments. Distraught at the sound of the bombs going off, she had rushed to the school and then to the town hospital, where she eventually found Alana smeared in blood, lying in a cot. But the blood was someone else's blood. Alana was in shock, but uninjured.

Such stories alleviated some of the horror. In *Sophie's Choice*, the 1979 William Styron novel later turned into a film, the Polish mother of that name has to let her daughter go to her death in a gas chamber in order to save her son. Zalina had also given up her daughter to be sure of her son's survival. Alana would have to spend the rest of her life knowing that she was the one her mother chose to abandon. But Alana had survived. That was the saving grace.

Back in Moscow, old routines offered distraction. A few months before the Beslan events, I had moved from my flat with Mike to the grand old Stalinist high-rise by a bend in the river south of the Kremlin, where I lived with my then-girlfriend Darya. I went for runs in Neskuchny Sad, the Not-Boring Garden, a wooded park on the other side of the bridge, and drank chilled vodka with friends in the kitchen, and wrote about other things.

It didn't work.

Ten days after I got home, Darya and I were getting ready for a night out and I was pulling on my socks when I began gabbling incoherently.

Darya was already standing in the hallway of the apartment, ready to step out of the door so we could walk to the metro. The light from the bedroom window caught the side of her face, sending shadows into her deep-set eyes. She was wearing a stylish, knee-length cream coat and carrying a handbag that dangled on long straps by her waist. She took a long look at me, back in the living room, and then unshouldered her handbag with a slender hand and carefully took off her coat.

She walked over to where I sat on our bed, my head down and my fingers laced over my neck in an attempt to stop them quivering.

'There were dead children under a sheet,' I said, lifting my head to look at her face. 'Their bare legs were poking out of the bottom. They were so young their feet were still domed and plump.'

Darya sat next to me. She nodded. She reached to brush my cheek with her thumb.

'I saw a man who was curled up in a ball, just overcome by terror,' I said. 'And there was this woman who found out that her child had been killed, and she made this unbelievable noise. I can't even describe it. Like the deepest, most animal sound of anguish you've ever heard.'

Darya put one arm around my shoulders and leaned her head against mine. My body was thrumming. 'It sounds completely awful,' she said.

I took her free hand and held it in mine until I felt her wince and noticed her fingers had gone white in my grasp. 'Sorry,' I said.

'It's OK.'

'The worst thing was not the bodies. I could cope with the bodies. The worst was the mothers' faces at the hospital. I just thought of my mum there, trying to find me or one of my brothers when we were small.'

The window in the bedroom was ajar and a cat yowled in the yard below as someone started a car engine.

'You've got to let it go,' said Darya.

I shook my head and said: 'That's just it. I don't know how to leave it behind.'

Darya tucked a wisp of brown hair behind her ear. 'I think you need to get away for a while on your own,' she said. 'Give yourself a break from all this.'

Darya was impulsive, fiercely intelligent, argumentative. I was mild, quiet and hated conflict. We would be together for only a couple more years. But I haven't forgotten her kindness that night. I took her advice and flew by myself to southern Kyrgyzstan, where I spent a week with Akmal the guide, circling the walnut forests on horseback. It was a balm of sorts, though not enough.

Unbeknown to me, Julius had already experienced PTSD from reporting on wars. He had appeared so calm during the hostage crisis: the morning after it ended, he stood by the brown sofa in our borrowed flat, smiling as he spoke to his grandmother on his mobile, congratulating her on her birthday and not saying a word about what we had witnessed: the charred bodies, the mothers seeking their children. 'Yes, Grandma, I'm very well,' he said. 'No, no, I'm not going out drinking pints right now, it's a bit early in the day for that. Yes, I love you too.'

We all have our ways of coping. Within months of Beslan, Julius gave up his job and moved from Russia to Canada, where he bought a cabin in the Rockies with his wife and set up a business running bear-watching tours. 'I thought: This has to be a changing point in my life,' he would admit. 'I can't do this anymore.' Julius didn't come back. He found solace in the remote location of his forest home, and in learning how to predict the approach of bears from changes in birdsong as he padded over the pine needles next to the river behind his cabin. Julius was mending himself in a grand tradition of traumatized men, by immersing himself in the wild.

BEGINNINGS

As for me, the nightmares gradually became less frequent, but they refused to go away. Every now and then, there she was, the mother of the dead child: tumbling, grappling, falling through my dreams in muffled horror.

No one would have questioned it – not colleagues, not relatives, not friends – if I did not go back to the Caucasus. The truth is, that was never an option. I had been captivated by the region ever since I first visited, and by the time Beslan happened, I was a regular. The North Caucasus had cast a spell over me that no place has matched, before or since.

Why had the Caucasus got under my skin? One reason was that I had come to love and respect a group of activists working for the Russian human rights group Memorial in Ingushetia, the Muslim republic next to Chechnya.

Vladikavkaz in North Ossetia had touches of colonial splendour, but barely fifteen miles away, Nazran, the main town of tiny Ingushetia, felt more like rural Turkey. Cars bumped over pitted roads through a scrim of dust, and cows munched on garbage. I would stay at the Assa hotel, next to a fetid lake, where guests were protected by Ingush soldiers of dubious loyalty who lounged in the lobby with Kalashnikovs in their laps. Ingushetia was convulsed by almost daily violence: conflict had spilled over from Chechnya, and Islamist gunmen carried out attacks on policemen and officials. In turn, the FSB – the KGB's successor agency – kidnapped, tortured or 'liquidated' young men suspected of the attacks, often because they had simply attended prayer meetings at mosques that were labelled extremist. Many victims were innocent, and the FSB's behaviour was one of the reasons young men joined the rebels in the first place – to avenge their lost fathers and brothers.

Stealer of Hearts

Much of this was only known because of the efforts of the *memorialtsy*, as the Memorial campaigners were known. They meticulously recorded testimony about abuses by the Russian security services from a cramped little office above a clothes shop in Nazran. Sometimes the corpses of the missing were discovered, dumped in the countryside, bearing signs of beating and electric shocks. Sometimes the abductees disappeared without trace. Occasionally, the *memorialtsy* would track them down and manage to extract them from some cellar or police station, to the utter relief of relatives.

This work was done in the teeth of slander and threats – and, incredibly, with exceptional good humour. On arrival, climbing the tiled steps into the little Memorial office, you would be invited to the kitchen for tea and pastries. As a kettle jittered on a gas hob, crumbs were swept from the table and the latest gossip was discussed over endless cups of black tea, sucked through sugar cubes held in the mouth.

Compared to the chicanery and cynicism of politicians in Moscow, the *memorialtsy* seemed like paragons of poise and quiet courage. I treasured their company and looked forward to every trip to Nazran. Among the Ingush and Chechen employees was Katya, a young Russian from St Petersburg whom I met on one of my early visits. The Memorial staff had arranged for me to stay in a room on the first floor of a half-built supermarket, which belonged to a family who had run out of funds to complete it. Katya had also just arrived and was staying in another room. Tall, with dolorous eyes, she had put her career as a political scientist on hold to work as an activist for Memorial in this dangerous outpost. I remember her tucking up her legs in an armchair, her soft, urgent voice echoing through the tiled building as we sat up late and she told me about her PhD dissertation on the events that led to the First Chechen War of 1994–6.

Katya was supposed to come to Nazran for three months but ended up staying five years. She never bought a corkscrew for her apartment, telling a visiting friend, 'There's no need, I'm leaving in a few weeks,' so many times that it became a standing joke. When she made calls to her parents in St Petersburg, she gave vague explanations of being on assignment while failing to tell them where she actually lived. The Caucasus could do this to you: pull you in and hold you tight.

It was Katya or Akhmed, a gentle Ingush in his late twenties, who would take me to meet abductees' families. Our driver, in his Lada jeep, was Israil, a cheery, round-shouldered colossus with huge hands and gold teeth. Israil had acquired his wife in a bride-kidnapping – in his case, a version of the custom that played out as a kind of elopement, agreed in secret between suitor and bride-to-be.

Through my friends at Memorial, I first met Chechens at the refugee camps in Ingushetia in the winter of 2002. Tens of thousands of people had fled there after Russia launched its second war in a decade on the separatists in Chechnya. In Ingushetia, the Chechens lived in canvas tents fringed with icicles in fields of petrified mud. Inside each tent, a single light bulb shed a choleric glimmer on the family's possessions. The tents had a gas supply for heat and cooking on a stove, but officials sometimes turned it off in sub-zero temperatures as a means of pressuring the inhabitants to go home. The refugees were an inconvenience: they reminded the world there was war in Chechnya. At night, the tent-dwellers woke to gunfire across the border. Nobody wanted to return to a war zone.

Stealer of Hearts

Later, I went to Grozny, the Chechen capital, where the stumps of shelled apartment blocks lined the streets, as if smashed with a giant sledgehammer. The buildings had been hit by wave after wave of shelling and aerial bombing in 1994 and 1999, as the Russian army tried to quell the separatists. Thousands of civilians perished, and the survivors lived for years among the ruins. I could never quite comprehend the barbarity. How did you do that to a part of your own country? How did you rain bombs and artillery on blocks of apartments on which the residents, in desperation, had painted the words *Zdes zhivut lyudi!* ('People live here!'). Where children lay in bed and grandmothers sat in kitchens? What went on in your mind?

Memorial also had an office in Grozny, and just a few months after Beslan I was back there. Among the activists were two remarkable people, Natasha Estemirova and Shamil Tangiyev, whom I had come to know on previous visits. Shamil's motivation was clear: both of his parents had been murdered by Russian soldiers. Natasha had been born in the Urals to a Chechen father and a Russian mother, and had moved to Chechnya to study as a young woman. She then became a history teacher, before joining Memorial in 2000.

Shamil and Natasha sat like two people on a bus, their desks one behind the other in a narrow room, with a handful of colleagues occupying another room next door. In her forties, with scarlet lipstick and a mane of auburn hair, Natasha was a striking presence. Loved by everyone, she was passionate, hard-working, funny, incontinently open and not very accomplished at admin. She adored good coffee and entertaining friends, and always looked stylish despite her modest means. She was, everyone agreed, the heart and soul of the Memorial operation. The first time I met her, she invited me to the office kitchen for tea and recounted the latest crimes against humanity with cheerful outrage.

From the beginning, Natasha had plunged into investigating the worst atrocities committed by Russian soldiers and police against the civilian population. She made risky journeys to devastated villages – once on horseback – to record the crimes. She drove colleagues spare by ignoring all the security protocols, scolding officials like schoolchildren and gaily telling strangers the pseudonym she had been given to protect her identity when writing about atrocities in the *Novaya Gazeta* newspaper.

Natasha was a single mother to Lana, a lively girl entering teenagehood. A typical day would see Natasha rising at 5 a.m. to write a report, taking her daughter to school, travelling to a remote village to investigate an extrajudicial killing, picking up Lana and then returning home to continue a seemingly permanent refurbishment of their tenth-floor apartment. Natasha had become fixated on decorating her daughter's bedroom with exotic wallpaper showing dolphins leaping from a tropical sea. Initially, she managed to get the dolphins upside down, before repapering with a fresh layer. The paper was too thin, and Lana's cat Reddie scratched it off within days. No matter. The struggle was the thing; that was Natasha's approach. Try to do something, try to improve the situation, even if you might fail. She was incapable of working secretly. If she saw an injustice, she spoke up, she harangued, she sought an answer. 'How can this be?' was her most common expression. She was something more than a human rights defender: a people's champion. Her badgering got results, it got men released from prisons and torture pits; not always, but once would have been enough.

After Beslan, Chechnya became my focus. A new power was rising: a former rebel by the name of Ramzan Kadyrov, whom

Putin installed as de facto leader of the republic to meet the insurgency head-on. As Kadyrov's militia ran out of control, attacking and kidnapping civilians, Natasha was my guide through the madness.

There was something else. If you look at Russia on a globe, Siberia and the Arctic seem to smother half the world in tracts of forest and frozen tundra. But at its bottom-left corner, the country dashes headlong towards the gap between two inland seas, thawing with every mile, trailing in its wake the lands of raw herring and fur hats and placid Slavic ways, accelerating over the steppe, warming, revelling in sunshine, until it begins to buckle and rupture, and finally soars into a kaleidoscope of snow and rock: the Caucasus mountains.

On summer evenings as I drove into Vladikavkaz, the sky turned a delicate shade of violet above the peaks and the Terek gurgled in its stony bed. Coming out of the hills fast and turbid and shallow, the river splashed the arches of the city's bridges and swept past the minarets of the Mukhtarov mosque. Only beyond the city would it feint to the left, before, slowing and widening, turning east towards the Caspian.

In *The Cossacks*, Tolstoy's hero, Olenin, becomes punch-drunk as he breathes in the 'hot, scented air' in a glade next to the Terek in Chechnya, where he is searching for the lair of a stag. One September afternoon, I felt a similar exhilaration. A village headman had invited me and two guests to his holiday cottage in the Chechen foothills. The wooden cottage was submerged in wild flowers and grasses, and bees thumped drowsily against the sunlit balustrade as we sat on the veranda. There was an enchantment about the place, heightened by the courtesy of our hosts. Despite observing the Ramadan fast, they insisted on grilling us lamb kebabs, watching politely as we ate, the fat dribbling down our chins.

The other guests were two Russian women. I don't remember now what they were doing in Chechnya. One, Olga, was a stout woman in her fifties wearing a brilliant white blouse and large-framed sunglasses. The other, Yulia, was in her twenties, with a tight dress cinched at the waist by a stylish, narrow belt.

For Yulia, the exoticism was almost too much to bear. Russians tend to see the Caucasus as bandit country, full of wild high-landers: barbarous, proud and over-sexed. Olga and Yulia spent the day teasing me with coquettish looks, fanning their flustered, excited faces with their hands as if they might swoon, and gasping melodramatically as we climbed a track to inspect an ancient stone tower.

Later, the headman said goodbye and put us in a car with one of his bodyguards for the ride back to Grozny. The bodyguard was a muscular young man in a black cap, a tight black T-shirt and camouflage trousers. We motored down a road that was cut from the side of the Argun gorge. Rockfaces bulged and splintered on either side. Between the patches of cliff, steep slopes covered by trees fell to the edge of a sheer canyon. Far below, the river boiled towards the flatlands. In places, the gorge widened and then tightened again, so that sometimes the lip of the canyon on the other side was no more than thirty metres away. At one such spot, a breeze was splaying clumps of white flowers by a patch of scree. Someone, I thought lazily as I laid my forearm on the open window, is beating a tin roof with a stick. How rapidly they did so, and with such metronomic precision. But why? And where, in this wild spot, was a roof? The pleasing rat-tat-tat was interspersed with whines and whizzes. Extraordinary, I thought, leaning back against the headrest and closing my eyes for a moment. Then

I realized. It was bursts of automatic gunfire ricocheting across the cliffs.

Our guard pulled over quickly. 'Could be militants,' he said. I opened my mouth to ask, 'Why are we stopping, then?' but before I could speak, he had picked up his sawn-off Tyulpan (Tulip) Kalashnikov from beside the gear stick, opened the driver's door and jumped outside. Through the back of my seat, I felt a wriggle of knees.

'Ooh,' said Yulia, with a squeak of delight. 'This is where we get sold into slavery.'

A rapid patter of shots seemed to come from the other side of the gorge and then stop. We stayed in the car, exchanging nervous glances. The sun burned hot on the dashboard, and the scent of thyme came through the window. The guard had walked back up the road a little and was looking across the river. The threat of abduction was very real. A Dutch aid worker had recently spent two years in a cellar in Dagestan before his NGO paid one million dollars to get him free.

We strained our ears, but there were no more shots. The body-guard leaned through from outside. 'Nothing serious,' he said. He got back in and placed the Tyulpan in my lap as he restarted the car. 'If anything happens, you shoot through the window while I drive,' he said.

I looked at the weapon, alarmed. I couldn't think of the Russian word for safety catch. 'How do you turn it on?' I said.

In the back, Olga and Yulia collapsed into peals of giggles, their hair threshing through the windows. 'How will you save us, Tom, if you can't turn it on?' shrieked Yulia.

The bodyguard, too, was grinning. Once we had descended from the hills onto the plain, he pressed the accelerator to the floor and the car hammered down the uneven road, its wheels whumping into the chassis. I had recently been on a 'hostile environments' training course for reporters back in England with ex-Marines. One of the tutors had told us that the most dangerous thing in war zones was not snipers or falling shells; it was local drivers who went too fast and caused accidents because Westerners were too polite to ask them to slow down.

'Let's cool it a bit,' I said.

The bodyguard smirked and kept up his speed. 'Don't be afraid,' he replied. 'Everything's normal.'

'Yes, keep going!' Yulia shouted.

I said nothing and stared ahead with my jaw clamped, feeling grumpy about being a coward, as Olga and Yulia laughed and talked above the roar of the engine, having the time of their lives. They didn't stop tittering all the way to Grozny.

Captivity, and the fear of it, is a persistent motif of the Caucasus. Alexander Pushkin's 1822 narrative poem *The Prisoner of the Caucasus* tells the story of a disillusioned Russian aristocrat who seeks adventure in the region, only to be captured and dragged on a rope to a mountain village. There, he falls in love with a highland girl who sets him free, taking her own life in the act. Leo Tolstoy, who served in the Russian army in Chechnya from 1851 to 1854 as a young cadet, wrote a novella with the same title, based on the true story of two officers he knew who fell into captivity.

The American anthropologist Bruce Grant has explored how these tales of captivity in the Caucasus played into a narrative of Russian sacrifice for higher causes. In the nineteenth century, Russians were puzzled that the highlanders spurned their offer of civilization, sheathed as it was in the glove of conquest. But they were also enthralled by their spirited adversaries. The Caucasus was at once savage and seductive: a stealer of hearts as well as a stealer of people. Its allure was only doubled by the terrain of soaring peaks and gushing torrents.

A delight in the sensuous press of nature had certainly gone missing in my own life, where I was surrounded for much of the time by a vista of shabby Moscow high-rises. I longed to leave these grey tableaux behind and rediscover a feeling from early childhood.

That stemmed from the moment in 1978 when my parents bought a dilapidated farmhouse with about seven acres of land on the marshes by the Waveney, the slow, meandering river that throws silver loops between the rural counties of Norfolk and Suffolk. Low Tree Farm was down a lane fringed with cow parsley at the back of Wortwell, a village with a pub, a grocery store and a string of flooded gravel pits known for good fishing.

I was five, and the farm and its environs were to be the arena for my first adventures. After school and at weekends, I would head off down the loke, a grassy track leading half a mile to the riverbank through bramble thickets and stands of crack willow.

Low Tree Farm itself had few trappings of modern life. Instead of a fridge, we had a chilly brick-floored pantry the size of a small bedroom, where my father salted pork. Our television was an antique black-and-white affair that took several minutes to warm up – and one day contrived to self-combust while I was watching The A-Team.

The farmhouse was more of a porous membrane than a border with the surrounding countryside. When the wind blew, its seventeenth-century timber frame creaked like a sailing ship in a squall. My mother stuffed newspapers into gaps in the window frames in an attempt to keep out the rain and draughts. Mice scuttled at will in the pantry, and at night, deathwatch beetles tapped inside the wooden joists above my bed, occasionally waking me up. The walls were made from wattle and daub – a mix of dried cow shit, mud and twigs that was prone to rupturing. Once, there was a small explosion of dust, like a puffball exhaling spores, and a fissure opened in the wall by my window. At the heart of the house, in the living room, like the reactor in a nuclear submarine, my father had installed a Norwegian wood-burning stove that pumped out heat that was soporific within a radius of three metres; beyond that, the temperature rapidly dropped, reaching near-Arctic conditions in the bathroom and other extremities of the house. In winter, I lay in bed breathing out long strips of water vapour and pretending to be a dragon.

That trip to the foothills of Chechnya reminded me of summer days in Wortwell, when I would lie on my back in the hay meadow behind the farm, watching clouds scud across the enormous sky and breathing in the symphony of smells. My father had pointed out orchids and yellow rattle among the myriad grasses; there was always the rotting whiff of the dykes to take the edge off the flowers' sweetness. Our house had been a hippie commune when we bought it, and the former owner, Benny, stayed on for months after the purchase, having apparently forgotten to find a new place to live. He was given to roaming around in the meadows, and once appeared at the back door, covered head to toe in stinking mud, after falling off a log into a dyke. 'Benny, no!' roared my father as he made to step into the hall. We sluiced Benny off at the outdoor tap before he was allowed inside.

It was many years since we had left Wortwell, and I had been to university and travelled abroad before arriving in Russia. But I missed my childhood life of the senses; of colour and texture and touch.

*

Stealer of Hearts

Could I walk across the North Caucasus?

The thought came one day, unexpected, as I did the washing-up at home in Moscow.

For me, walking was a means of knowing a place by stealth, of creeping into its bones. I was now in my mid-thirties. A decade earlier, during university holidays, I had spent months cycling and walking through the Balkans with friends, staying in monasteries and woodsmen's huts, or camping wild. Albania became a particular obsession. In the hill villages of the Accursed Mountains on the border with Serbia, we drank endless rounds of raki and tiny cups of coffee, lassoed everywhere we went by the ancient laws of hospitality. In one home, the host stooped to delicately untie our shoelaces on the beaten-earth floor and offered a bowl of water to bathe our feet. Later, he and his relatives sang beautiful polyphonic chants, and smiled patiently until we responded with discordant renditions of 'The Happy Wanderer' and Billy Bragg's 'Sexuality'. There were families still locked in blood feuds, their homes barricaded with steel shutters and sandbags – protection from vengeful neighbours. Further afield, at a homestead in the mountains of Iranian Kurdistan, locals took us in and fed us on mutton bones in the firelight, while in the Nepal Himalayas, a pass at 5,500 metres snatched air from our lungs and proffered a descent into Mustang, where trick riders at a horse festival swung down from their saddles to pluck handkerchiefs from the mud.

Back then, long walks in far-off places were all that I wished for: the physical exertion, the sensual high and the promise of the unknown. Every year, I took part-time and holiday jobs in order to scrabble together the cash for next summer's adventure. I worked in a book warehouse, pressed components in an electronics factory and flogged credit cards at a supermarket. I did the Christmas 'turkey run' at a poultry plant, skidding on spilled gizzards in white wellies and a hairnet. On a farm in Norfolk, I got stuck in a tractor cab, pitched at a drunken angle, after reversing the back wheel over a trailer hitch (I had said I could drive; I couldn't).

My heroes at the time were writers like Patrick Leigh Fermor and Eric Newby, and mountaineers like Hamish MacInnes and Don Whillans, climbing Himalayan peaks with a Boy Scout tent, pipe-fitters' gloves from the Barras in Glasgow and a sack of potatoes. We too went on a shoestring, with kit from charity shops and hand-me-downs from friends, living off pasta and cheese and tomatoes, with the odd stick of alarmingly pink Eastern European salami.

In Moscow, the spirit of those early travels had slipped away with the demand to make a living and build a career, but their serendipity stuck in the memory. Experience told me that walking makes you approachable and versatile. It has its own cadence: a liquid rhythm that frees the mind in a way that eludes the car traveller. There is no way of fleeing the unpleasant encounter, of stepping away. You are forced to be vulnerable, to use your charm and sometimes your guile: to engage. It is impossible to close your eyes.

So why not go? I thought now, as I stood at the sink, my hand frozen mid-wipe on a plate. Why not light out for the territory one more time? My life in Moscow had become a grind and, three years after Beslan, the nightmare of the falling woman was still paying its occasional visits. Politics had been reduced to a shadow play as the country edged, somnambulant, towards the end of Putin's second term. Dragging myself to interviews and press conferences, I craved to be truly alive again. It was connection I sought as much as escape. The journey I had begun to imagine was neither a sporting endeavour, nor a feat of technical mountaineering. It would be entirely meaningless without the people I met along the way. A long walk, I thought, might serve a twofold purpose: to dilute the memories of Beslan by seeing another side of the Caucasus, and yet, simultaneously, to help me try to understand what lay beneath the terror – the ground from which it had sprouted – and to write about that on my return.

Once planted, the idea germinated quickly. Through a friend, I tracked down a man who had a licence to acquire large-scale topographical maps produced by the Soviet army. He sold me all the sheets between the Black Sea and the Caspian. Each sheet was stamped at the top with the words 'Generalny Shtab', or General Headquarters. 'Cut that off if you take them anywhere,' said the map man. To my later chagrin, I promptly forgot this advice.

I was still living in the flat on the thirteenth floor overlooking the Moscow river, but now with my future wife, Masha. She was a journalist too: we had met when I was on assignment in her home town of Yekaterinburg. Masha had begun work at sixteen, and studied for a degree at the same time. She had long brown hair that fell in skeins, and beautiful teeth. She was impossibly smart and vivacious and fun, and sometimes moody. She played football and read F. Scott Fitzgerald and ate condensed milk with a spoon so that bits stuck on her face. I loved her then and I love her still.

Our flat retained its original warped parquet, smelling sweetly of floorwax, its floral wallpaper and two lamps with shades like enormous jellyfish. In our living room, while Masha was at work, I spread the maps between the iron radiator by the window and the end of the divan. Looking closer, I could see the best walking route was west to east, across the northern flanks of the Greater Caucasus mountains, a dragon-back range linking the two seas. This had a kind of neat logic to it. I could start in the modern resort town of Sochi, by forests of the subtropical Black Sea coast, and finish in Derbent, the ancient fortress city on the Caspian, one of the oldest settlements in the world. Entirely inside Russia, this route between the two inland seas led into primeval woodland, over high passes at the necks of the towering central peaks, across the steppe, and finally through the dry, rugged highlands of the east Caucasus, cut through with gorges and canyons. After Sochi's Krasnodar region, such a journey would take me through seven republics: Adygea, Karachay-Cherkessia, Kabardino-Balkaria, North Ossetia, Ingushetia, Chechnya and Dagestan. All except Dagestan were named after the principal nationalities that lived there, and each of these North Caucasus republics was a constituent part of the country: one of the more than eighty regions – or 'subjects' – that make up the Russian Federation. Chechnya, the most notorious, was about two-thirds of the way across.

The highlands themselves, I thought, exerted their influence on the fate of the Caucasus. Their guises were many: a home, a refuge, a marker of absence, a screen on which outsiders could project their fantasies. Landscape shaped destiny. To tread the mountains, I thought, promised new understanding.

My mind was made up. The pieces were falling into place. I was awarded a grant by the Royal Geographical Society to attempt the journey. Without it, I could never have afforded the expense and the time off work.

I decided to start with a detour into Abkhazia. This 110-mile sliver of mountains and subtropical littoral abutted Russia on the Black Sea coast. Formally a part of Georgia but de facto an independent statelet with its own president and army, Abkhazia had seceded from Georgia in a brief but especially vicious war in the early 1990s. Legally it was in limbo, unrecognized by the international community, and the Georgians desperately wanted it back.

My main route would take me across Russia, on the northern side of the Greater Caucasus range. Yet while it was on the southern side of the mountains, Abkhazia had strong cultural and historic ties with the Russian republics to the north, and it received political support from the Kremlin. A journey across the North Caucasus would be incomplete without a visit.

It was April 2008, and in Moscow winter was finally drawing to an end. The sun threw its first warmth on my windowsill. Running in Neskuchny Sad, I splashed through pools of water in the melting snow. The journey had set firm. I reckoned on three months to complete it, maybe four in case of mishaps: the four hundred and fifty miles from Sochi to Derbent as the crow flies would be greatly increased by circuitous routes over mountain terrain: the 'wiggle factor', as one acquaintance put it. I wanted to walk every step.

People I knew were disturbed. 'Are you sure it's a good idea?' they asked. Masha accepted that I had to go, but thought it was crazy. 'What do you want to get mixed up with that lot for?' she said. 'You'll only get shot or kidnapped.' She liked to tease me with stereotypes about the Caucasus to provoke me into a froth of Western political correctness – something extremely funny to many Russians. But it was clear she believed in the peril. A climber said: 'You should watch out for bandits crossing over from Georgia if you go near the high passes. I don't advise you to go to Ingushetia, Chechnya or Dagestan. But that's your decision.'

Others were more positive. One of the Soviet Union's most popular films, the 1967 *Kidnapping, Caucasian Style*, was another iteration of the captivity trope. The hero, Shurik, is a naïve young Russian who sets out for the Caucasus to collect examples of toasts and other pieces of folklore, prompting hilarious encounters with the locals. 'Yes, you will be a new Shurik,' said several of my friends.

I read the UK Foreign Office's travel advice. It was predictably downbeat, advising against travel to six of the eight regions I wanted to visit because of the high risk of armed conflict, terrorism and kidnapping (Krasnodar and Adygea were excepted). Further violence in the North Caucasus was, it said, 'likely'.

One night, I met two diplomats from the British embassy at a friend's dinner party in Moscow. One locked his fingers together when I told him my plans.

'Yes,' he said. 'Fascinating idea. You do know, of course, what we'll be able to do to help? If anything goes wrong down there, I mean.'

'No?' I replied, curious.

'Absolutely nothing.'

WEST

3

The Gift of Empire

APRIL, MAY

A line of dented minibus taxis idled by a palm outside the airport in Sochi. I took a seat in one and a group of holidaymakers
climbed in after me, clattering my knees with their suitcases. The
minibus disgorged us in the city centre.

Most of the people here were ethnic Russian, but I knew there
were a few indigenous Circassians and small communities of
Greeks and Jews. Everyone looked equally hard-faced and weary.

Sochi is the western tent peg of the Caucasus, on the shore
of the Black Sea. Blessed with a subtropical climate, it flourished
as a seaside resort in Soviet times, when workers from across the
USSR could save to come here on a one-off *putyovka* – a package
trip – sold by their trade union. The huge sanatoria that fact-
ories had built for their employees were still here, their stairways
curling down to the pavements, all lumpy grandeur and flaking
balustrades.

I spoke to no one, enjoying the secret of my impending journey. The last weeks before leaving Moscow had been a rush of
goodbyes and errands. Now I felt calm. The Abkhazia leg of my
walk was about to begin. It was late April but already warm. Up
the hill at the back of the city, the feeling was of the hot, happy

mess of Greece: narrow, winding lanes, cars parked up steep little concrete slopes, and oriental-looking cats slinking under fences. Whiffs of dog shit and bougainvillea filled the air. A sign on a door said 'Rooms to rent'. A woman with a broom ushered me in and gave me a room with a ceiling so low I had to walk around the bed with my head bent to one side. I dumped my pack and went out to explore.

Since the Soviet break-up, Sochi had developed a reputation for bars, beaches and casual sex — a kind of balmy Blackpool or Coney Island. That evening, I ate meat rissoles and potatoes in the corner of a gloomy amusement arcade, where young men pulled on one-armed bandits. On the way back to the guesthouse, I came across a trail of blood on the pavement — great, full splashes on the flagstones — and felt compelled to follow. It meandered for fifty metres, climbing onto a low wall in coagulated globs, splashing over a bush and lurching towards a fence, before ending in a scarlet pool next to a lamp post. Nobody paid it the slightest notice. What had happened? Some assault, some awful accident? Was it a bad omen? In my shoebox room, I tried to forget the blood trail by emptying my rucksack and checking the contents. I sewed two pockets that I had cut from an old pair of trousers inside the waistband of each of my two pairs of underwear. Here was a hiding place for a few hundred dollars in cash, a bank card and a copy of my passport.

At dawn, the hissing of rain came through the window. I pulled on my waterproofs and stepped outside. I was on my way.

On the streets, damp people were standing at bus stops. I marched past a botanic garden and out of the city, under a flyover and up onto the busy coast road. My aim was to head south along the coast and reach the Psou border crossing between Russia and

The Gift of Empire

Abkhazia by the following morning. I wanted to keep road-walking to a minimum, but near towns and in a few other places, it would be unavoidable. Passing cars covered me in a fine spray of grit. Soon, a thorny bank offered a chance to scramble down to a lane running alongside the beach.

'Are you local? Do you know where the cemetery is?' asked a voice. Two men had fallen in beside me. They had the look of Steinbeck's George and Lennie in *Of Mice and Men*, two working men trudging purposefully somewhere in mid-morning, if not to work. 'We're going there to *otdykhat*,' explained the smaller man, using the universal Russian word for 'to relax', which can mean anything from a nap to a hard-drinking session. Only then did I notice he was carrying a bag that clinked with the sound of two bottles.

The smaller man, wearing a tracksuit and plastic loafers, was Sergei, a Russian in his fifties. His vodka partner was Niko, a big, tough-looking Georgian with a broken nose. They were construction workers, out of a job, they said. Niko, a plasterer, had been sacked for not having the right papers; Sergei after refusing to pay a bribe.

I asked Niko where he was from. 'You don't know it. Shenako village in Tusheti,' he said, naming a remote mountain region of Georgia near Chechnya.

'I was in Shenako a couple of years ago,' I said. 'I went there from Telavi in an UAZik with a guy called Temazi. I stayed in a house near the church.' It was a village of perhaps two hundred people.

Niko looked astonished. 'Yes, yes, I know Temazi,' he said quietly.

We walked on, Sergei jabbering and Niko and I sharing dumb smiles at the sublime coincidence and the happy thought of

47

Shenako – his home far away from this drizzle-misted shoreline, a sprinkle of stone cottages on a knoll surrounded by hills in Georgia, that country of warmth and vitality and wine.

After a mile, we reached a split in the path. My new friends implored me to join them in their liquid picnic, but I was keen to make progress. We said our goodbyes, clapping each other on the back, and they pointed out the way south along the top of some sea defences that curled around a headland. As I turned to leave, Sergei drew me aside and asked directly but politely for ten roubles 'to buy bread'. It was about twenty pence. Niko overhead and rushed over, waggling his forefingers and crying, 'No, no, he is a traveller, he needs it himself!' But I had enough time to slip a hundred-rouble note into Sergei's grateful hand. Then they were gone, clink-clink into the bushes, with a wave and a cry of 'Good luck!' In the distance, I heard Niko's voice one last time, incredulous: 'He was in my village!'

I stayed a night in a guest house by the bazaar in the town of Adler, then walked on south. A path led along the top of a sandy beach, the Black Sea lapping gently to my right. Ahead and to the left were the first snow-girt peaks of the Greater Caucasus, leading east. Only a narrow, lowland gap separated the sea from the forest-covered spurs that stabbed down from the midriff of the mountains. This was the entrance to Abkhazia.

Back on the coast road, the border neared and stores and workshops began to appear. Each business displayed its goods in the strip of dusty ground out front, by the road. Abkhazian families who had driven across the border into Russia were fossicking among sacks of salt and flour, bathroom fittings, car parts, garishly upholstered armchairs and blank gravestones.

The Gift of Empire

The shoppers looked at me with curiosity. 'We don't only come to buy,' said one, a man in jeans. 'In the summer, we bring our own things to sell. Tangerines, mainly.' At the end of winter, Abkhazian women would trek across the border to sell armfuls of mimosa blossom for a few roubles to the Russians.

The heat was rising. I paced on, squinting and shifting the rucksack on my back, already damp with sweat. All the way from Sochi, cars had passed me heading north: people were leaving Abkhazia, but hardly anybody was going in. There had been reports that Georgia was massing troops in the Kodori gorge, a valley about ninety miles to the southeast that linked Georgia to Abkhazia, with troops of the opposing sides stationed at either end. After the 1992–3 war, in which Abkhazia had seceded from Georgia with Russian connivance, Russia had continued to support Abkhazia militarily and issued passports to the Abkhazians, allowing them to cross the border I now approached in order to shop and trade, avoiding the blockade that Georgia imposed at the other end of the republic. Georgia's young president, Mikheil Saakashvili, had often blustered about bringing Abkhazia back under Tbilisi's control. The thought that he might do something rash made me nervous.

By the border, someone pointed out the track that led past cottages to the pedestrian crossing. Old men and women were hurrying back and forth, dragging little trolleys loaded with holdalls. These were Abkhaz 'shuttle traders', making numerous trips to and from Russia to haul back merchandise to sell in the markets at home.

At passport control, a Russian immigration officer scrutinized my passport for ten minutes, flipping back and forth through the pages of stamps. A rivulet of sweat trickled down the centre of my back. The officer called over a colleague with a beaky nose. He examined my invitation letter from the Abkhazian government and then finally waved me on. An iron bridge crossed to the other side, where an Abkhazian officer was waiting for me. We followed a footpath under the bridge, past a billy goat chewing on a tussock, to a stifling immigration building.

I had been to Abkhazia once before. It had not been a trouble-free visit. The Abkhazian authorities took umbrage at an article I wrote about a quantity of highly enriched uranium that had allegedly gone missing from a nuclear research centre in Sukhum, the Abkhazian capital. Would the officer know? He had taken a seat at a desk and removed his cap, leaving strands of hair plastered over his forehead. A fan vibrated uselessly in the background. He began writing my details in a logbook.

'Where are you going?' he asked, mopping his neck with a handkerchief.

'I want to walk down the coast to Sukhum,' I said, 'then make a loop back to here through the highlands and return to Russia.'

A stamp in my passport gave evidence of the earlier visit. I thought the officer might be suspicious when he saw it. Instead, he was pleased at the thought of a foreigner making a second trip to his republic. 'So, you are a friend of Abkhazia?' he said, looking up.

'Of course,' I replied, smiling.

'That's good,' he said, snapping the logbook shut and showing me to the door. 'We need friends.'

Outside the immigration building, it was as if I had passed into another world. There were no shops, no houses, no people. Tightening my shoulder straps, I moved off down the only road, which cut south through lush fields fringed with groves of trees. To the right, the Black Sea stretched out to meet the skyline in an iridescent haze. From somewhere came the sound of excited geese, except they weren't geese; they were frogs in ditches, putting up a cacophony of croaks. A heron disengaged from a pond choked by reeds. All around was a feeling of moist fecundity. Yet the landscape was painfully empty of human life. A lone boy standing at the mouth of a lane let out a snort of laughter, and the odd saloon sped north towards the border. Only two old men on bicycles completed the scene.

The road climbed and traversed a steep hillside of frothing undergrowth. Plant tendrils corkscrewed down, brushing my face. Soon, the coastal strip narrowed as the mountains muscled down to the water, their steep sides offering no hope of getting off the road. Presently, there was a bridge where a river flowed out from a gorge with a sheer cliff on one side. As I stood watching the water, a heavy lady in a headscarf approached, puffing and moving with difficulty. She stopped and eyed me closely. 'So you are walking everywhere, that's it?' she said, once she had caught her breath. 'Good lad! You're still young. Walk! When you get old like me, you won't like walking so much anymore.' And she waddled on across the bridge.

Joseph Stalin bestrides the Caucasus like one of its mythical giants.

He was born Ioseb Dzhugashvili in 1878 in Gori, a small Georgian town, then part of the Russian empire. The son of a cobbler, he trained as a priest as a young man. In the North Caucasus, he is best known – and despised – for deporting whole nations to the steppes of Central Asia. But the Abkhazians hate Stalin for another misdeed: forcibly adding their territory to the republic of Georgia in 1931, when previously they had enjoyed the status of a separate republic within the USSR.

WEST

In the 1930s, Stalin became a regular visitor to the Black Sea riviera. The great *vozhd*, the chieftain, suffered from psoriasis, sore joints and a withered arm: he liked to soak his fleshy, aching body in the therapeutic spas near the coast. Stalin's main retreat was State Dacha Number 9 in Sochi, but he had at least three other dachas in Abkhazia: one in the mountains at Lake Ritsa, where he liked to make wine; one on the edge of the capital, Sukhum; and the third at Kholodnaya rechka (Cold Stream).

It was this last residence that I now glimpsed high above me, on a clifftop surrounded by pines: a fantastic eyrie overlooking the sea. Soon, there was a little gatehouse by the side of the road. Inside, two old men were munching salted cucumbers, which they picked off a piece of newspaper spread on a table. One of them called up to the dacha, and after some to and fro they gave me permission to ascend a track that switchbacked through trees up the back of the cliff. On a shortcut between the hairpins, water sprayed down my neck from the overhanging foliage, and at the top, there was a set of steel gates set into the hillside. I pressed a buzzer. After some minutes, footsteps echoed, the gates opened a crack and a soldier poked out his head. My request was hardly out of my mouth when he cut me short with a hiss: 'We have a delegation. Hide in the forest and we'll see what's what in twenty minutes.'

Feeling satisfyingly clandestine, I scuttled further up the slope and crouched behind a tree stump, out of sight of the entrance. After some time, there was the sound of engines and then a low whistle came from below. I crept down to find the soldier waiting. His name was Arkady, he said. The visitors had gone. Normally a tour had to be requested officially through the Abkhazian government. Only for a seven-hundred rouble bribe could he risk showing me around. It was too much, but I relented.

The Gift of Empire

The gates opened into a carport like a short tunnel. Since Stalin's death in 1953, explained Arkady, the dacha had rarely been used, and was guarded by a small security detail. Through the tunnel was a little garden; beyond that, the lime-green dacha itself on a terrace of flagstones. It was two storeys high, large but not extravagant. We stepped inside.

I was to encounter Stalin again and again on my journey: in people's stories of bitter anger, in others' words of praise, in a revered bust or a hated portrait. There is a common misunderstanding that the USSR deep-froze ancient enmities between nations; hatreds that thawed and sparked once it was gone. In fact, the Communist system incubated many of the bloody conflicts of the 1990s – particularly in the Caucasus - by promoting ethnic elites, granting them symbols and political power on defined territories, tools that nationalists used to rally support in the vacuum after the Soviet collapse.

The entrance hall smelled of warm dust. The dacha, Arkady explained, had been built by Miron Merzhanov, Stalin's favoured architect, and everything was preserved just as it had been at the time of the dictator's last visit. We walked through room after deserted room, with heavy furniture and panelling in varying shades – pine, walnut, African redwood.

'The concept was a labyrinth with many entrances and exits, where no visitor would feel totally at ease,' said Arkady. He kept up his spiel as we walked: here was an 1876 Bechstein grand piano, a war trophy from Germany that was played by Stalin's daughter, Svetlana; here were windows like portholes made from French crystal; here was Stalin's bathroom, with a special short tub, double-skinned to preserve the temperature of the sea water in which he bathed, pumped up from the sea 350 metres below; here was a projector room where Stalin watched

Charlie Chaplin movies with local children. 'Charlie Chaplin?' I asked. Arkady nodded. The idea seemed absurd.

Upstairs were several chambers with short beds covered in red and gold counterpanes. The mattresses had been stuffed with dried seaweed on Stalin's orders to ensure deep sleep. Stalin changed bedrooms constantly, so no staff knew where he was spending the night. Each room had an emergency buzzer to call his bodyguard, Vlasik. Stalin's paranoia extended even to the billiards room downstairs, where he installed a clear glass window in the lavatory door so he could look out and make sure his opponent was not nudging a ball towards a pocket as he relieved himself.

I asked Arkady what he thought about Stalin. He paused and took off his cap. 'He was loved, he was hated,' he said in a hushed voice. 'He held such power over people. But you can say what you like. I saw myself on TV what he left behind when he died. Fifteen cups, one of them chipped. Nothing!'

It was a familiar theme: the frugal Stalin, the workaholic undermined by the machinations of lesser mortals. I had met a woman once, a gulag survivor in the far north of Russia, who slaved for years in a coal mine and slept at night in a bunker that she and other inmates had carved by hand out of the permafrost. Did she blame Stalin for her suffering? 'No, no,' she replied. 'He didn't know about my imprisonment. The system was to blame, not Stalin. He did the right thing for the Soviet Union.'

Beyond the Kholodnaya rechka dacha, the coastal sierra shouldered even closer to the shore and the road climbed high above the sea, following the contours of wooded spurs that plunged down to the waterfront. The road was supported on pilings that lifted it above the treetops. I passed marble plaques engraved with men's faces. They bore the inscription 'Died for the Motherland' and dates in 1992 and 1993.

Gagra appeared, the first town on the coast. The main street was lined with eucalyptus trees: in a rare enlightened moment, Stalin's henchman Lavrenty Beria had had them planted to suck up moisture from the malarial marshes. An old man stood in his yard breaking up a concrete patio with a metal pole. I asked if he knew somewhere where I could stay the night.

'Come in,' he said, pointing at his gate. Upstairs in his cottage, he showed me a simple room.

'How much?' I asked.

'How much did you pay in Sochi?'

'Three hundred roubles per night.' That was true: ten dollars.

'Here, it's two hundred,' he said with a triumphant look, and gave me a key.

I lay down to rest. I had walked twenty-eight miles from Adler to Gagra, and my lower legs were pulsing with pain. Later, I hobbled out and found a café where the chairs were a row of old cinema seats propped against a wall. I ate spicy bean soup and was the only customer all night.

The next evening in Gagra, my host, Zhora, invited me for tea and spoons of plum jam in his kitchen. His wife was 'on death's doorstep' because of cancer, he said, and would not join us. She sat pale and silent in an adjacent room, watching television at high volume with two of their three daughters. Zhora was in his early seventies, a member of Abkhazia's large Armenian minority, with a sweep of carefully combed silver hair. He too had cancer, in his neck. It had made him deaf in one ear and damaged a nerve so the right side of his face hung motionless, tugging at his mouth and right eye. But he did not feel sorry for himself, and asked many questions with interest, touching my arm.

I asked Zhora what had happened during the war with Georgia in the 1990s. It was well known that groups of volunteers from across the North Caucasus republics had travelled from Russia to help the Abkhazians. One was a young Chechen, Shamil Basayev, whose troops played a key role in retaking Gagra. Basayev's men were rumoured to have decapitated captured Georgian soldiers and played football with their heads in the town stadium.

'I don't know anything about that,' said Zhora, spooning more jam onto my saucer. 'Probably it's lies. But I did hear the Georgians gutted a pregnant woman like a fish in Sukhum. Can you imagine? The beasts!'

Such stories, widely believed but rarely backed up with evidence, were still the currency of hatred. Zhora and most other Armenians had sided with the Abkhazians in 1992 to protect their homeland. He had owned a little restaurant by the sea that was destroyed by bombing. 'The Georgian soldiers were nothing but looters,' he said. One day they came to his house, taking clothes and a sack of sugar. 'They went from home to home, gathering up their booty on the beach and taking it away by ship.

'The Chechens were another matter, real fighters,' Zhora went on. 'When the Georgians heard the Chechens were coming, they began to shake and run away.' He looked pleased. 'Yes, our thanks to Basayev, he saved us.' He shook his head. 'Wah, you should have seen them in all their kit! Real men!'

Blue-black night had descended, and the kitchen was lit by a single bulb. A sea breeze came through the window, turning a flypaper above a trestle that was stacked with crockery.

Zhora and I watched the news on television. I was shocked when the newscaster spoke of impending war. While I had been at Stalin's dacha, Russia had sent a column of military hardware and a thousand more troops down the coast road from Sochi into Abkhazia, to bolster the Abkhazians 'against aggression'. The Georgians were expected to attack through the Kodori gorge at any moment.

A real man! I thought as I lay in bed that night, kept awake by the creaking frame. That bastard, Shamil Basayev, a real man!

It was extraordinary how allegiances shifted. In 1992, the twenty-seven-year-old Basayev was already a supporter of the separatist leader of Chechnya, Dzhokhar Dudayev, who wanted his republic to break away from Russia. The previous year, Basayev had hijacked a plane flying to Turkey to bring attention to the Chechens' cause. But when he brought his men across the Caucasus to fight the Georgians in Abkhazia, the Russians had let them through without a glance. Moscow supported the Abkhazians, and so, for a moment at least, Basayev was an ally – or, at least, a useful pawn: the man who would soon be despised and hunted as Russia's Enemy Number One.

Basayev first used his terrorist tactic of mass hostage-taking three years after the Abkhazia fight, in 1995, when he led a team of militants who took 1,500 people captive at a hospital in Budyonnovsk in southern Russia. That was a forerunner of the Beslan operation, which Basayev orchestrated without being present. I had seen images from the hospital in Budyonnovsk, where he wore a cloth hat like some kind of modern-day bushwhacker. The security forces' rescue attempt was a shambles, leaving many hostages dead in the crossfire. In all, at least 140 people were killed. After four days, an agreement was reached to release the remaining hostages in exchange for a cessation of hostilities in Chechnya. Incredibly, Basayev and his men were allowed safe passage home.

Next day, the mountains stepped back from the coast and the road cut inland through a landscape ablaze with chestnut, elder and acacia blossom.

Already, I was developing routines. I calculated I could cover a kilometre in eleven minutes over flat terrain. When the walking became monotonous, I timed myself, marking off the distance to my next rest or food stop. A squeak in the hip belt of my rucksack acted as metronome.

On my walks a decade earlier, I had always travelled with one or two of my childhood friends, Mike and Joe. Mike was a countryside ranger, Joe an environmental scientist. Mike was intensely practical, steady, kind, funny; Joe more volatile but possessed of enormous gusto. I had often fallen back on their nous. Here, I missed their company and their laughter. To be alone intensified the experience. At times, it unmoored me. I had a simple mobile phone with no internet, but the signal was unreliable and I could rarely speak to Masha in Moscow.

On the road in Abkhazia, there was nobody in sight. Wild flowers and ferns grew untrammelled on the verge. I stomped on, drifting in thought. What was it that had pushed Shamil Basayev to inflict such suffering at Beslan? He had surfaced again in my mind's eye; his high forehead and long, narrow nose, his mouth curled by mirth, ever ready to taunt the Russian public. Basayev had remained on the run for almost two years after the events at Beslan, before finally dying in 2006 in a mysterious explosion. Did he ever question what he had done?

For me, escaping the nightmare of the woman near the school had so far proved impossible. Even now, as I recalled Beslan, it flickered across my mind, her slowly convulsing body replacing, for a moment, Basayev's gleeful face. It was at once a disturbing memory and a trifle compared to the suffering of survivors and relatives of the dead. Basayev, the orchestrator of the hostage-taking, claimed to have a clear conscience, blaming 'the Kremlin vampire' – Putin – for the deaths at its climax. Well, yes, I thought, there were many questions about the storming of the school. But Basayev's reasoning denied a simple truth: that it was he who had sent men to seize hundreds of children; he who had put them in mortal danger.

Dotted along the roadside beyond Gagra stood monuments to young men who had died in car crashes, on which an etched illustration of the victim would be fixed to a metal pole, often covered by a little roof and with a shelf below the image. Religion is worn lightly among the Abkhazians – they have been both Christian and Muslim, while polytheistic and animist beliefs persist. Mourners left half-smoked cigarettes, cartons of juice or boiled sweets on the shelves as an offering. I could not under-stand how the collisions happened. There were rarely two vehicles on the road at the same time.

I wanted to talk to people, but even the occasional houses were reticent, set in trees away from the road. I saw no one on foot. All around was unfettered nature. Most fields were not cultivated, and groups of ponies cantered freely back and forth over the road. Across the republic, there were swaths of landscape slowly returning to wildness; rotting villages, whole suburbs of towns thick with weeds. After the Georgian population fled at the end of the war in 1993, the Abkhazians had become 'masters in their own home', in Neal Ascherson's memorable phrase, 'but the house was roofless, and they wandered lonely through its desolate rooms'.

At lunchtime, I stopped under a tree in a meadow of butter-cups to eat some bread and cheese. Further on, a man sat alone on a bench by the road. He wore a flat cap and held a stick. He invited me to rest. I sat down next to him and asked what people did around here. 'Nobody grows anything anymore,' he said. He was small with grey stubble, in his late fifties and robust. 'We used to have tobacco, tea. Now there's only livestock.'

I knew there was some larger-scale harvesting in places – hazelnuts and citrus fruits – but in the absence of any real industry, many Abkhazians were scraping survival.

'Soon there'll be war, and everything will improve,' the man declared.

'Why?'

'It'll fill in all the holes.'

What could he mean? Before I could ask, a train came into view a few hundred metres away, partly obscured by trees. Grinding to a halt, it blasted frantically on its whistle. 'The Moscow–Sukhum express!' exclaimed my new friend, leaping to his feet and running up a hillock next to the bench. 'The cows must have got on the line,' he cried, squinting anxiously and brandishing his stick.

In a few moments, he relaxed. 'Good lad, good lad. At least he's stopping.' He returned to the bench. I could see through a gap that his cows had ambled off the tracks and the engine was pick-ing up speed. 'Thank God,' he said, wiping his brow and taking a seat. 'Driver could have just squashed them to fuck!'

It seemed almost comical, the small peasant waving his stick at the train, but later I thought: those animals are his livelihood.

On the fourth day, a cluster of golden domes glowed distantly as I rounded a corner. I was anxious to press on to the Abkhazian capital, Sukhum, to find out what was happening in the conflict with Georgia, but this was somewhere I could not miss: the Novy Afon monastery.

Russia's advance into the Caucasus during the nineteenth century had a strong religious bent. That so many of the 'small peoples' of the region had converted to Islam under the influence of Turks and Persians was seen as a sign that they had failed to preserve their true custom and faith: the Byzantine Christianity that penetrated parts of the region at the end of the first millennium. In 1860, Emperor Alexander II decided to put things straight by founding a Society for the Restoration of Christianity in the Caucasus. Fifteen years later, a group of Russian monks who had left Mount Athos after a dispute with their Greek hosts arrived in Abkhazia to find a new home and spread the word of God. After months of searching, they chose a spot by the ruins of an ancient city, Anakopiya, and the remains of a tenth-century church dedicated to Simon the Canaanite, the apostle said to have visited Abkhazia in the first century AD. Here they built Novy Afon – New Athos – which I now approached.

A path led up to the monastery, which stood among cypresses on a shelf of hillside overlooking the sea. There, I found a three-storey quad enclosing a cobbled yard with a large cathedral set at its centre: a neo-Byzantine confection of yellow and terra-cotta stripes topped by five cupolas.

In the glare of the yard, heat reflected from every surface. A pair of monks strode past before I could think what to ask. Then another, a scowling dwarf who did not break step. I waited, but no one else came.

Near the entrance was a shop selling icons. An assistant there gave me vague directions to the cell of a monk called Father Feofan, who 'dealt with foreigners'. I could not find it. In the yard, I spied the only entrance that appeared to be in use. It had a notice pinned on it: 'Please leave the monks in peace.' A ruddy-faced man in an electric blue shirt shot out of the doorway, followed by a woman in high heels and a short skirt. Russian tourists. I had seen a tour bus down at the roadside. 'I shouldn't go in there looking for help,' cried the man as he passed. 'They'll tear you a new asshole.'

But there was no choice. I entered the corridor and knocked on a door. The dwarf opened it.

'What do you want?' He looked even grumpier.

'I'm really sorry to disturb you. I'm a writer, and I wanted to ask if it was possible to stay here and find out a bit more about the monastery.'

The dwarf sighed theatrically, rolled his eyes and flounced off. I presumed to follow. Across the yard, he entered a vestibule I had not seen and rapped on a door. After some seconds, a young man stepped out. Like the other monks, he wore an ankle-length habit and a long beard. His hair was tied in a ponytail. 'I am Father Feofan,' he said. 'Welcome.' The dwarf disappeared without a word.

Father Feofan lived in a tiny cell with a cot, a bookshelf and a few icons. He found me an unused cell just down the corridor, where I left my pack.

'This is so kind,' I said.

He flapped his hand. 'Come on, I'll give you a tour.'

As we walked, I asked Father Feofan about himself and he answered freely. He was thirty years old and had been at the monastery for five years, he said. 'I'm a Russian from Karaganda in Kazakhstan. When I was a boy, we moved to Izhevsk in the Urals, and my mother worked there in a secret weapons facility.' Out in the world, his name had been Andrei. By his teens, he was a petty criminal, 'a fraudster', he said. 'I had to get away from that life. I went to study law and then dropped out to become a monk.'

The Gift of Empire

I liked Father Feofan immediately. Together, we looked at the frescos in the cathedral and then inspected the basement, where underground streams had caused the floor to swell and burst. Then we climbed the bell tower.

'Wonderful view,' I said as we reached the top via a narrow staircase.

'Yes,' said Father Feofan. 'Especially on New Year's Eve, when everyone's firing all around: rifles, automatics, the traffic police down there in the village send up some flares.' His eyes danced. 'Then there's a crump and a flash from the Kodori gorge, and you know the soldiers are letting off some heavy artillery.'

'What will you do if Georgia attacks Abkhazia?' I asked, surprised. There were ten monks at the monastery.

'We are monks, but we can and will fight if we must,' he said.

It wasn't so hard to conjure the image: a tooled-up Father Feofan, like those Greek Orthodox priests in the Cypriot home guard in the 1960s, all blackness and beards, striding about with shotguns over their shoulders.

That afternoon, we went for a walk behind the monastery, where a footpath followed a mountain stream overhung by trees. Abruptly, Father Feofan stepped onto stones at the edge of the stream and pulled his habit over his head. His body looked simultaneously podgy and firm, and was totally white, like a grub. Around his neck was a wooden cross. He was clad in nothing but a pair of shapeless grey boxer shorts. Seeing my surprise, he said: 'Here in this stream, the apostle Simon the Canaanite was martyred. Traces of his blood are visible on the stone, but they are underwater, so we must dive to see them. Take off your clothes.'

There was no dissenting. I stripped off, remembering at the last minute to pull out the money hidden inside my pants and stuff it into a boot. The stream was hemmed in by three-metre walls of rock that descended below the surface. We advanced through the torrent to a spot close to one wall and crouched down. The water was throat-tighteningly cold. We plunged our heads under. Father Feofan pointed out the red staining on the rocks in front of us. The 'blood' looked like lichen, but I nodded appreciatively when we emerged: 'Yes, I saw it!' Teeth chattering, we slithered over boulders and branches to the other side of the stream, where there were more traces on the rock face.

Father Feofan said he and the other monks came often to bathe in summer, when temperatures climbed to the mid-forties centigrade. They tore off their stifling habits and wedged themselves between rocks to be blasted by the torrent, which was icy and invigorating. It was true: the cold water sent endorphins racing around your body. The sensation was delicious as I slipped back into the sun-heated clothes that I had left on a stone.

I couldn't help finding Father Feofan excellent company, even when his more alarming views became clear. We were roughly the same age; back in his days as a young hood, he had listened to East 17, one of the British pop groups that I had despised energetically as a pretentious photography student in Edinburgh.

As an Orthodox monk, he was a determined Slavophile and monarchist, but he was not enamoured of the later tsars. That night, after dark, we talked alone over dinner in the monastery kitchen. When he was not praying or studying, his job was to bake bread. We sat at a steel table squeezed between his dough-mixing machines: the tangy smell reminded me of the six months I'd spent as a teenager working in a village bakery. Father Feofan served pasta with a tomato sauce, boiled eggs and a tin pan full of adjika, a spicy relish made from peppers, garlic and blue fenugreek.

Peter the Great, the tsar who established St Petersburg on the Baltic coast as his imperial capital in 1703, was the worst culprit, claimed Father Feofan. 'He planted the bomb that led to the revolution, with all his love of the West,' he said, with contempt. 'Before him, the tsars were all devout believers who prayed constantly and wore long caftans. Peter closed hundreds of monasteries, six hundred out of the nine hundred in Russia. Men started walking around – to put it bluntly – like half-queers, in wigs and tights.' The Bolsheviks finished the job, said Father Feofan. Seventy years of Communism had had a devastating effect on behaviour and mentality. Yet one leader had his respect. 'Stalin killed many people, but he understood the Russian people; he realized they needed a tsar, and they needed religion,' he said.

'But he had thousands of priests murdered,' I blurted.

Father Feofan nodded. 'Yes, but he was a national patriot. During the war, he ended meetings with the words "Glory to the great Russian nation!" rather than the usual praise of Marx and Lenin. When the Nazis drew close to Moscow, icons were paraded around the city. It was not cynicism. If we had Stalin now, the West would not dare to treat us as it does, bombing Serbia, recognizing Kosovo.'

It was not an unusual opinion among Russians, but still surprising to hear it from the mouth of a monk. Spreading adjika on an egg, I asked him what he thought of Russia's post-Soviet leadership.

'Under Yeltsin, we were humiliated,' said Father Feofan, rootling in his beard. 'He was a disaster. He let the West take control and pillage us. No other country would allow foreign states such a big role in controlling strategic assets.' He meant Western firms exploiting oil fields in Siberia. 'Putin at least introduced a little order. But he is not a real patriot. I'm sure he and his people represent the Masonic clan in the country.'

We said goodnight in the yard, and I walked down a long, gloomy corridor to my cell, which was lit by a single bulb. There was nothing inside except a dirty old mattress. I did not mind: it was warm and dry. The door had no lock, so I propped my rucksack against it. Drifting off in my sleeping bag, I cast my eyes over the images scrawled on the wall. There was a naïve depiction of Golgotha, the Orthodox cross planted above a skull and cross-bones representing the remains of Adam. Below it was written in Russian: 'Lord! Jesus Christ, the Son and the Word of God! Forgive me in my heart my loathsomeness and desolation!' On the back of the door was a scribbled prayer: 'I deny you, Satan, I deny your pride and refuse your service; rather, I go with you, Jesus Christ, in the name of the Father, the Son and the Holy Ghost! Amen.' This exaltation cheered me up until I saw the grim coda beneath: 'The hour of death will find us too, and it cannot be avoided.' I slept fitfully to the sound of footsteps creaking up and down outside my door.

The next morning, Father Feofan came to collect me at 11 a.m., after prayers. We had agreed to climb the hill behind the monastery to look at the remains of Anakopiya, the ancient settlement where Abkhazian forces repelled Arab invaders in the eighth century. But first it was time for an early lunch.

Across the yard, a pair of handsome doors opened into the monks' refectory. Inside, there were windows set with stained-glass crosses and banners reaching down to the floor from a high ceiling. During the Soviet period, Novy Afon was turned into a holiday camp. I had read the account of a foreign visitor on an organized tour in the 1980s. He found caravans parked in the courtyard and the monks' cells used as dormitories. This refectory had been converted into a self-service cafeteria, its frescos defaced, with electrical conduits running straight through patri-archs' faces and a plug positioned on an apostle's stomach. Some of the frescos had been restored since the Soviet collapse, but several were still obscured by whitewash.

In the centre of the hall was a broad table with benches either side. We took up positions with the rest of the monks, facing an altar at the head of the table. A monk at a lectern behind us read out a prayer. The dwarf was there and seemed in a better mood: he even nodded to me as we sat down. One of the monks served while the prayer-reader continued to recite a religious text. We ate in silence from tin bowls, although Father Feofan showed appreciation by smacking his lips. The food was wholesome and plentiful: chunks of white fish with mashed potato and salad. I was the only guest.

Little was left of Anakopiya, but on top of a beech-cloaked hill behind the monastery were the remains of its citadel, dating back to the fifth century. After lunch in the refectory, we climbed there on a path with a canopy of leaves like a vaulted ceiling of the brightest green.

Walking without my pack, I felt like a bullock released into a spring field, despite niggling aches to hips and shoulders. On a bare part of the hill was a first line of defence: a circular tower with a massive collapsed column inside. Two cows had found refuge there from the heat. Father Feofan and I got talking about science. 'Orthodoxy and science are uniting to deal a blow against superstition, Satanism and all forms of occultism,' he announced, squatting on the sill behind an embrasure. 'Together we are dis-proving this nonsense.' I asked him what he thought about Harry Potter. 'A perfect advert for occultism,' he replied, deadpan, as a cow ambled between us. 'All those wizards and witches.'

Orthodoxy, said Father Feofan, was the strongest weapon in

the fight against dark forces. The different branches of Christianity were always arguing over which is superior, which holds the absolute truth. Well, the best way to prove that Orthodoxy was superior was to conduct a simple experiment. Under scientific conditions, keep two glasses of water, one blessed by an Orthodox priest, the other by a Catholic. After a couple of years, the Orthodox holy water would be as fresh as the first day. It would not spoil. 'But the Catholic water does not do that,' he said. 'It turns rank.' I nodded, unsure how to respond. Father Feofan took heart. 'Of course, Darwin has been almost completely discredited,' he announced abruptly, a little later, watching me gleefully out of the corner of his eye.

At the hilltop were ruins of the citadel's heart: a square tower, a roofless stone chapel and the tumbledown cells that monks had built up from the ruins when they arrived from Athos. We sat in a small patch of shade under a fig tree. The sun was out and a warm breeze caressed the grass. It was hard to grant that war could be only a few days away. Father Feofan twizzled a grass stalk in his mouth and talked about life. 'Be careful of Russian women,' he advised. 'Don't become a victim. They will be nice as pie, but once they get their claws in you – especially a foreigner – then watch out!' I asked him to tell me more about his past. 'I was in a gang,' he said. 'I was part of the criminal world. It was lucky it didn't end in prosecution. I moved in on someone, got caught out, and they only backed off because my brother was a crime boss. After that, I thought deeply and realized I was not living my life in the right way.'

We sat on in the sun. 'By the way,' said Father Feofan. 'I know that you have criminal areas in England.'

'Where, for example?'

'East 17 in London,' he said. 'Same as the group.'

The Gift of Empire

'Ah, Walthamstow.'

'Volfam-sto?' he wrapped his tongue around the unfamiliar sounds.

'Yes,' I replied.

Father Feofan nodded, and as we walked down the hill, he murmured contentedly to himself, 'Volfam-sto, Volfam-sto.'

That evening, Father Feofan and I visited an Abkhazian family with whom he was friendly. They lived in a house at the foot of the hill, under the monastery. We drank the Georgian grappa known as chacha – monks are not obliged to abstain – and ate plates of polenta made from maize flour with slabs of cheese poked into it. There were delicious side dishes of chicken in walnut sauce, spicy red beans and adjika.

Our hosts were deferential to Father Feofan. He was warm and polite, but I detected a hint of superiority in his voice: they were lucky to know him. I thought: it's the old idea of the 'gift of empire'. Abkhazia was once again in Russia's grasp. The first monks who came here from Athos would have thought the same: we are civilizing these people and they should be grateful. Father Feofan's Slavophile heart, I suspected, was set on continuing the mission of the Society for the Restoration of Christianity in the Caucasus. That meant corralling the fickle Abkhazians – strays from the path with their pagan rituals and Muslim minority – in an Orthodox faith that affirmed Moscow's status as its last true protector; as the Third Rome, the remaining bulwark against Islam after the collapse of the dissipated western Roman empire and the fall of Byzantium.

Someone switched on the television. A newsreader was saying that two unmanned Georgian spy drones had been shot down earlier in the day in the south of Abkhazia. Tbilisi was clearly trying to monitor the movements of the new Russian troops who had entered the republic while I was at Stalin's dacha. Shards of the drones were shown scattered on a floor. Abkhazian and Russian cameramen circled them, filming, before soldiers scooped the fragments into a sack.

'Israeli technology, American money,' said Father Feofan, the weapons enthusiast, sucking his fingers and pouring more *chacha*.

The next morning, rain streaked down the cell window as I packed. Father Feofan cracked open his door to say goodbye. He handed me a crucifix that he had carved from boxwood, with a tiny figure of Christ. 'Bring me some books on English history if you ever come back,' he said.

4

Paradise Lost

On the edge of the village beyond the monastery, two men hailed me at a food kiosk. One was the owner, the other a customer with chest hair gouting out of his shirt. An open bottle of vodka stood between them on the counter.

'Where are you hurrying off to, my dear?' shouted the hairy man. 'There's no rush! Come and *otdykhat* for five minutes.' They poured me two drinks in a row and gave me iced buns, refusing payment. 'Tell the world there's no war in Abkhazia,' called the kiosk owner as I waved goodbye. 'The Georgians do something every year to scare off the tourists.'

The road made a long, hairpinning climb through dripping woods and then descended to a bridge spanning a ravine over the Gumista river, high above the water. On the far side of the bridge stood a dozen marble memorials etched with men's faces. The bridge had been a battleground during the 1992–3 war, where Abkhazian forces prevented Georgian troops reaching Sukhum from the north. In front of the memorial stones stood a half-empty champagne bottle, an open tin of olives and an orange. These were votive offerings, not picnic litter, left by relatives who had come to sit a while and honour their deceased.

Sukhum appeared without warning at the top of a rise. Its

71

first buildings were apartment blocks freckled with bullet holes. I made my way to the centre down a boulevard next to a tram-line and past the city's decrepit train station. People stared at my rucksack and muddied trousers. 'Where did you get lost?' cried one passer-by in disbelief.

Sukhum felt provincial and half-deserted, which it was. After the war in 1993, almost all the Georgians – forty per cent of the population – had fled. The city lay on a scrap of lowland curled around a bay, with a maze of hills behind it. Some houses damaged in the fighting had been restored, but many stood gutted and abandoned, or pitted by gunfire. On the seafront, the grand Hotel Abkhazia, where Ho Chi Minh and Fidel Castro had stayed in Soviet times, was an empty shell surrounded by palm trees. Nearby, the hulk of a rusting ship lay across the pebble beach.

Looking inland, the city seemed half-consumed by vegetation, like a Mayan ruin being sucked into the jungle. Eucalyptus and black ash spread their fronds high above the streets. Torpor hung over everything: there were only a handful of shops in the centre, and people loitered everywhere on street corners, talking in groups; nowhere to go, nothing to do. Young men constantly asked me for cigarettes – not beggars, but opportunists who broke off conversations to try me, just in case.

I found a place to rent in an Armenian family's house on a back street. It was a large upstairs room with shelves of Soviet books and a musty carpet. One of the trouser pockets in my pants had come loose, so that night I set to work with needle and thread in the light of a reading lamp.

It seemed wise to establish contact with the authorities: their sanction might be useful in the current febrile atmosphere. Plus, I needed a visa.

Paradise Lost

At the cabinet of ministers, a guard at the entrance issued me a pass to visit the foreign ministry, which occupied a handful of rooms on the second floor. The place was deserted: two opened umbrellas drying in the corridor were the only sign of life. There was a door marked 'Protocol', and another marked 'Minister'. No one answered when I knocked. The sound of triumphal music drifted from an open doorway further down. There, I discovered almost the entire staff of the foreign ministry – about fifteen people – in one room, watching the inauguration of Russia's new president, Dmitry Medvedev, on television. They were laughing and joking. Seeing as they all held Russian passports and Abkhazia itself was effectively a protectorate of Russia, Medvedev was their leader too.

Maxim Gunjia, the thirty-two-year-old deputy foreign minister, rose to greet me. 'We were amusing ourselves wondering what Putin will do next,' he said, chuckling. 'I have this theory he will go on a spiritual quest to Tibet and come back a changed man.'

Having no official intergovernmental contacts with any country in the world, the ministry's function was something close to that of a PR agency. Maxim, a fluent English-speaker with a relaxed manner, was deployed to charm Western officials. He gave me the visa I needed to replace my invitation letter. It was a loose slip of card: because the country did not exist, Abkhaz visas could not be stuck in passports. Maxim invited me into the cramped office he shared with a colleague and I asked him what was going on. He said Abkhazia had intelligence that Georgia had moved about seven thousand troops into the 'security zone' – the upper Kodori gorge and the southern border of Abkhazia with the rest of Georgia along the Enguri river. The Georgians had also opened new military hospitals in an eastern district, were using more spy drones and had accelerated a 'military preparation programme'. 'In short, it looks like they're preparing an attack,' he said.

I said the boosting of the Russian contingent of troops in Abkhazia must have been reassuring. 'Yes,' he said. 'But seeing that column arrive was also a terrible thing. It's still militarization. It's tension. Of course, we rely on the Russians and hope they will be a deterrent. But still, we could have avoided all this. Bringing in troops is one thing, but one day the question of them leaving will have to be raised. And withdrawal is so much harder than deployment.'

I spent a couple of days wandering around the city: it was small and invited reconnaissance on foot. Near the esplanade, where magnolias bloomed under slender palms, a whole street had been restored, and the Hotel Ritsa was a stuccoed gleam of white against the deep blue sky. A few Russian tourists sprawled on the beach and Abkhaz men played backgammon in the shadows. Someone had built a wine bar at the end of one of the three crumbling piers, where liners had lain at anchor when Abkhazia was part of the Soviet riviera. But away from the sea, there were few signs of enterprise. Houses hit during the war lay folded in ruin and stray dogs roamed on wasteland strewn with rubble. At the end of a street stood the republic's former SovMin (Soviet of Ministers): twelve storeys high, square, windowless, burned – like a great smoke-flamed waffle stood on end.

One afternoon, I met a young man named Anton who worked in the botanical gardens. Anton spent his time travelling around the republic, collecting samples of plants and flowers: they were dried and pressed, then stored between sheets of paper in stacks of cardboard boxes outside his office. Once, high up a cliff face near Lake Ritsa, he had discovered a rare bellflower endemic to Abkhazia.

I envied Anton this gentle, thoughtful work. But even his life was shaded by the memory of the 1992–3 war.

Paradise Lost

'Look at this,' he said, as we sat talking in his office. He pulled from a shelf a leather-bound book published in 1880, full of templates of orchids. A stray bullet had come through Anton's window and ripped right through it, chewing every page. We examined a laboratory in a pre-revolutionary annexe that lay wrecked and abandoned, its exterior wall gashed open to the elements. Tables covered with flasks and test tubes in racks were buried under a layer of dust and fallen plaster.

'Why hasn't it been renovated?' I asked.

'No money,' said Anton. 'And no one wants to be around that for long.' He pointed at a metal cylinder wedged into the ceiling. 'Unexploded Grad rocket,' he explained.

The road to Kodori was so broken that in places it was little more than a track. Tanks and military trucks heading for the gorge had buckled the asphalt and spalled its edges. I stepped gingerly over the fragments. The odd car passed, once an hour or so. For the first few miles beyond the edge of Sukhum, there were cottages by the road, with washing hanging in their gardens and other signs of life, but soon they became fewer and further apart. Then there were only disintegrating houses – seemingly abandoned rather than damaged in fighting, for I saw no signs of bullets or shelling. Bits of guttering tottered over caved-in ceilings and rotting window frames. In two half-deserted villages, horses grazed on the verge. A lithe animal sprinted away and peeped at me from behind a tree. A pine marten, I think. There was barely a soul around. Once, outside one of the few intact homes, I saw a small table laid with a brilliant white cloth and a vase of flowers. A handful of men stood by it, stiffly. What had happened? I was curious, but there was no obvious reason to introduce myself and the men did not look my way.

I had told Maxim at the foreign ministry that I wanted to walk to the Kodori gorge to see how the people living there were coping with the threat of invasion, as Georgian troops reportedly massed a few miles away. The looming conflict was impossible to ignore, so why not get to the heart of things? From the gorge, I planned to strike though the Abkhazian highlands, looping back to the border crossing with Russia at Psou, where I had entered the republic. Maxim said it would be fine to go to the mouth of the gorge, where Russian troops were stationed.

Close to the wayside ran a shallow river. It split and joined over shoals of pebbles. House martins with lovely blue backs dipped and dived, snapping up insects in the morning light. The road, blasted out of the cliff, began to gain height and the water stayed far below in a defile. Striated escarpments plunged steeply downwards on either side. All but their upper reaches were covered in trees thrusting out into the nothingness, like a great cataract of forest petrified in downward flight. Overnight, large rocks had loosened and tumbled onto the road in scatterings of ochre earth. Lianas dangled from overhangs. I spotted beech, oak and hazel in the cascading forest. The edge of the gorge was a tangle of fig trees, brambles, dog roses and orchids.

In the afternoon, the defile opened into a green bowl of landscape furrowed by low ridges. At the far side was a notch draped with cloud – the way to Kodori. Goats and horses grazed, and pigs rootled in bushes, unattended. Soon, houses were visible among trees away from the road. This was Tsebelda, or Zebelda, as the English mountaineer Florence Craufurd Grove called it when he passed through in 1874. His book, *The Frosty Caucasus*, was one of the nineteenth-century travelogues that I had read in Moscow before departure. At the time of Grove's journey, Tsebelda was home to a hospital serving the Russian garrison further on in the village of Lata, for the 'teeming vegetation raises the subtle miasma so often found in places of rare beauty, and the magnificent valley of the Kodor is full of malaria . . . [It] is to no small number in truth the Valley of the Shadow of Death.' When Grove visited the hospital, he found 'poor wan ghosts of men hovering about, their pitiful weakness telling only too clearly of the poison which is breathed in the air'.

Three men were talking in a yard below the road. When I called out to ask their advice, they climbed some steps to see me. Only then did I realize they were in military fatigues. I had hoped to keep my distance from soldiers, but it was too late to backtrack. 'I'm walking to Lata,' I said. That was the village where the Abkhazian part of the gorge ended and the Georgian part began. 'I'm looking for a place to stay or pitch my tent,' I said. 'Could you suggest somewhere?'

'Come in,' said the older man, pointing at the gate. His name was Todar, and he explained that they were Abkhazian servicemen who patrolled the area close to the Kodori gorge. He was from another region and had served here for eight years, buying the house in the yard so he could tend some cows and supplement his pitiful army pay. The men had a small headquarters across the road, which I had not noticed. Russian forces with heavy weapons were stationed further up the valley, said Todar, just as they had been in the nineteenth century when Grove passed through. He shook his head as he led me inside. 'The Russians won't let you walk to Lata, I'm sure of it,' he said. This was a blow, but I was hopeful I might still find a way to go on.

Life here was simple: the house was shabby and almost bare. Todar's wife sat on the floor in a back room, peeling potatoes. She did not get up. Todar pointed us to a table and cut pieces of white cheese. 'I'm sorry, it's all we have because our supplies have been delayed,' he said. I pulled out bread and a *kolbasa* sausage from my pack to add to our meal. A bottle of vodka appeared. Toasts were made. Givi, a small man in camouflage trousers who appeared to be Todar's deputy, said I could stay the night in his house next door.

'Thank you. I'm happy to pay,' I said.

'Of course not,' said Givi.

The atmosphere was friendly. That changed suddenly when a tough-looking man in his thirties entered the room, his face twisted into a scowl. 'Where is the spy?' he demanded.

He had a handsome, weather-beaten face covered in stubble, and a bulky frame. He wore a black cap, a shirt with rolled sleeves and jeans with turn-ups. Everyone in the room seemed to shrink. The man had entered uninvited, and now he crashed across the room and pulled up a chair next to me. His breath smelled of alcohol but he was not drunk. His bare forearms were scarred and thick. He exuded brute force: not the steroid strength of a body-builder, but the solid strength of a blacksmith or a farmworker. 'You are a spy,' he said, stabbing me in the chest with a finger. The other men said nothing, looking down.

'No, I'm not,' I replied. 'I'm a journalist. I came here to find out what it's like for the Abkhazians in Kodori. For the people who would be on the frontline if Georgia invades.'

He was unimpressed. 'I've caught you, spy. You won't get out of here,' he said. He leaned forward. 'Who sent you? Why did you come?' He did not wait for an answer. 'I'll hand you over to the military prosecutor. American, French, English – no difference. You're a spy for Georgia.'

I tried to laugh it off and continued a halting conversation with the other men, who still looked cowed. But he drew closer and sat gripping my arm, fixing me with a blank stare. 'If you are a friend' – he kissed the tips of his fingers on his free hand and pressed them to his chest – 'but if I find out you're a traitor, I'll kill you. You're no Englishman, you're an American spy. You're a snake in the grass.'

He turned to the men: 'Let me take him home. He might stab me in the back during the night, but I'll have my eye on him.' The others shrugged and said I had already been invited to stay with Givi. But I was not confident they were going to stand up for me. I could see their innate sense of hospitality in protecting me as a guest had been tainted by doubt: maybe I was really a spy; maybe they were getting themselves in trouble by helping me.

The brute turned to me again. 'Who sent you here? Who's paying? You won't go any further, I won't let you through. Now, let's find out who you really are. Give me some contacts. Who knows you?'

'I'm a friend of Maxim Gunjia, the deputy foreign minister. Contact him if you like. He knows I'm here.'

His expression did not change. 'We'll find out who you are, spy. I'm a military man, a partisan. What did you plan to get here? Where were you going, and why?'

'I told you. I wanted to go to Lata and talk to people who live there.'

'There's only one family in Lata, and no one will let you that far,' he snarled.

'It's strange that Maxim didn't mention that,' I said. 'He said I could go as far as Lata—'

'FUCK MAXIM!' he shouted. 'Where was your Maxim when we were fighting the Georgians? Go back to Sukhum and tell your Maxim that I FUCK HIS MOTHER.' He smashed an open palm on top of his fist. 'I FUCK HER BRAINS OUT!'

'Calm down, he's no spy,' said Givi quietly.

'FUCK YOUR MOTHER TOO! See this dick between my legs? I fuck your mother with it, you useless bastard!'

For several minutes, Todar had kept his vodka glass raised in the air, pleading with the brute in low tones to drink a toast of reconciliation. I felt strangely calm, but I had never been in a fix quite like this before, and I did not know what would happen next. It was one of those moments when I cravenly hoped my Western status would afford some protection. In my years in Russia, I had faced other stand-offs with hostile locals. Usually, I felt that we were entering a little charade where we played out our roles, without any real likelihood of things slipping out of control. However much I was despised, the potential consequences of attacking a foreigner with money and possible influence mitigated against violence. I wanted to believe the same was true now. Surely, doing me in would create more of a scandal than it was worth for these low-ranking soldiers? Yet such a calculation was far from the partisan's mind. His focus narrowed by rage, he saw only an interloper, a fifth columnist for his enemy.

'What do you know about us? It's all here,' he was shouting, staring into my eyes and slamming a hand on his heart. 'We are Abkhazians! Not Russian, not Chechen, not Circassian. Abkhazians! This is our land. We have nothing but a little maize in our hands' – he rubbed his work-fattened fingers together – 'that's it. But this land is ours. We want to live in peace. I'm sick of killing, of pain, of fear, of war. But we will fight to the death to protect our land.'

I said I didn't doubt it – and I really didn't. He fell silent. For a few strange moments, normal conversation was awkwardly resurrected. The brute watched me menacingly. Then he butted in: 'You're holding up well, spy. Drink to the bottom, none of your nancy-boy sipping. That's it, like a *kavkazets*! I don't know what they taught you in spy school in France, but I caught you.'

'I'm not French, I'm English.'

'What fucking difference—'

I decided to take a risk. 'What, like Russian and Abkhazian – what's the difference?'

'WHAT?!' he roared.

'We English are also a nation, with our own land, our history, our pride,' I said.

A horrible smile played across his lips. He reached over and crooked an arm around my neck, heavy as a millstone. His hand dangled on my chest. I looked down at its splintered fingernails edged with dirt. It was not clear if it was a mock-embrace or if he was about to snap my neck. 'You're still a spy,' he hissed. 'You're no Englishman.'

The situation felt critical. A thought appeared: if it came to it, how fast could I get my knife out of my pocket and into his stomach? It was a moment before I caught the absurdity of what I was contemplating. For a start, I had no idea how to strike some-one with a knife, and I doubted I had the guts. What's more, I am a wiry man who tries to keep fit with the odd jog and handful of press-ups, but I would be no match for this titan. If I retali-ated, his fists would come down on me like a sledgehammer on a matchstick battleship. I could picture my ridiculous penknife spinning to the floor, useless. Also, if I didn't fight back, I might get away with a lighter beating. And survive. The best tactic was to keep calm and try to prevent things reaching a climax.

After what seemed like ages, the partisan lifted the millstone arm from my neck. He got up from the table, whispered some-thing to Givi and said to the room, 'I'll be back.' Then, to me: 'I'm not your Russian Ivan to get drunk and fall asleep. I'm watching you.'

Once he had gone, Givi said: 'Don't worry. He's mad when he drinks. But he's my relative. No harm will be done to you here. I am your host; I will protect you.'

I felt a little reassured. But I remembered how meek the men had looked around the brute. 'Why does he call himself a partisan?' I asked, hearing a quaver in my voice.

'Because he comes out on patrol with us sometimes,' Givi replied.

We drifted back towards normal conversation, discussing my route. The men said it would be impossible for me to cut through the mountains back towards Sochi from here, because there were no paths through the dense forest and I could easily fall off a cliff.

I had just begun to relax when the partisan returned. He took a seat and raised a toast to Givi, calling him 'uncle'. After watching me sullenly for a while, he got up to go again. 'Don't give in to a provocation,' he said to Givi. Then he turned to me as he stepped through the door. 'You're a spy,' he spat. 'Here at our table, you are a guest. If you kill my relative and come to me as a guest, I will feed you and give you drink in my home. But remember: once you are a hundred metres down the road, I'll shoot you.'

It was late. Givi lived next door in a semi-ruined house. Two rooms at the back had no glass in the windows and no floor. He lived in a single room at the front with two iron beds. His uniforms hung from hooks on the wall. It was cool outside, but the room was suffocatingly hot. A makeshift heater – a naked electric element set in a cinder block – glowed red in the darkness.

Givi saw that I was tense. 'Do not be concerned,' he repeated. 'No one can hurt you here. I have a pistol under my mattress.'

Paradise Lost

Later, when he went out to the toilet at the back of the yard, I looked under his mattress. There was nothing there except a couple of cigarette lighters, a safety razor and a bar of soap.

That night, Givi muttered and shouted in his sleep, lying on top of his sleeping bag in his fatigues. I was wakeful, following every snuffle and twig-snap that came through the window.

It seemed pointless to push on down the valley when feelings were running so high and there was little chance of reaching Lata. At dawn, I got up and left to walk back to Sukhum as Givi went to feed his cow. Until now, I had been inside the fortress of obligatory hospitality, protected from violent behaviour. Would the partisan be waiting in a hedge just beyond his hundred-metre mark? I quick-stepped out of the village, throwing glances over my shoulder.

On the road through the half-deserted villages, I passed the garden with the table covered in white linen. A man was hammering a stake into the ground. The sound of a woman wailing in grief came from the house. For a moment, I thought of the white cloth over the teacher's body in Beslan, and of her mother cupping her head in the open coffin. A smudge of the daughter's funereal rouge had marked the base of the mother's thumb.

Had I passed some kind of test with the partisan? Was the important thing to hold your nerve? It was hard to parse what he must have been thinking. I felt bitter about the way I'd been treated. Hadn't I come in peace to look and sympathize? But part of me understood his resentment. For a man who had probably spent all his life tilling the soil, the idea of his land being snatched away must have filled him with rage. I recognized that emotion:

the feeling of intense belonging to your place of birth, the will to defend it.

I made one more attempt to walk through the mountains back to Psou, on the border with Russia. My map indicated a path heading north through hills above Sukhum and climbing over a pass to reach Pskhu, an isolated village known as a kind of repository of traditional highland life. Monks from the Novy Afon monastery had fled there during the Soviet religious persecutions in the 1920s and 1930s. From Pskhu, I could attempt another high pass, if it wasn't still blocked by snow, to reach Lake Ritsa, where Stalin had kept his second dacha. From there, I hoped, I could descend to Psou.

After two days of walking through dense forest, fording numerous streams and dodging patches of abandoned minefield, I got lost and found myself at the remote cabin of a hermit who lived off hunting and beekeeping, and professed to be an escaped murderer. He and a friend promised to take me to the first pass, but drank so much that I doubted they could make it. In fact, I worried they might do something altogether worse with me. The rivers were in full spate and the way was unclear. A group of loggers who turned up by the cabin urged me to leave for my own safety rather than go with the hermit. Reluctantly, I gave in, and went back to Sukhum with them on their truck.

Besik, one of the men I had met in the forest, offered to put me up in Sukhum. It turned out he was not a woodsman like the others, but an old friend of Daur, their leader. Besik had joined them on a trip to the forest out of curiosity. He was well built and striking and, at thirty-four, the same age as me.

We dropped in at the timber yard to dump a piece of equipment the team had salvaged. The men sold beech timber to furniture manufacturers in Turkey, and there was a large territory where the wood was cut and processed. Hearing my story, a mechanic at the yard said there was a light aircraft going to Pskhu, the isolated mountain community, in three days' time. Why didn't I fly there? It seemed a good idea. As I had been forced to come back to Sukhum on the loggers' truck, my plan not to use transport was already dashed. But maybe I could still continue my walk from the village via Lake Ritsa. The men promised to help me find out about the flight.

Besik lived with his parents, his wife and their three-year-old son in a well-appointed house in a suburb of Sukhum with a walled courtyard. They owned a small biscuit factory attached to the house. The family welcomed me without question, whisking away my boots to be cleaned and giving me my own bedroom.

Waiting for news about the plane, I spent the next three days hanging out with Besik. Talk of an immediate attack by Georgia had receded, but the ink-smudged four- and six-page newspapers sold in roadside kiosks were still full of dark prophecies of war.

There was little to do in Sukhum. Besik and his friends spent much of their time driving around in their cars, bumping over the dusty, potholed streets and gazing about proprietarily through dark glasses. When relatives or acquaintances were encountered in their vehicles, the cars ground to a halt in the middle of the road and handshakes were exchanged through the open windows. At one of these stops, a man passed a new Czech shotgun through the window for us to admire.

In company, I was warmly received, although there was usually at least one person who accused me of being – as a Westerner – some kind of Georgian secret agent. Abkhazian men, it seemed, were eaten up with bitterness: at the loss of relatives in the war, at the injustice of their isolation, at the destruction of the happier life they remembered from Soviet times. All this was exacerbated by a constant fear of invasion. Daur and Besik's friends spent their nights sitting in a street café on the waterfront, griping and disputing history. One had lost an arm in the war with Georgia; a rigid prosthetic limb dangled uselessly at his side. Another, Rusik, a slim young man with reddish hair, summed up the mood as we lounged one sultry night in the café. 'This is our land; it's not much, but it's ours,' he said. 'We have been here for thousands of years. We won't give it up. We'd rather stay here and die on our own soil than give it up. OK, there are not many of us, only a hundred thousand. In this terrain, it's enough to defend against a bigger attacker.'

In reality, Abkhazia could not survive without Russia, but people were clearly ambivalent about the support. 'Russia is our ally, that's the way it turned out,' said Rusik. 'We don't love Russia. That place near Sochi, Krasnaya Polyana, where they will hold the Olympics – that's the spot where they butchered our ancestors.' He was talking about the victory of tsarist troops over Circassian and Abkhazian tribes near Sochi in 1864, at the end of the Caucasian War, which saw Russia complete its conquest of the highland peoples of the North Caucasus. 'But Russia supports us, so we accept their help,' Rusik went on. 'How else could we survive under blockade? And with this aggressor, Georgia, as our neighbour? We are not asking for much: to live in peace on our own land. Maybe Britain wants to be our ally? We are ready to bargain! We can't work out why the West ignores us.'

The sense of impotence seemed valid. These people had a right to their grievances. But there was also something jarring. When I looked across at the wrecked cafés and the rusty boat lying on the beach, I felt like saying, 'Instead of sitting here drinking beer and moaning, why don't you get that lot cleared up, for a start?'

Paradise Lost

Any visitor would surely feel sympathy for the Abkhazians: it was hard to do otherwise when you contemplated what they had been through. The Georgians, too: they had their own story of suffering. But you also got weary of the endless rehashing of past wrongs, a wider trait across the North Caucasus, and one that stifled action. As I surveyed the scruffy beach, I became aware of a shrill little exclamation of protest trying to jump out of my mouth: 'A British NCO would get that sorted out in three days!'

Thankfully, I bit my tongue.

At the airport, Besik had spoken to a pilot friend, who said I should have no problems joining the flight to Pskhu, the remote mountain village. Besik and one of the woodcutters, Alkhas, took me there well before departure time.

A man in uniform was standing near the runway with a manifest, surrounded by a handful of others smoking cigarettes. It was silent. Sukhum airport is closed to international flights, and only a few light aircraft make short trips across the handkerchief of territory that is Abkhazia. The official had not heard of Alkhas's friend. To join the half-hour flight, I would need a permit from the state security service, the SGB, he said. We might just make it if we hurried. Alkhas drove fast and we found the local branch of the SGB in the small settlement near the airport. There, an officer shaped like a bullfrog stared at us impassively from behind a desk and said we would have to go to the national headquarters in Sukhum. There was no point in arguing.

The headquarters was a faceless building on a side street near the waterfront. At this point, I still had hope, although the Soviet reek of dust and fried rissoles that reached up around my throat as we stepped through the door should have been a warning. A guard behind a screen examined our documents and asked us to wait. Presently, a stout man in a pinstriped suit rushed into the foyer. He wore the pointy-nosed dress shoes favoured by provincial bureaucrats and small-time businessmen. This was another bad sign, as was the fact that he was spluttering something about 'the forestry unit' amid streams of *mat*, the supple and copious language of oaths in Russian that can replace all parts of speech with endlessly varied vulgarity. Besik looked at this apparently deranged character with equanimity and suggested he might get the information he needed from the officer behind the screen. However, the pinstriped madman, it transpired, was looking for us. The bullfrog had obviously called ahead and mentioned Alkhas's work with the woodcutting team. Pinstripes was a senior officer with the SGB.

'Upstairs!' he barked. It was not a request. Glumly, we climbed to his office, two other agents slipping into the room behind us. Pinstripes, I thought with a stab of unease, was old enough to be a KGB veteran. He pointed to a chair and took a seat opposite me, behind his desk. A foot-high statuette at its corner was ominous. It was Felix Dzerzhinsky, Lenin's head of secret police and the orchestrator of the Red Terror, the Bolsheviks' campaign of mass killings during the Russian civil war, from 1918 to 1922.

Still cursing, Pinstripes placed a file in front of himself and reached to light a cigarette, blowing the smoke towards me. 'I was told to speak to Vladimir Borisovich,' I said, before he could begin speaking. 'May I ask if that is you?'

He looked up for moment, his face covered in a light sheen of sweat, and held my gaze. 'If you want it to be,' he said.

The file before him was made of thick brown paper. Pinstripes now threw it open to reveal a sheaf of printed pages. I caught sight of a headline in English. It was, I realized with distaste, a file on me. He began to read aloud from a Russian translation of the article that I had written five years earlier about radioactive materials that had gone missing from an institute in Sukhum. 'A cheap smear against Abkhazia,' he said as he finished, swearing and sucking on his cigarette. 'And you call us separatists. Separatists – people who want to live on their own land.' Picking another page, he read from it, mockingly. It was the letter I had written to the Abkhazian government asking for permission to walk through the republic. This letter, he said, was 'irrelevant'. Alkhas and Besik sat like spanked schoolboys on the other side of the room, staring at the floor. Pinstripes turned to me. 'You're with MI6, aren't you?' he said. 'What's your rank?'

'I'm a correspondent,' I said. 'I'm carrying out a journey on foot that was described in detail in my visa application and discussed with your foreign ministry.'

He shook his head. 'The fucking foreign ministry, they give a visa to anyone. You're not a correspondent, you're one of us.' He patted his shoulder to indicate a secret service officer's epaulettes.

All hopes of a permit were lost. This was an interrogation. Pinstripes ordered Alkhas and Besik to leave, and they trooped out of the room without a glance. He called the head of the consular section of the foreign ministry and abused him over the phone for giving me a visa. Then his manner softened. 'So, tell me about yourself,' he said, listening attentively as I talked about my journey and where I wanted to go from Pskhu. Then he made notes and asked for details of diplomats that I knew at the British embassy in Moscow. I denied knowing any except the press officer.

'It's all clear. I trust you, Tom,' he said finally, laying down his pen. In an aside to one of the other agents who entered the room, he added: 'A good lad, he's travelled all over the world.' But it was a ploy. Just as I began to relax and anticipate my release, Pinstripes passed me to another officer, a smooth young man in a dark suit and a fake gold ring called Astemir. I was taken downstairs to a different room.

Brushes with the security services are part of the territory of being a Western reporter in the former Soviet Union. I've been cajoled and threatened and toyed with on several occasions. It often feels like a performance you have to go through: another suspicious foreigner apprehended and interrogated, another mark in the ledger of patriotism. The sight of a discomfited Briton squirming in front of them is pleasing to some denizens of the old regime, brought up on tales of English perfidy and subterfuge.

In the room in Sukhum, the hazard felt greater. I was fairly sure Pinstripes and his subordinates did not really believe I was a spy. But with Georgian troops massed by the border, there was a danger that I could be put to use in the information war with Tbilisi and publicly denounced as a Georgian-sponsored infiltrator. Guilty or not, it wouldn't matter in the atmosphere of fear and paranoia.

Tugging at his collar in the heat, Astemir repeated Pinstripes' questions as another agent searched my rucksack. Then the pair drove me to the house where I had stayed. They wanted to talk to the landlady, but she was out, so we went back to the headquarters, where I was left in the foyer. There were bars on the windows and the guard was instructed not to let me out. He shouted out at me when I sat down to rest on a windowsill. I was, I realized, a prisoner. After an hour and a half, I was taken in again and questioned in turn by two more operatives. When I slumped onto one elbow on the couch where I sat, a senior officer looked round the door and snarled at me to sit up straight, saying sarcastically: 'Maybe you'd like me to bring you some bedding?' I wanted to snap back that that would be great, but kept quiet. Surely this was all part of an interrogation tactic to unsettle me? I had nothing to hide. And I wanted to stay calm for fear of provoking further suspicion.

In the early evening, I was returned to Astemir, who reluctantly agreed to take me to a café across the road from the spy HQ to get something to eat. I paid for some disgusting pelmeni for us both. I resented paying for him, but said nothing.

'You know, you're in a lot of trouble,' he said, shooting his cuffs. 'Your documents are not in order. Things are piling up. We're going to have to decide what to do with you.'

We walked back to the SGB building. It was not looking good. Had I been mad to continue my journey? I had learned of the troop build-up before I even reached the Novy Afon monastery. I could so easily have turned back.

In the room again, other priorities shifted into focus. Astemir was now fingering my possessions. 'What an excellent camera, maybe you'd like to give it to me as a present?' he said, prodding its buttons. I declined. One more agent, who looked like a hard-boiled Glasgow detective, came in to 'have a chat while we are waiting'. My nerves were fraying, and I told him to get the answers to his questions from his colleagues. He shrugged and asked in detail about my grant from the Royal Geographical Society, which I had stupidly mentioned to Pinstripes. Such groups – foreign NGOs, charities, professional organizations – are widely seen in the former Soviet Union as fronts for Western intelligence, so that had only deepened his suspicions. Astemir returned and said his bosses were still deciding what to do with me. 'The camera would be such a good present,' he added. I did not want to give in: handing over a bribe could be used to snare me as evidence I had tried to corrupt an official. We waited on, smiling coldly at each other, as he picked over my things on the desk.

Finally, Astemir got up. I had been interrogated for eight hours. Ordering me to leave my rucksack and passport at the HQ, he drove me to a cheap hotel on the edge of Sukhum. In the lobby, he asked me for five hundred roubles to pay for the room, because 'they're bound to cheat you if they find out you're a foreigner'. I was too tired to argue. He left me in the hotel room, saying the interrogation would continue the next day. I was not to go out. Later, I asked the women at reception how much a room cost. It was 250 roubles. Astemir had pocketed the rest − about five pounds.

From the hotel, I managed to call my colleagues in Moscow and get the mobile phone number of Sergei Shamba, Abkhazia's foreign minister. Shamba was the number two person in the republic after President Bagapsh, and the chief ideologue of the independence movement.

Shamba said the security officers had informed him that I had 'confirmed' I was planning to cross a pass over the main Caucasus range from Abkhazia into Russia without going through a border checkpoint. 'That's a lie,' I protested. 'I never said any such thing.' He promised to find out what was going on.

At night, my stomach churned and I could not sleep. There was no point in fleeing without my passport. The high passes into Russia were blocked with snow and, anyway, I risked getting shot. On the other hand, it was not clear whether Shamba had any influence over the security forces. It would be easy now for them to plant something suspicious in my rucksack and then 'discover' it. Would they make an example of me?

*

In the morning, Astemir brought my belongings to the hotel. I had wolfed down a large breakfast, expecting another day of questioning. But as he handed over my rucksack and documents, he simply said: 'We no longer have any questions for you.' Shamba had pulled a string. Suddenly, the dread receded. I asked Astemir if I could fly to the mountains after all. 'No,' he said. 'Don't start all that again.'

There was no apology, nor could Astemir say why permission could not be granted. Before he drove off, he laid out my possessions on the car seat so that I could check nothing was missing. 'Maybe you would at least give me that,' he said in a wheedling voice, pointing at a new memory card for my camera, still in its packaging. I handed it to him wordlessly.

I called Besik and met him on the waterfront. He did not get out to greet me when I walked up to his car: something I knew would be an insult between Abkhazian friends. He handed the notebooks I had left at his house through the window and I gave him a toy truck that I had bought for his son. He answered my questions in a monotone. It was clear he had been frightened by the whole experience with the SGB and believed we were still under surveillance. He wanted nothing more to do with me. I felt angry that our friendship had been ruined. I'd imagined that Besik and I would stay in touch, but we never spoke again. Three magical, thrilling and occasionally scary weeks in Abkhazia had ended in sadness.

The next day, I rose early and took the bus back to Russia.

5

Circassian Requiem

Russia is strewn with roads and railways built on bones, with soldiers' corpses still gripped by sandy soil, with execution pits yet unearthed.

In open steppe outside Volgograd, I once saw a group of volunteers scrape carefully with knives and fingers to reveal the remains of a Red Army lieutenant seven decades after his death. Two of them eased the skeleton free, along with bullets, a compass, a phial of chlorine for killing bacteria and the broken neck of a glass water flask. In Tomsk in Siberia, a young man pointed at a snowy ravine and said: 'There are many of them in there, I'm sure.' By combing archives in the local FSB headquarters, a clerk peering over his shoulder, he had managed to identify the men who executed his great-grandfather in Stalin's purges of the 1930s, and the place they buried him alongside scores of other victims. Gulag inmates who toiled on infrastructure projects like the White Sea Canal or the Salekhard to Igarka railway were often interred where they fell, to be lost under gravel and sleepers.

The traces of life before me now were fainter still.

I had tramped up the road out of Sochi that morning: a ribbon of sticky asphalt that sent heat through the soles of my boots.

Circassian Requiem

Towards evening, the road curved and rose to a viewpoint over the Shakhe river, flowing from the east, grey and fast and shallow.

The sight made me gasp. It was June and a shagpile of forest covered every inch of the hills that receded into the distance, blurring the sharper edges of ridges and crags into rounded contours, and glowing in the evening light. Trees and undergrowth crowded down to the banks of the river, its course divided by spits of gravel as it twisted its way through the tangled greenery.

Here, at the western end of the Greater Caucasus, my journey – the main part from the Black Sea towards the Caspian, hundreds of miles away to the east – was about to begin.

After the messy side-trip into Abkhazia, I had gone back to Moscow for a week to take stock and then returned to Sochi. Now I was both elated and perturbed. The forest ahead looked impenetrable. Would I find a way? The Abkhazia section of the walk had shown up my poor navigation, but there was something else: a nervousness about treading a landscape that felt like a memorial. Because the wild panorama beyond the Shakhe spoke of absence and of longing; of a people disappeared.

Today, they are all but forgotten, but in the nineteenth century, the Western eye found few nations more thrilling than the Circassians. In the months of snow and slush the previous winter, I had begun to research the history of the North Caucasus and the people I expected to meet. Reading material grew in piles on the edge of my desk at home: printouts of academic papers, newspaper articles, hardbacks with forbidding titles like *The North Caucasus Barrier* and *Russia's Islamic Threat*. I had a collection of Russian-language history and ethnography books from specialist regional publishers; last-minute purchases from Caucasus airports as I took planes home after assignments. Most had been relegated to the far end of a bookshelf and quickly forgotten. I blew the dust from the tops of their pages and started to read.

What I discovered both intrigued and appalled me. Living in the northwest and central Caucasus since before the Middle Ages, I learned, the Circassians had developed a finely calibrated hierarchical society with a caste of princes known as *pshi*, who ruled over nobles, commoners and slaves. The tribes close to the Black Sea dwelt in settlements strung along rivers like the Shakhe, where orchards and groves of walnut enfolded their homesteads. Besides farming, they hunted game and rustled each other's cattle. Many lived down trails, far into the forest.

Muslims, though not long converted, the Circassians told stories about a mythical race of heroes called the Narts, who were warriors, hunters and sorcerers. These sagas were suffused with the Circassians' love for their native forest; one spoke of a tree in the giant semi-human form of a princess who spread her foliage into the heavens and gave the Narts the Milky Way to light their path during raids. Groves or specific trees – often individual oaks – were considered sacred: a passer-by carrying firewood would leave a few pieces at the base of the trunk as an offering.

The Circassians also worshipped a god of thunder named Shible. They treated death by lightning as fortuitous, the victim's coffin buried on the spot or hoisted into branches overhead. Leonty Lyulye, a Russian ethnographer, witnessed locals dancing and singing around a high dais on which they placed three goats killed by lightning. Celebrants dragged more goats to the spot for sacrifice, raising their heads on stakes.

Dressed in clothes of hemp, wool and goat hair, the Circassians struck guests from the West as the finest of noble savages. They carried light guns and sabres that hung on silk cords in the Turkish fashion, while silver and gold inlay flashed on the hafts of their daggers. Some warriors even galloped into battle in vests of chain mail, stirring fanciful theories of descent from lost Crusaders. A favourite trick was to perforate the bonnet of a comrade with a pistol shot if it flew off while riding. Arriving on the Circassian coast, foreigners would spy warriors emerging from the forest to meet them, jumping nimbly across rocks on the beach. 'They suddenly came before the sight as though the oaks and pines had turned into men,' noted George Leighton Ditson, an American traveller.

It was these stories that sprang to mind as I moved up the road from the viewpoint over the river. On his journey in 1837, a Dundee-born adventurer named James Stanislaus Bell had stopped in the valley of the Shakhe, a little downstream towards the sea from where I now walked. At that time, the river was dotted with Circassian settlements up to its higher reaches. Kept inside by bad weather, Bell feasted on cakes and millet porridge brought by a Russian prisoner who was his hosts' servant. Houses like the one where Bell stayed were not situated on the valley floor as it broadened near the sea, he wrote, but 'lurk in clusters in the wooded dells above – a consequence, probably, of the war so long waged on this coast'.

I imagined these homes, embosomed by trees, as I stumbled, footsore, to the end of the road from Sochi, where a village materialized. It was twilight and too late to find a secluded spot to pitch my tent, or so I told myself. A man fixing his car emerged from the chiaroscuro of his garage into the softer gloaming outside and pointed me to a holiday camp next to the Shakhe, where I rented the upper floor of a chalet at eye-watering expense. From the back of the complex came a grinding noise. It was some moments before I realized it was the sound of boulders being pushed along the bed of the river by the sheer force of the water.

Adoring the Circassians became a kind of competitive sport in Europe and the United States.

In the early nineteenth century, as the Russian empire expanded, tsarist troops began to move beyond the 'line' of Cossack frontier settlements already established on the Caucasus steppe. There had been uprisings in Chechnya as Russia edged southwards in the late 1700s, and the highlanders stood accused of constant raiding into Cossack territory. Now a war of conquest was launched on two fronts. Once taken, the area would act as a buffer against Iran and the Ottoman empire.

But this Caucasian War did not end quickly. Stretching from about 1817 to 1864, it would be the defining moment in the history of the hitherto-independent mountain peoples, most of them followers of Islam. In the east, toward the Caspian, the tsars' troops collided with Chechens and Avars led by Imam Shamil, a tenacious Sufi commander. In the west, they faced various Circassian tribes without a unifying leader. Separating these two focal points of resistance was the mostly peaceable central Caucasus, where Russia had an ally in the Christian Ossetians and controlled the road over the mountains via the Pass of the Cross into Georgia, which had joined the empire in 1801.

The Circassians, so attractive in their forceful defence of their homeland, had admirers in London who saw them as a potential brake on Russian encroachment in the Near East. Amid the fighting, a series of British adventurers – covert agents in all but name – sailed from Turkey to Circassia's Black Sea coast to meet the plucky highlanders and encourage them to strive on against dominion.

Circassian Requiem

In London, sympathy for the Circassians was born out of a genuine concern for their plight, mixed with a desire to stymie Russian expansion towards Britain's assets in India. There was also a creepy obsession with the native body. Accounts of warriors' physiques extolled their lithe and majestic figures, while male visitors to Circassia could barely restrain their erotic fantasies at the sight of beautiful maidens whom relatives or traders shipped to Ottoman seraglios. 'When these fair creatures are brought into what is called the slave market, the sensualist casts his eyes on the rounded limbs, the fairly developed form of the mountain maid, and purchases her at any price,' wrote Ditson.

Beyond the holiday camp a track led past a tea plantation – 'The most northerly in the world,' a woman assured me over a fence – and along the Shakhe river into the trees. Sunlight and shadow played on the track beneath a tracery of leaves. Everywhere, spring snow-melt warbled its way down the sides of the valley. It was a glorious morning; the annoying expense of the chalet was soon forgotten.

Suddenly, a man drew up beside me, matching step. He introduced himself as Vladimir, a Russian who had driven up from Sochi and parked near the holiday camp. 'I had a heart attack a year ago,' he explained, taking rapid strides. 'I'm keeping fit with walks in the woods.' We moved on together, crossing footbridges over streams that purled into the river, their banks plush with ferns. Vladimir was trim, in his early fifties, with an air of assurance. The idea of my walk to the Caspian pleased him and he asked lots of questions. In his youth, he had been obsessed with mountaineering, he said. Now he ran a tree surgery team.

A pair of men appeared on the track, hurrying towards us, each carrying a rifle and an oblong leather satchel. 'Rangers,' murmured Vladimir, and I stiffened. We were entering a national park. In Sochi, I had requested permission for this first part of my journey at the park's headquarters. The staff had demanded I take a guide and a packhorse provided at an exorbitant price that I suspected was tailored to the bulging wallet they imagined I owned. Without a permit as I was, these rangers in the forest could mean trouble.

They paused as they arrived in front of us: burly fellows who looked like they would brook no argument. Was I about to be detained again? My heart sank. Not now. Not so early. But the men were in a rush. Just as one opened his mouth to ask a question, Vladimir launched into a florid account of me and my trip: the hike towards Elbrus, the sublime Russian landscapes that would surely be met on the way, the 'friendship of the peoples' that could not help but be engendered. The ranger was nodding and trying to interrupt. His partner had started to move on. He wavered for a moment, and then, signalling defeat with a flap of his hand at the blethering Vladimir, dropped to one knee and wrote out a five-day pass for five hundred roubles. It was an eighth of the daily fee the staff in Sochi had demanded. In a moment, he was standing up, handing me the pass and jogging on down the path after his comrade.

'They're not bad lads,' said Vladimir, after the rangers had passed out of sight. 'They do what they must to stay alive. When you earn four thousand roubles a month, you've got no choice.' That was about eighty pounds. 'Oh, taking bribes from poachers or going hunting themselves,' Vladimir replied, when I asked what he meant. 'Why else would they need those high-powered rifles? They shoot bears and sell the fat for people to rub on their chests when they're ill. Or they send the gall bladders to the Chinese. Those can fetch a lot.'

Circassian Requiem

There was a drone above the foliage and two helicopters passed overhead, each carrying a load slung on a cable. Vladimir said they were building a luxury dacha in the hills, maybe for the Russian president, whose summer residence was in Sochi. The site was not far from where I was headed, and the helicopters were the only way to bring in materials, at enormous cost.

'For the president?' I said. 'For Medvedev?'

'Yes, probably,' said Vladimir. 'Sometimes there are FSBshniki at the pass who turn people back.' He meant officers from the federal security service. As that moment, a young hiker came down the track wearing an old-fashioned knapsack and a pair of rubber boots. He stopped to exchange a few words.

'Any FSB guys on the pass?' Vladimir asked him.

'Didn't see any.'

'What about snow?'

'Plenty,' the young man replied over his shoulder, casting a sceptical glance at my thin cotton trousers and leather boots. It was the beginning of June: still early for the mountains. I smiled nervously.

Much later, I realized Vladimir and the man in rubber boots were the only people I met during my entire journey who were walking for pleasure. Just two in a thousand miles.

As the Circassian tribes began to capitulate in 1863, Tsar Alexander II offered the beaten highlanders a choice: to go into exile or to be relocated among Cossack settlements, inland by the Kuban river.

Up to 100,000 Circassians did move to the lowlands, where they could be better controlled and taxed, rather than going abroad. The rest refused. In response, and as sporadic resistance continued, the Russians focused their energies on deportation. In the space of five years, at least 370,000 Circassians – some think a million or more – would be forced to depart on boats for the Ottoman empire.

Evictions were deliberately conducted over the winter of 1863–4, when the destruction of houses and food could have their cruellest effect. Hundreds of thousands died, and of those, only a tenth from bullets, according to one Russian general; the rest perished 'in blizzards in the woods, or on open slopes'. The strategy was clear: the Black Sea coast had to be purged of its native inhabitants to prevent them offering a toehold to Russia's rivals, principally the Turks.

Whether they died or departed was immaterial. Droves of civilians were herded to the coast, their homes torched. The weak succumbed to typhoid and smallpox. Ivan Drozdov, a Russian officer, would later recall the 'implacable, merciless severity' with which tsarist troops burned villages and trampled grain.

It was ethnic cleansing on an immense, pitiless scale. At the coast, huge numbers of refugees gathered in bays waiting to be taken across the sea to Constantinople and Trebizond. Russian and Turkish ships carried them away, but long delays meant thousands of the refugees died of hunger and disease while sleeping in the open. Eyewitnesses spoke of an infant still sucking the breast of its dead mother, and of bodies frozen solid in huddles where they had tried to eke the last warmth from each other.

Boat captains, paid per passenger, dangerously overloaded their craft, some of which sank. Few Circassians could write, so first-hand accounts are scarce. One child who survived and later became a Turkish army officer recalled:

> We were flung like dogs onto sailing boats: choking, hungry, ragged. We waited for death as the best outcome. Nothing

was taken into account, not old age, not disease, not pregnancy... They treated us like cattle, thrown on a galley boat in our hundreds with no heed of health or sickness and then dumped on the nearest Turkish shore. Many of us died, the rest found shelter where they could.

On 21 May 1864, the Russian army declared final victory over the Circassians at Qbaada, a ravine about thirty miles to the southeast of where I was now moving down the path by the Shakhe river. In the east, in Dagestan, Imam Shamil had surrendered five years earlier. It was the end of the war. Russia had conquered the Caucasus.

Yomping down a wrong turn through the trees lost me several hours before I retraced my steps and found the path I needed: across the Shakhe on a rickety bridge and up the hill on the north bank. The break in Moscow had slackened my limbs a little, and now they protested at the extra work, a twinge in both thighs. A steady climb led to a cluster of wooden cottages in a clearing: the rangers' base. There was no one around. Further on, there was a stretch of forest where great oaks unfurled their crowns and the earth was soft and tamarind-brown, and a beast emerged on the path.

A beast?

It took a moment to process. Yes, my eyes told me, a beast. It was black, waist-high and five metres away. It scowled at me and snorted. I stared at it dumbly. Things seemed to have gone into slow motion. I was observing the scene as if at a distance, removed from reality. There was time to note, with wholly inappropriate leisure, that the animal's ears were rounded and bristly – and somewhat amusing in this rounded bristliness. Huh, I thought. Then a more sober idea took shape. *Wild boar.*

I froze.

Sharp tusks protruded from either side of the boar's long snout, which it was moving slightly from side to side. Now I was focused, and this didn't look so funny. The boar was facing directly towards me. It planted its legs wider apart and lowered its head.

As we contemplated each other, an image jumped into my mind. It was Gena, a poacher I had met in Abkhazia. He was pointing to a four-inch gash in the flank of his hunting dog with a cord of muscle rippling deep in the wound. 'A *kaban* charged him,' Gena was saying. 'They don't like it when you surprise them.'

Something dark was shifting in a thicket behind the boar. If it was a female accompanied by its young, it would surely be doubly prone to attack. It kept its gaze fixed on me.

Lowering my eyes, I lifted my left foot and began to move it infinitesimally, a few inches to the left. Then I repeated with the right. Then the left. Then the right. The boar watched. It huffed and rocked back a little.

By increments, I shuffled behind a hazel bush at the edge of the path. I glanced up and met the boar's eyes through the branches; a dull, animal stare that gave nothing away. Then I turned on my heel and legged it.

This was, it occurred to me as I galloped between the trees, almost certainly the wrong thing to do. Wouldn't it only provoke pursuit? The top of my rucksack plunged up and down in ridiculous fashion above my head.

After thirty seconds, I looked back over my shoulder and, seeing nothing, dived into a hollow behind a tree. The forest was still. I panted and grovelled in the dirt, waiting for the inevitable squeal, the tearing of flesh.

Another minute passed before I dared raise my head. Was it coming? Was it adjusting its line of attack? There was another shimmer in the thicket.

Fifteen minutes must have gone by, and my heart was still thudding, when the boar, another adult and three piglets emerged from a patch of rhododendron a hundred metres away and tripped off down a slope. I watched with my nose pressed to the dirt at the lip of the hollow. They were grunting quietly. Chortling, in fact. The piglets were striped yellow and brown, a festive livery, like little rodeo clowns.

Now I felt sheepish. Had I imagined an evil intent in the boar's eyes? Maybe it had been merely curious, and bemused by me running away.

Only my pride was hurt. But the encounter had given me a jolt. That night, I pitched my tent on a shelf on the hillside, at the point where the path began a switchbacking climb over damp leaf litter and exposed tree roots. From not far off came the sound of a large beast – surely bigger than a boar – smashing about in undergrowth. What could it be? A moose? A bison? A bear?

Back in Moscow, I had laughed when friends who knew the Caucasus suggested carrying a weapon to deal with wild animals. I didn't have a gun, but I'd spent weeks trekking in heavyweight mammal country like the Canadian Rockies. Avoiding confrontation was, I thought, a question of using the kind of methods I'd learned in Canada. Singing to warn of your approach or wearing a bell on your boot, wrapping up food at night and hoisting it into a tree: that sort of thing.

The problem was I had blithely failed to do any of this. Worse, I was sketchy on survival tactics. Don't run if you see a bear, that I remembered. Lie down and play dead if it gets close. I remembered that too, although it seemed preposterous. Black bears can climb trees; grizzlies can't. That had stuck. But what about Caucasian bears? Would it be worth scrambling up the twelve-foot lightning-blackened stump by my tent in case of an attack? I was astonished to find I did not know. (In fact, there are several subspecies of brown bear in the Caucasus. Most cannot climb trees because of their weight.)

Unnerved, I resolved to pack my food in plastic bags each night. Was that another noise from the bushes? My only weapon was a small knife. I'd read recently about an Australian swimmer fending off a shark by poking it in the eye with his finger. I laid my titanium walking stick by the tent entrance, telescoped into a short baton with its handle at one end and pointed ferrule at the other. Perhaps it would serve to discourage a hungry bear?

Dozing off, I woke with a start to the sound of scuffling. The moment of reckoning had come so early, I thought groggily. A wave of panic passed over me. I reached for the stick, bracing myself for a claw to rend the wall of the tent.

Agonizing moments followed, until all became clear. The scratching noise was my unshaved chin rubbing against the hem of my sleeping bag.

Since the Soviet break-up, the tract of landscape ahead of me had avoided much of the violence that now convulsed the Russian republics further east, where I was headed. Between the forests of the northwest Caucasus and Mount Elbrus, about a third of the way along the range, only isolated jihadi cells were active, and they were likely to operate at lower altitude, from towns on the steppe.

Yet I felt I was already tiptoeing through a landscape drenched in blood and sorrow.

Circassian Requiem

After the Circassians' forced exodus in 1864, their homes and hunting grounds were abandoned. The Shakhe valley and the surrounding hills fell silent.

The path next morning was indistinct but waymarked here and there by fading smears of red paint on tree trunks. I couldn't help but think of the highlanders' retreat to the shores of the Black Sea: wounded fighters, children, women, dragging a few bundles, the twigs catching at their ragged clothes. The sheer depravity made me remember the mothers and fathers in the school in Beslan; their children still within arm's reach, but that parental right, that privilege, of providing food and safety extinguished by circumstances over which they could exert no control.

'The inhabitants of the *auls* came running out of all the places where they had lived, which were subsequently occupied by the Russians, and their starving parties went through the country in different directions, leaving their sick and dying on the path,' wrote Alexander Fonville, a French military envoy to the Circassians who witnessed the carnage. 'Occasionally, entire groups of migrants froze to death or were carried away by snowstorms, and we frequently noticed their bloody trails as we passed. Wolves and bears were digging in the snow and pulling out human corpses.'

Before me, groves of beeches came into view, pale and etiolated from the altitude. Their slender trunks curved at the base, as if they had set out to grow perpendicular to the mountainside and only then remembered to go up straight.

I was still feeling jumpy after the encounter with the boar and the sound of the beast in the forest. The incident with my beard chafing the sleeping bag had added a comic touch. But I was gripped, now, by a genuine fear that I had not anticipated, thinking myself immune. The slightest sounds in the forest

107

snapped my head to and fro. My body felt like it was coursing with espressos.

Being alone was part of the problem. On a fishing trip in Canada, my friend Joe and I had once leapt into a lake to escape a grizzly that emerged from behind a tree and made bold steps towards us. Young and carefree, we laughed it off, and slept untroubled in a cabin in the woods without a door – an open invitation to passing bears. Fortunately, they did not sniff out our carp-smeared clothes. Now I was older and I knew what physical violence could do to a body; how it could pulp it, shred it, turn it inside out. The corpses of the dead at Beslan had shown the frightening vulnerability of human flesh, torn by bullets and shrapnel; a mauling of its own bestial intensity.

Between the beeches, there were soon chutes of crusty snow. It took most of the day to slog through the forest to the first pass, at 1,800 metres. I'm not a climber and none of my route through the Caucasus was technically challenging. But slithering on those chutes of snow, I wondered if a wiser walker would have stowed a pair of crampons.

At the pass, there was no sign of the FSBshniki – or anyone else. The trees had thinned. Ahead and to the left reared the huge rock torso of Mount Fisht, one of the Caucasus's major westerly peaks, obscured by cloud. To the right was a gently sloping area with a group of A-frame shepherd huts at its centre. Beyond that rose the next pass at the neck of a ridge running southeast from Fisht.

Glad to be in the open, I plodded down through a field of glacial boulders where the snow between spurs was deep, scored by rivulets of water. In places, drifts of older grey snow were edged by fresh deposits like brilliant white fox furs. Where the snow had melted, primroses sprang up amid patches of grass. But it was June; still too early to bring sheep up from the valleys to these high pastures. The shepherd dwellings were empty; a door banged and a piece of tarpaulin snapped in the breeze. High to the left, beyond a buttress at the corner of Fisht, a tur – a wild goat with extravagant horns – climbed the slopes. In the stillness, the sound of the stones dislodged by its feet could be heard half a mile away.

This stretch of open country between the forests made it easier to see the way ahead. On the next pass, there was a blue metal obelisk and boulders the size of cars fixed with plaques. They commemorated not the Circassian exodus but a border guard regiment that had 'twice destroyed the fascists trying to break through to Sochi' here in autumn 1942. Who could doubt the heroism – but why were there no reminders of the nineteenth-century war? It was as if it had been erased from memory. Wiping the plaques clean with my sleeve, I continued my descent. Dusk was approaching, and I hoped to get to a walkers' refuge that I had heard about. Rain was now falling in splashes. From the centre of a double-headed embattlement of rock on the flank of Fisht, streaked snow spewed like an alluvial fan. The path led down through patches of mixed beech and pine forest. There were more gullies to cross, some alarmingly steep, and each filled with hardened snow. Fatigue was taking its toll. To traverse the tongues of snow in the gullies at their narrowest point, the only option was to descend the slippery, scrubby spurs between them, edge across and then fight back up to the path through stands of hazel, my rucksack constantly snared by branches. Once I lost my footing and glissaded on my back down a river of ice before cannoning into a tree stump forty metres below.

A tin roof showed through the trees, and after a few more minutes, I was standing on the flat, open floor of the valley, exhausted. The refuge was a pair of simple two-storey buildings surrounded by pools of water and melting snow.

Half-hopeful for a hearty welcome, I pushed open a door that led into a kitchen. No luck. On the table lay unwashed plates, open food tins and a piece of cheese spiked on a fork. Coats and dungarees hung on hooks and an axe was propped by a stove full of ash. But the stove was cold and no answer met my call of greeting. This was clearly the warden's quarters. Maybe the occupants were out for the day?

In the other building was a grimy dormitory with sleeping platforms and a pile of mouldering blankets. On a bench lay a visitors' book with a stern warning 'not to spoil this book with your impressions'. In the past two months, only four groups of walkers had stopped at the refuge; the last, five days before me.

Upstairs were more platforms, a few discarded packets of noodles and a broken guitar propped in a corner. The place was empty. Disappointed, I smashed up the guitar for firewood, set the shards alight in a saucepan and heated the noodles in my tin mug over the flames. The warm food was a bonus. I was not carrying a stove in order to save weight, and my diet in the days to come would consist of tinned meat and fish, salami, nuts and dried fruit that I had bought from a supermarket in Sochi.

Outside, darkness was falling. Through the flat middle of the valley ran a stream, and a giant screen of limestone crags towered behind the refuge. There was an acute sense of isolation. Nobody had returned to the lodge, which seemed odd considering the half-finished meal. Several times, it felt as if someone was watching from afar. A mantle of cloud settled lower and lower.

It was early in the season for other visitors, but the feeling was inescapable: the lodge was a *Marie Celeste*, a deserted ship set adrift on a deserted sea. This was a country emptied of people and never repopulated.

Circassian Requiem

Natural exits out of the valley slipped from view. The slopes all around were lagged in forest, concealing the route to the next pass. A chill had entered the air.

Fully dressed inside my sleeping bag on the first floor, I dreamt of winged boar rising out of the stream and of being trapped alone in the valley, endlessly treading its muted greys and greens in search of a way out.

Unexpectedly, morning brought bright sunshine. Mount Oshten, the next along in the chain from Fisht, and the pass below it stood distinct against a blue sky, as if to say: 'What were you worried about? Here we are.' I threw my belongings together and stepped out of the door.

On the other side of the stream, a path that had eluded me the night before meandered into the woods under the pass. It soon melted away in fallen leaves, but the route was clear because of graffiti in Russian carved on tree trunks. One inscription read: 'S. Penkosky, 28.06.68', the large letters distorted by age.

I tried to envisage this Soviet walker forty years before me, descending the path that I was climbing. What was his first name? Stepan? A solid fellow with thick wool socks, bulging calves and a canvas rucksack. A lathe operator from the Urals, let's say, a member of the outdoor club in his factory. Before my departure from Moscow, I had scoured old maps and guidebooks and learned that in Communist times, there was a well-maintained network of walking routes in the Caucasus. Vigorous exercise and fresh air were seen as ideal ways of revitalizing the bodies and minds of Soviet citizens. Turizm, as hiking was called, was not an individual escape; it was a pursuit to be done collectively, like calisthenics or work. Every year, trade unions across the country sent tens of thousands of people to the mountains to join treks led by professional guides.

They'd known the route I was now climbing through splendid beeches as the Jolly Descent. It would have been thronged during the summer months as groups marched in the opposite direction to me, down towards the seaside, where the lucky ones would finish their vacation in a spa. Soviet hikers were a hardy sort, scorning those who preferred to lounge at base camps as *pizhamniki* (pyjama people). There was Stepan, pounding down through the trees with his carolling comrades, stopping to pull out his knife and press its point to the bark. Did he have any idea of what had happened here, a century before his trip? That fleeing Circassians had been harried down such paths to the squalid chaos of the coast, where thousands upon thousands of the survivors had tried to board ships to Turkey on the other side of the Black Sea? It seemed likely he didn't. The date of his graffiti prompted another thought: what did he know of the events unfolding as he took his holiday? June 1968 was the height of the Prague Spring, when Soviet tanks rolled into Czechoslovakia to crush a nascent democracy movement, shocking the world.

Was I any better, knowing that this was haunted ground? At least I was alone, and silent. Somehow, that felt less of a blasphemy. Since the Soviet collapse, the number of walkers had dwindled. There was no longer an organized system of holiday-making, and the beaches of Egypt and Turkey held greater allure than a fortnight of hard climbs and damp tents. There was no fresh graffiti on the trees.

Beyond the pass and then another, I moved beneath the cliffs of Oshten. To the southeast, chains of mountains stretched away towards the main range, blue in the morning light and garlanded with cloud. Before them, an open sward of landscape dotted with purple fritillaries fell away to a valley where a river tinkled, unseen. I stole over streams covered by caps of snow, rapt at the beauty of it all.

On the eastern side of Oshten, a long escarpment guided me down open slopes to the edge of more forest. Ten minutes into the trees, a voice hollered. I had seen no one for two days, but in a moment four men were at my side, crying greetings. They were Russians, all dressed in caps and camouflage, who had come from Krasnodar, the main city on the plain to the north. 'We're here to otdykhat for a week or so in the woods,' said one of the two older men. There was that word again. This 'relaxing' probably meant hunting, fishing and drinking, but I avoided the subject because we were still in the reserve, and I doubted they had a permit.

The men tugged out a bottle of vodka, sloshed some into my tin mug, found their own, and we toasted our meeting. I sat with them for a time as they cut saplings and began to lash them together to make a shelter. Two of them worked while the others sat and smoked. One of the younger men, Volodya, was wearing a pair of velveteen slippers with his military smock and trousers, as if he was at home in his living room. He laughed when I glanced at them. 'Couldn't be bothered to get my boots out of my pack,' he explained. 'Wish I had, though. Had to walk two hours in these from where we left the car.'

Volodya asked me what I was doing, and I began to explain: my recent departure from Sochi, the journey ahead to Elbrus, and from there on to Chechnya and Dagestan and the shore of the Caspian. Drawing on his cigarette, Volodya interrupted: 'Aren't you afraid on your own? I'd be afraid.' I said that I wasn't; not yet, at least. Without taking his eyes from his work, the second older man said: 'You'll be OK. Just watch out for the chyornye. It's them you can't trust.'

Chyornye, or 'blacks', was a term I had heard often in Moscow. It was not the only epithet that Russians used for people of the Caucasus nations. There were others that corresponded to the worst insults used against Black people in America and Europe. (Black people of African origin were usually called *negr*, a term that sounds jarring to foreign ears but that many in Russia consider neutral, although now it is sometimes rejected in favour of *tyomnokozhy* – dark-skinned.)

I left the Russian men in the wood soon after the conversation took this ugly turn, but I knew there was a long history of such pejorative and inaccurate language. In the nineteenth century, the terms 'Circassian' in English and 'Çerkes' in Turkish were often erroneously used for all people from the North Caucasus, regardless of ethnicity. In fact, Circassian was only correct as the collective name for that nation's various constituent tribes, living in the west and centre of the North Caucasus. In post-Soviet Russia, the distortions continued: skinheads and football fans often use *khachiki*, from a common Armenian first name, to describe someone from the Caucasus, whatever their nationality or religion.

As for physical appearance, many of the *kavkaztsy* (people from the Caucasus) I knew had dark hair and brown eyes, but there was a whole spectrum of looks and shade of skin. And the Russians' use of 'black' to describe them was ironic considering the historical use of the word 'Caucasian' in English to denote a white person.

It was a German scholar in the late eighteenth century who popularized this usage. Johann Friedrich Blumenbach devised one of the earliest racial classifications of mankind, naming five principal 'varieties', based partly on skin colour and partly on complex measurements of human skulls: Caucasian, Mongolian, Malayan, Negroid and American. Blumenbach was especially

Prometheus chained to the rocks of the Caucasus, a sixteenth-century image by Dutch engraver Cornelis Cort.

Novy Afon (New Athos) monastery in Abkhazia in the early twentieth century.

Father Feofan at the place of martyrdom of Simon the Canaanite.

An Abkhazian hermit with the head of a wild boar he had killed.

The beach in Sukhum.

Heavily wooded slopes in the northwest Caucasus.

Me in Karachay-Cherkessia.

A Circassian warrior.

Tales of alluring slave-girls from the Caucasus led to fake 'Circassian beauties' like this one being ogled at shows in the United States.

Shepherds of the North Caucasus: resourceful, tough, my constant helpers.

A high pasture ground in the central Caucasus.

Soviet tourism poster.

Seypul, a Karachay victim of the deportations.

struck by the 'beautiful' skull that he had observed of a young Georgian woman from the South Caucasus: the skull was passed to him by colleagues in St Petersburg after she was taken captive by Russian forces who brought her back to Moscow, where she died of venereal disease. More broadly, Blumenbach was engaged by the mythological and symbolic charm of the word 'Caucasian'. While his skull measurements were considered scientific at the time, his assessment of skin colour assumed that brilliant white skin and rosy cheeks (especially those of women) carried a 'vernal beauty' that darker shades could not match. That perception chimed with travellers' stories he had read of milky-faced Circassian slave girls.

The term 'Caucasian' now appears to be losing favour in the West, except to describe light-skinned crime suspects. Oddly, Russian police have inverted the meaning, using *litso kavkazskoy nationalnosti* (a person of Caucasian nationality) as a term to identify suspected criminals. Because the word *litso* means both 'face' and 'person', the implication is that the individuals concerned are un-Slavic in appearance, or un-white.

I met Mehmet in Guzeripl, the first village I reached when I came out of the woods into Adygea, the tiny enclave in Krasnodar region that is one of the republics where Circassians remain in Russia.

Mehmet was moustached and thick-waisted, but his exuberance and the clipped hair on the back of his head gave him the air of a schoolboy. The four men I had met in the forest would have called him a *chyorny*.

He had called me over as I walked past a table where he sat in a friend's front garden with his wife, Tamara, and their two young children, a boy and a girl. On the table were plates of smoked cheese, bread and sliced tomatoes.

'I am a Circassian born in Turkey,' said Mehmet, loading me a plateful of food. He spoke mangled Russian, which made even his children wince.

'When I was young in 1991, I saw the Soviet Union fall,' he went on. 'I felt something in my chest, maybe patriotism. I knew that I had to leave Anatolia and come to Russia right away, to the historical motherland of my people.' He shrugged and smiled. 'I never went back.'

Mehmet's story had its roots in the calamity of 1864, when his ancestors had climbed into boats on the Black Sea coast, heading into exile in the Ottoman empire. 'It was a genocide, of course,' said Mehmet. 'Even now, people in the diaspora do not eat fish from the Black Sea as a sign of respect for the dead.'

Mehmet's forefathers had gone to Turkey. Others ended up in Jordan. In time, the Circassians gained influence in their adopted homelands, taking pride in their martial tradition and securing high-ranking posts in the army and civil service. Later, following the collapse of the Ottoman empire, Kemal Atatürk's assimilation policies suppressed their language, but after the Second World War, an ethnic revival began, peaking in the 1970s before it was pegged back by military rule. By the time the Soviet Union unravelled, Circassians in Turkey were on the rise again.

Mehmet and his family lived in Maykop, the drab little capital of Adygea about forty miles to the north, and had driven down to visit Guzeripl for the day. 'Kakoy krasot!' he exclaimed in his appalling Russian. Tamara was a local, descended from Circassians who had stayed behind, and the family normally used their native language. Mehmet was gesturing at the hills. How beautiful, he had said. But there was a note of regret in his voice. Only a few thousand Turkish Circassians had joined his risky enterprise of returning 'home' to the Caucasus in the 1990s and 2000s. 'It's mostly Russians who live here now,' he said, pointing at the wooden cottages across the street, where chickens pecked near a fence. 'People in the diaspora missed their chance. A few years ago, you could buy land here for kopecks.' He rubbed his fingers together and pouted his lips. 'Now it's going off the scale.'

Mehmet made a living by organizing heritage tours for the descendants of exiles who came from Turkey and the Middle East to see the motherland. The quaint traditions they had learned from folklore and dance groups in the diaspora were little in evidence in this corner of modern Russia. Circassians were only in the majority in Kabardino-Balkaria, the republic further east beyond Mount Elbrus. The fervent nationalism that enthralled some diaspora groups barely existed here.

Mehmet seemed a tragic figure, for all his audacity in coming 'home'. Yet he had not lost hope. He wanted to send his children to a Turkish school in Abkhazia, where they would 'learn all the languages'. 'They will be international citizens, but they must know their native tongue,' he said. 'It's terrible how many Circassian children are already growing up without it.'

After lunch, Mehmet and his family said goodbye and got in their car to drive back to Maykop, while I went to Guzeripl's tiny museum. Inside, there were some mangy stuffed bears and a vast bison in a cabinet. Black-and-white photographs stretched along the walls, captioned in French. They showed Grand Duke Sergei Mikhailovich – a first cousin of Tsar Alexander III – near the village with a series of hunting parties in 1906.

The grand duke was a tall, elegant man surrounded by bearded Cossacks. In one picture, his retainers grasped stag heads with impressive antlers. In another, there were phalanxes of men holding rifles; eighty or more. Curious, I thought. How could there be enough game to support such an army of hunters? Then it dawned on me. Only forty years before the grand duke's visit, the Circassians had been forced out of their land. 'In the mountains of Kuban Oblast now, you might run into a bear or a wolf, but not a highlander,' the Russian officer Ivan Drozdov had written, concluding his account of the Caucasian War. The Circassians' deserted orchards and homesteads had been quickly sucked back into nature. By the census of 1897, three decades after the slaughter and exodus to Turkey, there were still no more than sixty thousand people living on the entire Circassian coast, of whom only fifteen thousand had been born there. The area must have been full of wild beasts; ideal for hunting.

A deliberate evil had wrought this wilderness; a campaign of extirpation against a people living on their own soil. I was glad to be here, but a sense of guilt for enjoying the place was inescapable. It was an Arcadia born in terror.

CENTRAL

6

Cossack Country

It had taken three long days to reach Guzeripl from the coast. I rented an expensive room in a local man's house for the sake of a hot shower, in which I scrubbed my clothes as well as myself. Valya, the owner, gave me a bottle of warm milk fresh from his cow, which I glugged with pleasure as I lay on my bed, surrounded by steaming clothes.

I had wanted to find a way through the tree-covered hills to the east, emerging on bare higher slopes close to the main Caucasus range about forty miles away. From there, I thought, I could strike on towards Elbrus, the dead volcano which is Europe's highest mountain. (Mont Blanc in the Alps is often mistakenly thought to be the continent's biggest; in fact, the Caucasus chain has about a dozen peaks that are higher.) But locals in Guzeripl told me that paths had fallen into disuse and grown over, and there was a risk of getting hopelessly lost. A detour above the forest belt was the only answer.

For four days, I walked on stony tracks and roads, making a loop to the north. The blisters I had acquired on my toes as I tramped up the baking road from Sochi on the first afternoon were beginning to harden. Shoulders and leg muscles settled.

CENTRAL

In villages that I passed through, a single kottedzh often reared among smaller houses – confusingly, in Russian this word, borrowed from the English 'cottage', designates a large, modern villa. The kottedzhi, execrable in taste, were the property of the village's most successful son, usually a businessman or a state official. Locals told me stories about their owners. 'Oh, he's in gold mining in Kazakhstan and he owns a pig farm,' said a woman as we contemplated a pink monstrosity with strange, geometric windows.

Since coming out of the forest, I had begun to lose my anxiety about hungry predators. There were still patches of woodland, offering an easy way to conceal my tent from prying human eyes. One night, I camped among trees where shrews scurried in dead leaves on the ground. On another, I set up in a dell that fell away a few feet from the verge. It was dank and thick with slender trunks. I found a handkerchief of flat, slimy ground and, pushing in the tent pegs, felt a sense of unease. It reminded me of the sensation I'd had as a child when entering a copse near our farmhouse in Norfolk, where my father had spotted a muntjac, a small deer with pointed canines that frightened me with the idea of its flitting presence.

It was early the next morning in the Caucasus dell when I woke to the sound of powerful limbs breaking through undergrowth close to the tent. A chorus of howls broke out, answered by more howling deeper into the trees. Wolves. The fear came back in a rush. I lay rigid on my back, imagining the creatures rushing forwards, their ears up, their tails out and mouths parted to suck in the crisp morning air. To my relief, they did not break step, ripping past with carnal energy, their thrashing legs seemingly an arm's length away. The sounds slowly faded. I kept still, staring at the dew-wetted fabric above my head as it glimmered with the first sign of dawn. It was a long time before I plucked up the courage to look outside. Besides a single broken twig, the wolves had left no trace.

The woods soon thinned into occasional fruit trees and rolling fields full of spindly cows. At the top of a rise that was knee-deep in grasses and wild flowers, I slept a night in a thicket. About thirty horses were grazing in the field. Concealed behind a hawthorn, I watched at dusk as a man on horseback rounded up the herd, driving them downhill. He uttered short cries and cracked a whip as they flew past, manes gilded by the falling sun. I felt as if I had seen few things more beautiful.

People I met were often friendly, but gave bad directions. The best map I had managed to get for the area in Moscow was 1:500,000 scale: almost useless for walking. Several times, I got lost. There is nothing worse than marching around through fields and overgrown orchards, getting hot and exhausted, without knowing if you are on the right road. In truth, it was impossible to describe to a stranger like me how to get somewhere on a network of faint and interconnecting paths that resembled a labyrinth. Nonetheless, it chafed the nerves to meet some fork in a footpath only five hundred metres after a gaggle of people had sworn blind there would be no turning for miles.

Locals in village grocery stores were surprised to meet an *anglichanin*, an Englishman. A woman behind a counter sighed: 'It's such a shame that your England is going to drown.' (Later, I found out there had been a documentary on Russian television predicting Britain would disappear under the North Sea. It claimed London had supported the NATO bombing of Yugoslavia in 1999 in order to carve out a territory there to replace the sunken UK.)

The owner of a little brick bakery said: 'I'm not happy with it yet. I want a lawn out front, like in England.' One elderly couple – he with a mouthful of gold teeth, she in a headscarf – were so keen to help me they almost came to blows when they could not agree on which path to recommend. I crept away as they exchanged volleys of abuse.

This was Kuban, a land of wheat-growing and rich, black soil, although many fields appeared to be lying fallow. In villages, geese and cows wandered on mud roads. Single-storey cottages made from wood or tin with corrugated asbestos roofs stood behind a narrow trench either side of the street, crossed by planks. The doors and window frames of the houses were painted in blues and pinks.

On the pastures above a village called Novosvobodnaya, a woman carrying a bottle of milk paused outside a small farm. She was well built, with strong arms and rounded pink features. 'My name is Tatyana,' she said in a commanding voice. 'I'm a Cossack.' Tatyana was the descendant of Zaporozhian Cossacks from Ukraine who were granted land in Kuban after serving heroically in the Russo-Turkish War of 1787–92. She and her husband lived at the farm and tended their herd of cows. Among themselves, they spoke a dialect of Ukrainian called *balachka*, she said (from the word the Russians originally used to denigrate this vernacular, *balakat*, to natter). In the past, Tatyana explained, Novosvobodnaya was named Tsarskoye after Tsar Alexander II. He had held talks with the Circassians on a nearby hilltop, she said, waving her hand in its direction. The tsar had also raised his army from surrounding villages. I told Tatyana about my close encounter with the pack of wolves. She looked like she could have beaten them away with her bare hands. Sure enough, she was unimpressed. 'Don't worry, it's already spring,' she said, evenly. 'They're not

hungry enough to attack people. There's plenty of prey around.'
I felt silly for having been afraid.

France has baguettes and berets; Italia has spaghetti and Vespas.
The Russians are convinced that England is enveloped in an
eternal pea-souper, calling the country *Tumanny Albion*, or Foggy
Albion.

Every nation suffers from both comic and hostile stereotypes,
pegged somewhere between truth and fiction. Russia, of course, is
the land of vodka, bears and gulag camps. In the Western mind,
the quintessential Russian is the Cossack, flinging out his legs in
a squat dance and cackling drunkenly before leaping on a horse
and riding into battle, waving his sabre.

I can't recall my first visual encounter with the Cossacks.
There's a vague black-and-white memory of men in great coats
falling repeatedly to their haunches and grinning gauchely at the
camera. Perhaps an archive reel of Pathé footage shown on television during my childhood.

As a group, their reputation for debauchery is not without
foundation. Modern-day Cossacks are descendants of Tatar groups
and runaway serfs who fled to Russia's borderlands and lived a
freebooting life in exchange for defending its frontiers. One of
Ernest Hemingway's 'ten best books of all time' was *Taras Bulba*,
Nikolai Gogol's romantic story of an old Cossack chief and his
two sons. I'd read it back in Moscow and been struck by an epi-
sode when Bulba stops to enjoy the sight of a splendid young
Zaporozhian Cossack slumbering on the road, his body stretched
out like a sleeping lion, his trousers of rich red cloth 'spotted with
tar, to show his utter disdain for them'. That image of youthful
vigour was so captivating; it reminded me of a Spaniard I'd met at
a house party in Edinburgh, a lean man with a husky voice who

scorned our British sipping of sangria, and showed how it should be drunk with abandon, spattering onto the floor.

In the northern hinterlands of the Black and Caspian Seas, in what is now southern Ukraine and Russia, the Cossacks ran their own communities and became an advanced guard for territorial expansion, giving military service to the state in exchange for a degree of autonomy and privilege. By the nineteenth century, their 'North Caucasus Line' of settlements became the base for the Russian conquest of the highlanders. Many Cossacks took part in the fight as their role in the army was increasingly formalized, and the Line was bolstered with forts.

Orthodox Christian Cossacks and Muslim highlanders are commonly imagined as bitter rivals. But there was also respect and understanding. The Cossacks' horsemanship and dress had much in common with that of the mountain nations – their lambskin hats and cherkeska tunics were direct copies of highland attire. There was a lively trade on the frontier: highlanders bought melons and sackcloth and cast-iron pots from the Cossacks, while selling them clothes, carts and weapons – the very weapons used against them in battle (150 years later, Russian soldiers would provide arms in the other direction, selling their guns and ammunition to Chechen rebels).

Cossacks and highland men – albeit those loyal to the tsar – were also known to become kunaks: blood brothers. Tolstoy had a kunak named Sado, who rescued him from a gambling debt by winning back the aristocrat's IOU from another card player.

In Russian national mythology, the Cossack is positioned somewhere between 'self' and 'other' – both familiar and strangely distant: at once a defender of the tsar and the Orthodox faith, and an unshackled pirate from far-off shores, a symbol of the country's own eternal identity crisis as a place adrift between Europe and Asia.

Now I was turning south, back towards the mountains.

It was warm again, my back slick with sweat against my pack, the sun branding a red stripe down my forearms as I rambled across the undulating steppe.

The walking was doing me good. I had missed it all those early years in Moscow, tearing across the country in aeroplanes, living the peripatetic life of the correspondent, stopping in places for a day or two and shuttling on again. Being on foot made you look properly; it made you slow down. I studied butterflies at rest stops. I felt the warm chips of asphalt under my legs when I sat on the edge of a deserted road.

Occasionally, I look back and think: *You were just enjoying a long holiday.* There's truth in that, of course. Not everyone can allow themselves a summer off, and few would not benefit from doing so.

Another truth is that walking heals. I've had reporter friends who suffered from PTSD, and I know I didn't have it after Beslan. The nightmare of the falling woman was distressing. It didn't cause a breakdown or prevent me from enjoying life. But there *had* been a cumulative effect from working in the Caucasus; from witnessing the evil that swaggered there.

The exhilaration I was now experiencing did not mean that that evil had gone away. It served, though, as a kind of affirmation that another Caucasus existed. And the very act of walking had restorative power.

Plodding down a quiet road across the plain, I received a call from Masha. We did not speak often because of the poor reception, so these moments were precious. I stepped off the road and lay down in the grasses. 'Everything's good, only you are missing,' I said.

'Same here,' she said. But I knew she was happy in Moscow, always a free spirit, with no need for me to prop her up.

We talked and laughed for a while, and I set off again, not into reminiscing or philosophical or even lustful thoughts, but into a fugue where my body seemed to dissolve into the heat and the scents of the steppe. Was this how a lizard felt on a sunny rock, doolally with heat?

The next morning, the sun burned off the haze and the jagged, snow-topped wall of the Greater Caucasus ran stark along the horizon, its lower slopes grading into the piedmont. A feeling of glee and apprehension tingled in my spine. I thought of the young Russian soldier, Olenin, approaching the range by cart in Tolstoy's *The Cossacks*:

> Suddenly he saw, about twenty paces away as it seemed to him at first glance, pure white gigantic masses with delicate contours, the distinct fantastic outlines of their summits showing sharply against the far-off sky. When he had realised the distance between himself and them and the sky and the whole immensity of the mountains, and felt the infinitude of all that beauty, he became afraid that it was but a phantasm or a dream.

That world did seem closer as I surveyed the peaks, rising huge and austere above the humdrum greens and browns of the rolling steppe. I had never been a mountaineer, but I had winter-walked in Scotland and Canada – enough to feel the thrill of high and icy places. One of my favourite pieces of mountain literature was Maurice Herzog's *Annapurna*, his account of climbing the

Himalayan peak in 1950. As he and a friend approached the summit, Herzog was transported to another realm: the landscape around him seemed diaphanous and pure, his steps became strangely easy, as if the world had been shorn of gravity. For a few short hours, he was 'living in a world of crystal', overcome by 'an astonishing happiness'.

The uncharitable think this poetic euphoria may have been caused by Herzog popping amphetamines. Some climbers did that in those days (he denied it). In any case, I had felt something of the same exultation in Crianlarich and Corrour: the joy of silent mornings on slopes of radiant white. On this journey, I would not be spending long above the snowline, but I hoped for more of those moments, however fleeting.

The tallest mountains were still days away. After a night at a crumbling Soviet-era holiday camp, I moved into trees and the narrow valley of the Bolshaya Laba and camped to the sound of the torrent. The next afternoon, by the dirt road that clung to the river, I was falling into daydream when a truck pulled over and three men leapt from the cab to say hello. Nazim was dark and elfin in a tracksuit and baseball cap. Ruslan was plump in a sheepskin coat. Albert, a rangy youth, had a horn-handled knife hanging from his belt. 'Woooh, what are you doing?' they cried. 'Why are you walking? Where are you from? *England?* You're joking. Get in, we'll give you a lift! Are you really from England?' Laughing, I explained that I could not use transport. Nazim struck his temple with his palm in disbelief as they climbed back into the cab and reluctantly drove away.

I was sad we had not spoken more, but hours later, I caught up with them. They had ramped the drab green truck on a knoll overlooking the river, and sat crouched around skewers of lamb, coaxing embers underneath. It was a celebration.

CENTRAL

'We just turned eighteen,' Albert said, grinning, throwing an arm around Ruslan's sheepskin-padded shoulder as they got up to greet me. The pair of them were leaving within days to start their military service. This trip into the hills was a last hurrah to see them off. Nazim, in the tracksuit, did a little timber hauling and had provided the truck. Sitting on a log by the fire, he called me over. 'Come, come, sit! I am the elder here, I'm in charge,' he said. 'I will not let anyone offend you or cheat you. This is the *Kavkaz*. You are our guest.'

The men poured vodka and we drank it with the *shashlyk* and *shorpa* made in a cauldron, a salty soup of boiled mutton which tasted sensational after days of living on tinned sardines. It was the third day of their bender, they explained. Who knew when it would end? Maybe they would push on through to the eve of the boys' departure.

The two recruits were already drunk. Albert gabbled and reeled around the fire with the legs of a newborn foal, and then pitched into the back of the truck. Ruslan, pumped up with thoughts of joining the army, shouted cheerily at me about the superiority of Russian weapons. 'If there is a war – you understand, a war? – and the Americans fire missiles at us – missiles, you understand, missiles? – then we can shoot them down with our own rockets before they reach us.' Soon, he too crawled off to the truck to doze.

Nazim smiled. 'I'm the old wolf, the only one who can take his drink,' he said, as he prodded the fire. He was twenty-six. Although he had grown up in Kyrgyzstan in Central Asia, his grandmother was a Karachay, the Turkic mountain people who lived on the high slopes to which I was headed. The sides of the valley rising steeply on either side of us were garbed in forest. Nazim had moved to the area two years earlier and started cutting timber, 'sometimes legally, sometimes illegally', he said. Logging trucks were the only vehicles that moved down the track, rattling empty to the south, then charging in the other direction later in the day, fully loaded with trunks a metre thick. Nazim knew many of the drivers. He shouted abuse or shook his fist at them in cod anger as they sped by, grinning and hollering back.

Drizzle had started to fall when Albert emerged, blurry-eyed. Uttering a cry, he stripped to his underpants, tore down the bank and plunged into the freezing shallows, roaring and pumping his arse up and down in exaggerated press-ups between the boulders. Then he ran back to the fire. We laughed as he repeated the ritual three times, holding himself under the water on the last press-up. I was already fond of the two recruits. How would this untamed soul fare in the army? Older soldiers in the Russian army frequently subjected draftees to beatings, a ritual known as dedovshchina, or 'reign of the grandfathers'. Doctors had recently been forced to amputate the legs and genitalia of Andrei Sychev, a nineteen-year-old from Yekaterinburg, after a sergeant beat him for four hours while he crouched with his hands tied behind his back. I had travelled to the Urals to interview him in the small apartment where Andrei lived alone with his mother: one more heroic woman holding a damaged family together through strength of will.

Yet in the army, men from Caucasus nations often stuck together. Sometimes they turned the tables to terrorize those around them.

The farewell party lasted until the early hours. After much vodka, we tumbled into sleep on the filthy bed of the truck. Next morning, I woke smeared in dirt with the sensation of a shashlyk skewer pushing into the back of my skull. Ruslan's heavy arm had fallen over my chest, like Queequeg's over Ishmael. Waking no one, I eased myself from under the arm, picked up my pack and climbed out into the chill of morning. Mist was rising like smoke off the river, black slabs of rock protruding from the torrent. I splashed my face in the water, drank deeply and set off down the track.

Ahead lay the high passes of the Central Caucasus. Physically, this promised to be the hardest part of the journey. A few isolated villages dotted the mountains; the only other inhabitants there were shepherds. The area was the home of two rarely studied Turkic peoples. Among the peaks between me and Elbrus lived the Karachays. To the east of Elbrus were the Balkars.

After years of land disputes, these highland nations were wary of the Cherkess and Kabardians, their Circassian neighbours – the ones who had not left in the nineteenth-century exodus – who occupied the hills and plains lower down, living mostly in towns. The Karachays and the Balkars share something else: a great injustice. Alongside the Chechens and the Ingush, they were deported en masse from the North Caucasus during the Second World War after Stalin accused them of collaborating with the German army, which had pushed deep into the Soviet Union in 1942. All told, at least 600,000 people from the four nations were packed in cattle wagons and sent to Central Asia in 1943 and 1944. Small groups of partisans did rise in support of the Nazis. The numbers were exaggerated and the effect was minimal. In revenge, the Kremlin punished entire nations. An estimated twenty-five per cent of the deportees died en route or succumbed to disease and starvation within five years of arrival.

To be ripped from one's hearth is tragic for anyone. For herders and farmers who rarely strayed beyond their villages, living off livestock and the land and tending the same plots for generations, it was a soul-lacerating calamity. Unlike the Circassians a century earlier, many Karachays and Balkars were allowed to return home in the late 1950s. But the scars had yet to smooth. A few months before I set out on my walk, guerrilla radicals in the North Caucasus had formed an alliance called the 'Caucasus Emirate', promising to expel Russians and create an Islamic state in the region. The security services had helped fill the guerrillas' ranks by torturing and murdering suspected extremists, who were often peaceful conservative Muslims. As for the historical pain of the deportations, that was a kind of deep background grievance, a throbbing ache. Shamil Basayev had once named the forced exile of the Chechens as a motive for his fight against Russia.

Starting me from my thoughts, two men in uniform came the opposite way down the track. They were small but nimble and tough-looking. Each carried an AK-47 and had a knife strapped to the webbing across his chest.

Russia strictly controls a buffer zone along the length of its frontier with Georgia and Azerbaijan. These were FSB border guards on patrol. 'Your papers,' said one. Back in Moscow, I had applied for a permit to walk through the zone, listing the valleys and passes I hoped to cross as I traversed the Russian Caucasus from west to east. Now I produced it. The guards studied the permit. One of them spoke into a walkie-talkie. 'We have met the foreigner whom we've been expecting for a long time,' he said. The reply was instant: 'Check his papers and move aside so he can't hear our conversation.' The guard gave a sheepish look and sidled up the track.

I felt nervous. After the debacle in Abkhazia, I was expecting trouble. The officers from the Abkhazian National Security Service who had arrested me in Sukhum would surely keep in close contact with their Russian allies in the FSB, on this side of the border. Had they passed on a message that I was a spy? The second guard stood close and watched me with placid curiosity. We waited for a few tense moments before his comrade returned. 'You can go on,' he said. I had not been detained: that was a start.

The track led on, flanked by crests topped with snow. Cloud was easing down into the valley and another, older border guard was tending horses in a meadow. 'Are you the foreigner they caught?' he asked eagerly. Word about me had clearly got around. He looked crestfallen on learning my papers were in order.

Now I was treading through woodland where the fronds of the fir trees were edged with soft new needles. A noise that sounded like cows wailing and mooing in distress came from somewhere in the trees. It was spine-chilling, and I never learned the source of this sound. Was it really cows? Were they being assailed by wolves?

The border guards' base appeared and, on a whim, I knocked on the gates, which were emblazoned with the motto 'Duty, Honour, Fatherland'. Two officers received me warily.

'You're the only person we can remember travelling alone in these mountains,' said one. 'What will you do if you meet a bear? It's still early in the season and there are not so many berries in the forest. They're hungry.'

I assured them I would be careful. The truth was that I was still not sure in my own mind how I would respond.

A sweaty hour passed as I plunged through knee-high mud and broken branches in a wood on the edge of a village, my hands covered in pine sap. The place had been recently logged and I could not find the way. In a filthy mood, I was about to return to the village when a faint footpath came into view on the hillside above the forest. It led all day down the V-shaped valley of the Pkhiya river.

After the detour onto the steppe, I had finally turned east

towards my destination, the faraway Caspian. For as far as I could, I planned to shadow the frosty crest of the Greater Caucasus, crossing the ridges that lay between it and, in the words of the climber Douglas William Freshfield, that 'great wall of limestone which is the mountains' first line of defence on the northern side of the range'. Such topography promised frequent climbs from low river to high pass and down again, as the torrents that sprang from glaciers under the high peaks flowed north, castellating the limestone wall, to the plain, where they turned either left to the Black Sea, or right, to the Caspian.

The path proceeded over grassy spurs where patches of giant hogweed sprouted between groves of conifers. That night, I pitched the tent on the lip of a ravine. At dusk, I spotted several bears. On close scrutiny through my monocular, they turned out to be a tree stump, a boulder and – distantly – a lump of horseshit.

The word 'shepherd' – pastukh in Russian – conjures something pastoral, serene. But the life of a Caucasus shepherd is full of privation and solitude. They must protect their flocks – and themselves – from bears, wolves and storms, living for weeks or months on remote and wind-whipped hillsides.

Transhumance is a phenomenon in mountain cultures worldwide: the tide of grazing animals that rise to the necks of the peaks in spring, only to subside to the valleys in autumn. For me, it is something magical. When I was a boy, my father showed me tumbledown shielings in Scotland where crofters had spent summers with their flocks before the clearances. In my twenties, walking in eastern Turkey, I had stayed at a yaylak below the fangs of the Kaçkar peaks, a mountain pasture ground where people from the village below passed the warmer months in handsome log cabins. In the Caucasus, the shepherds live in koshes, an old

Turkic word for a sheep pen and a simple shelter made of stone or timber, or planks covered in sheeting.

A dark ripple was advancing up the hillside: the first sheep being driven to the high pastures. Soon the flock was upon me, hundreds of reeking black sheep. Two *pastukhs* on horseback harried them forward, striking the ground with their whips. They were hard-faced men in camouflage smocks and knitted black hats. They called greetings to me but kept on the move. The sheep darted over the stones, nipping each other. A horse-drawn cart with a canvas cover brought up the rear, followed by two more men herding a group of cattle. Here, I saw my first Caucasian sheepdogs: enormous, with chewed ears and scarred faces. In an instant, two of them were flying across the ground, snarling, their noses wrinkled in fury, their hackles raised between bulging shoulders. A spasm of atavistic fear ran through me, like a caveman facing a smilodon. The dogs came on at vomitous speed. Raising my titanium stick above my head, I was bracing to strike when a voice rang out: a single, sharp word that I could not identify. It was the man at the reins of the cart. The effect was immediate. Like great juggernauts containing their massive power, the dogs shuddered to a halt ten metres away, their front paws ploughing into the earth, their back haunches thrown upwards by momentum. They snarled once more and turned, slinking back to the flock. One of the dogs gave a backward glance – regretful, as if sorry to have missed a tasty lunch.

I grinned weakly at the cart driver and waved. He gave a nod and turned back to his work.

That afternoon, I arrived in Arkhyz, a village ringed by rocky peaks. The locals here were Karachays, a Turkic people of disputed origins who populated the mountains all the way from here to Elbrus. Beyond that great peak lives their brother nation, the Balkars, whose language and customs have much in common.

Arkhyz felt like a real frontier settlement with its dirt streets and horses tied to railings. Russian tourists came here for a taste of the mountains, and here they were, dressed in brightly coloured cagoules and white trainers. Some rode past on horses led by lean, sun-blackened Karachay men. Others sat with their children at little shacks that served shashlyk, or khychiny, flat pies stuffed with meat. A group of tourists at one stall looked plump and ungainly next to the women serving them in black skirts and headscarves.

As I drank tea at one of the shacks, a Karachay boy of no more than ten came cantering bareback down the street on a stallion, whooping with delight. In full flight, he snapped off a twig from a tree and whipped the horse into a gallop. Seconds later, he was out of sight. The tourists went on munching their pies as if nothing had happened.

On a rise beyond the river in the centre of the settlement was a guesthouse. All the rooms were full, but the kindly owner let me stay in a vagonchik, a trailer that stood in the yard. Russian families had parked their Ladas in front of the hotel with the boots open, and were drinking beer and eating dried fish at picnic tables, with music blasting from their car radios. They did not seem to move all day.

'The worst is in July and August, when the mushroom collectors come,' said Tokhtar. He was a Karachay, the head of the mountain rescue team. 'They get lost in the forest and then they come down to the river,' he explained, as we sat on a bench by his house at the edge of the village. 'They huddle by the water, shivering all night long. They don't try to go up or down the river to find a way out. And next to the river, they can't hear a thing; they can't hear us shouting for them. They just freeze.' He shook his head. 'You can only find them if you shine a torch right in their eyes.'

Tokhtar, a lean veteran with a ruddy triangle of tanned skin at his throat, had many diverting stories. He spoke of rescues in the Abkhazian mountains. The gorges there were so deep that he and his team walked all day on the cliffs, unable to get down to the streams below and fill their flasks. Once they found a place where some wild boar had made a wallow to bathe. 'We were so thirsty that we drove them out of there and collected the water with spoons to boil for tea.'

I was about to enter a stretch of wilder country. Tokhtar wrote my name in his logbook and said he would send his deputy from the rescue team, Dima, to walk with me the next day and show me the way.

Dima was the only Russian ascetic I'd ever met. He was in his fifties but as lean as someone half his age. He didn't smoke or drink, and he practised yoga. He had shaved his head and wore a green cotton tunic and trousers he'd designed himself. He reminded me of one those Beat-era Buddhists like Gary Snyder who worked as fire lookouts in the North Cascades.

I found him waiting for me outside my *vagonchik* as morning light spilled over Arkhyz. He was carrying an enormous orange rucksack; regulation issue for the mountain rescue team. He was happy to join me, he said. A path behind the guesthouse climbed through pine forest. Dima charged up it, stopping once to point out the fresh paw print of a bear as big as my outstretched hand. Within an hour, we reached a saddle that Tokhtar had pointed out the day before. Save for scrub, it was bare, swept of trees in an avalanche. Beyond the saddle was a great dish of green landscape dotted with groves of birch. It stretched to the horizon. Past the rim of the dish was my goal: a rocky ridge cutting from north to south.

As we walked, I questioned Dima about his life. 'I was born in Perm in the Urals, to a Russian mother and a Belarusian father,' he said. Once, when skiing as a teenager, he had fallen asleep in the snow, looking at the stars. 'I lost consciousness and almost died of hypothermia. I began to suffer from angina and had to give up my studies.' He had been a student at a missile technology institute. He spent two years convalescing in Crimea, he said, and then moved here to Arkhyz on a friend's advice, seeking fresh air and exercise to curb his illness. He had worked 'as a farmer', he said, and then joined the mountain rescue team.

'I want to ask something about Britain,' he said abruptly. 'What can you tell me about your radio telescope for tracking UFOs? It's one of the most famous in the world.' I confessed I knew nothing of it. Dima looked disappointed. 'I've seen a UFO here three times,' he said. 'It was hovering above the ridge behind Arkhyz. It was long and cigar-shaped and it shone like the sun.'

We ate lunch by a stream. I wolfed down slabs of salami and cheese, while Dima took out a flatbread and a jam jar full of greens. 'I'm fifty-three and I feel wonderful,' he said. His escape to Arkhyz intrigued me. Here, he had reinvented himself, trans-forming the sickly youth into a dynamic hero who pulled climbers from snowdrifts and went hiking on his days off. I wanted to know why he had not gone home to the Urals. But Dima's mind was on other things.

'Do you ever really think about what motivates you beyond everyday instincts, desires?' he was asking. 'It serves to consider this. Next time you are dreaming, try to look in a mirror or look at your hands. Do you see imperfections? This will tell you a lot.'

What exactly, I could not fathom, and he was back on his feet and tearing across the grass before I could ask.

By early afternoon, we had climbed to the edge of the dish. On the far side of the next valley, teardrops of snow hung in the gullies that scored the ridge. Dima said he would go no further, but he pointed out a route to the top. 'You'll be alright,' he said, as if reassuring himself rather than me. 'If you get lost, ask the herders' advice. There's a good man down in the valley. Goodbye, and be careful.'

Below the pass, a flock of sheep pointed up the slope in a black chevron. I met their guardian on horseback, a simple lad from Siberia come to work for the summer in the hills. He had buck teeth and thanked me as we parted, as if grateful for the chance to tell of meeting a foreigner. Within a couple of hours, I was on the valley floor. There was an iron bridge spanning the Marukha river, which raced towards the plain. To the south, at the head of the valley, the peaks towards the main Caucasus range were smudged by cloud.

Besides Dima and the shepherd, I had seen no one all day. Now an UAZik came trundling up the track next to the river. The UAZik (pronounced Ooh-Ah-Zik) is Russia's answer to the Land Rover, a kind of supercharged four-wheel-drive minibus whose cute bread-loaf shape belies its pugilism. It is mostly used by the military. My heart sank as a team of border guards climbed out and headed to intercept me. We met on the bridge. But it was not what I had expected. The men checked my documents, suggested a different pass to the one I was planning to cross, and then piled into the UAZik and drove away.

Beyond the river, the next ridge rose steeply from a fringe of trees. The guards' directions had seemed clear, but I spent an hour chasing down paths that petered into undergrowth. Time was getting on and the sky had turned dark. Half a mile down the valley, I could see a cottage. Rain began to fall in sheets. Two teenage boys were standing on the doorstep, water pouring off plastic sacks that they wore like cloaks. They beckoned me over. 'Come and shelter,' said one of the boys.

Inside, the floor was strewn with old fleeces, bits of timber and tools. The cottage was falling apart, its window cavities covered with polythene. The boys opened a door to a room where there was a sleeping platform covered in blankets and a fire thrumming in a stove. The heat was delicious. We sat on the platform and the boys played cards. I was fighting sleep when the owner of the cottage returned. His name was Abubekir and the boys were friends of his son. He immediately invited me to stay the night. 'A traveller needs rest,' he said.

We ate yogurt and drank tea by the fire. In the evening, Abubekir and I moved to another room where there were iron beds and a table made from an old door. We talked in the darkness. In 1972, as a young paratrooper, he had been sent to Iran with a unit of Soviet special forces given the task of helping mujahideen resist the American-backed shah. 'The selection was tough, but I was a highlander, I had a good heart and lungs,' he explained. The army tried to keep him, but Abubekir refused. 'I said, "You've had two good years from me, now I'm going back to my family."'

Since then, he had lived in a village on the piedmont, coming to this remote cottage in summer to graze his cattle. He spoke wistfully of the Brezhnev era, a time remembered by many in Russia for a modest growth in prosperity among the poor. Back then, trade unions had sent groups of walkers to the valley. 'There were scores of people camping here every night in summer. They came from all over the Union. There were dances, there was a shop. Now I see only a handful of people every year.'

After the demise of the Soviet Union, things had begun to fall apart. The cheese factory just down the river, to which he had provided milk, closed. Suddenly, the North Caucasus was convulsed by nationalism. Many of Abubekir's fellow Karachays burned to create their own homeland. They wanted to live separately from the Circassians with whom they shared a republic – Karachay-Cherkessia – and who were settled mostly on the plains.

'It was a difficult time.' His detached voice came through the darkness. 'Some of the lads from round here went to fight in Chechnya against the federal troops. Russian soldiers started arriving in armoured cars and pointing guns at people. They did it to me once. I had a weapon; I could have taken them all out. But I didn't want to start a war.' Eventually, the campaign for a new republic waned and things calmed down. Then Abubekir suffered a new upset. Five years earlier, he had shattered his pelvis when he was riding as a passenger in a friend's truck that overturned. When he got out of hospital months later, he found his cottage had been ransacked. Even the window frames had been stolen.

I mentioned that Dima, the mountain rescuer, had shown me the way that morning. 'Oh, Dima, yes, I know him well,' said Abubekir, brightening. 'He's a good lad. He lived here for a while and worked for me. He needed to be off the map.'

'Oh, why?'

'He was involved in an accident in which someone ended up dead. It wasn't his fault, but the person turned out to be related to an important bureaucrat. Dima had to run away. That's why he came to Arkhyz.'

It completed the puzzle. The Caucasus has long been a place of exile; a halfway house on the road to redemption. Prometheus was fastened to a rock on Mount Kazbek, condemned to have his constantly regenerating liver pecked out every day by an eagle.

Cossack Country

Yet in the end, he was freed by Hercules. Pushkin was sent to the south as censure for his subversive poems, but felt liberated from the philistine society of St Petersburg.

In his own way, I thought, Dima too had shaken off his chains.

Abubekir served breakfast: a leg of mutton and a bag of boiled sweets. We walked back up the valley past the bridge, and he showed me the beginning of the path. I felt strong and rested, but sorry to say goodbye.

The path ascended steeply beside a stream and past a ruined stone kosh. It was a heart-thumping hour-long climb to the ridge. My right knee had begun to produce an unpleasant grinding noise when it was put under pressure; it did so now, but was not painful and did not inhibit my movement. The weeks in the hills were starting to pay off. I felt stamina building.

At the top, an ice-filled tarn lay in a cirque patched with snow. Swirls of sooty cloud unfurled over the bowl of rock. I descended quickly, expecting rain. High on the slope was a hut standing alone in a patch of mud. It was the size of a garden shed, made from planks and sheets of asphalt. Two galvanized buckets hung from nails on the wall and a ram's horn was stuck on a post. A pastukh was at the door.

'Come in,' he called. We stepped into the warm fug of the kosh. 'So, an Englishman,' he said, as he lowered a kettle onto a gas burner. 'Your racehorses are the best in the world.' He had a magnificently broken nose. It was splattered across his face.

We sat a while, sipping coffee as the pastukh told stories and fried pastries in a pan. 'I was walking up here one night, pitch black,' he said. 'I had a sack of belongings over my shoulder and a bottle of vodka in my pocket that I was swigging from. I was shining a little torch and I saw something black across the path.

I thought, "There shouldn't be anything black here." I almost stepped on it. It was a bear cub. Suddenly, there was a great roar. It was the mother bear. She had just crossed the path. She reared up on her hind legs. Massive, furious. I hurled the sack at her and threw myself down the hillside. I was tumbling head over heels – thank God I was drunk. When I got up, I was shaking all over. The bear had gone. The vodka too.'

Now he was waiting for his *naparnik* – what American cowboys would call a 'pardner' – to come up from the lowlands and join him. Most years, in spring, the two of them had to rebuild the *kosh*. 'We first put it up in 2002. In 2004, it was destroyed by an avalanche. In 2005, avalanche. In 2006, avalanche. The last two years, it's stood.'

He wrapped a pile of pastries and a knob of rubbery cheese in some paper and pressed them to my chest, then picked up his knapsack and crook – it was a good eight feet long – and we headed down the hill. The flock was scattered over the slopes. He had two Hungarian sheepdogs, and now they arrowed out to pick up the stragglers, racing over capillaries of paths, responding to his whistles and tirades of swearing. 'They're intelligent, like your collies, but sometimes they get so into it they don't know how to stop.' I left him standing on a knoll, a hardy little hero of the hills. He was Russian and we had talked briefly about politics. 'Those bastard oligarchs stole everything from us,' he said as we parted. 'Abramovich, who bought your Chelsea – let him come here and work just a day in the rain and the dirt.'

A swath of forest damaged by fire gave into a field of yellow flowers by the Aksaut, the next river flowing down from the main range. There was no bridge. In heavy rain, I followed the river north in search of a crossing. An hour had passed when a man appeared, coming up the track. 'We've been expecting you,' he said. 'The border guards told us there'd be someone coming over the pass. You'll stay with the watchmen at the children's camp.'

I was surprised but, tired and glad at the prospect of shelter, could think of no immediate reason to object. The camp – such as it was – lay in a fold in the hills: about thirty dilapidated huts in a sea of long grass and brambles. Two janitors, Anatoly and Sergei, lived in a *vagonchik* near the entrance. They were Kuban Cossacks from Nevinnomyssk, an industrial city near Stavropol, seventy miles to the north. Every autumn, they travelled here and stayed through to spring, Anatoly explained, to protect the huts from being stolen. There was no electricity and no running water. During winter, the snow reached to their waists. In the summer, they went home, and children from their city came on subsidized holidays to the camp.

'Did you say stolen?' The camp was miles from the nearest village, and the huts were mouldy prefabs.

'Oh yes,' said Anatoly. 'If it weren't for us, someone would have pinched the lot by now.'

Inside the *vagonchik*, drops of condensation fell hissing on an iron stove in the middle of the floor. There was just enough room to sit on one of the beds on either side of it without burning one's knees. This was how they spent the winter, melting pans of snow and eking out their supplies of potatoes and dried meat, like scientists at the North Pole.

Anatoly and Sergei had visitors: two border guards, one with a Kalashnikov in his lap. The five of us squeezed into the tiny space. The guests were polite and professed not to know of me. I could not tell if the FSB was monitoring my journey, or if these defenders of the frontier were being genuinely obliging. Perhaps both. In any case, they were not impeding my progress.

CENTRAL

When the guards had gone, Anatoly served lumps of salted pork fat and beetroot soup by the stove. Drops of sweat fell from my forehead into the bowl. Anatoly saw me notice pictures of half-naked women pinned above the beds. He laughed richly. 'This is how we live, Tom,' he said. 'Two Cossacks, alone, with tarts on the walls.'

I had thought him surly, but really he was droll. Anatoly was the senior of the two. Sergei wore a blue tracksuit and had a black eye, which gave him a browbeaten look. Anatoly had a shaven head, a bushy moustache and the bearing of a true Cossack. He wore camouflage trousers and the striped blue-and-white vest of a paratrooper. He reminded me of a Cossack ataman I had met in the city of Mineralnye Vody a few years earlier. The ataman sat at a desk under a picture of his forebears: a copy of Ilya Repin's painting of the Zaporozhian Cossacks writing to tell the Turkish sultan they would not submit to his demands ('You Babylonian scullion, Macedonian wheelwright, brewer of Jerusalem, goat-fucker of Alexandria...'). The ataman's body looked hard as a tree, and he spoke in clipped, declarative sentences. In the First Chechen War, he had served with a Cossack unit that he said was later disbanded for being too brutal: a unique distinction in that welter of depravity. Anatoly had the same straight back and brusque manner as the ataman.

The Cossacks are often antisemites and have wrought their own special breed of terror over the centuries. They are victims too. Large numbers of them, just like the highland nations, suffered persecution at the hands of the Soviets. After the Bolshevik Revolution, Cossacks in Nevinnomyssk – Sergei and Anatoly's home town – had joined the White Army to fight the Reds during the civil war that lasted until 1923. In the wake of defeat, thousands were executed, while many more succumbed to disease and starvation as their land was collectivized.

Above the door in the *vagonchik*, Anatoly had pasted a portrait of Vladimir Lenin with the letters 'VOR' underneath. 'Vozhd *oktyabrskoy revolyutsii*,' said Anatoly, smirking. Chief of the October Revolution. Yet the acronym spelled a word in Russian, and he knew it: vor, or thief.

To the left was a photograph of Joseph Stalin. 'Know your enemy by face,' said Anatoly. He pointed to the sole hero of the triptych, on the right. It was Alexander Suvorov, the brilliant eighteenth-century Russian general, in full ceremonial dress. 'A master tactician and a gentleman,' he said.

Anatoly and Sergei were repairing the huts in the camp, for the children from Nevinnomyssk would soon arrive for their holiday, and the two of them would go home. They found me a hut with a melanin bed and only a thin brown streak of damp on the ceiling. Once more, I fell into exhausted and grateful sleep.

Anatoly woke me at 6 a.m. He had promised to put me on the right track for the next pass. He was wearing a camouflage cap and overcoat to match his trousers, a pair of gigantic black boots and a knapsack. Fine binoculars hung around his neck, and in his right hand he held a staff. He looked formidable.

I pulled on my socks and threw my things into my pack. Anatoly strode down the track, planting his feet firmly in the mud. 'The country is going up the arse,' he said happily as we motored along the valley. 'The Jews and the magnates have pillaged everything. A pensioner gets three thousand roubles a month. Do you call that money?'

The fate of pensioners was a concern I could get behind, but

I didn't push back at the comments about the Jews, falling guiltily silent, too cowardly to confront the prejudice when I knew we were about to say goodbye.

We arrived at Krasny Karachay, a hamlet at the confluence of the Aksaut and a stream called the Marka. It was deserted save for three or four homes. Anatoly marched up to a door and bashed on it. 'Owner!' he roared. After some minutes, a bleary-eyed Karachay in boxer shorts opened the door and squinted at us with trepidation. Asked for directions, he pointed dumbly along the stream. 'Work-shy, this lot,' grumbled Anatoly loudly as we moved on. 'They could sleep all day.'

The stream gushed from a steep-sided glen with the path tight at its bank. At a footbridge, we stopped to wish each other well. Anatoly gave me a pulverizing handshake and said: 'Go with God.' When I looked back a few moments later, he was gazing through his binoculars into the crown of a tree.

7

High Caucasus

Slowly and with some apprehension, I was approaching Elbrus, the dead volcano which rises – massive, domed – a third of the way along the Greater Caucasus.

Sochi lay about a hundred miles behind me, although the walking distance, with twists and turns and detours, had worked out much greater. Here in the highlands, mileage meant little – it was the loss and gain of altitude that ruled my days. Ascents and descents from one valley to the next were getting bigger. The path from Krasny Karachay climbed high on the right side of the canyon, with the river roaring deep below in its bed. I stumbled over roots and damp rocks, feeling short of sleep.

After a couple of hours, the walls of the canyon retreated, the path fell and a bridge crossed to a meadow studded with boulders. To the north, ribs of rock slanted across a brutish ridge. Rags of cloud hung in the sky and three huge birds – griffon vultures, I later discovered – passed overhead, their tattered wings mowing through the air, vvvvvvv!

In two days, I crossed two passes, my head always tugged to the right by sights of the high peaks, resplendent in their mantles of snow. Once I got lost in a pine forest, and near the small town of Teberda, wardens with guns detained me for not having a permit to

149

walk through the nature reserve surrounding it (we disagreed over the boundary). The wardens took pity, withholding a fine and letting me stay for free for a night in a lodge near their headquarters.

On the first pass, a *pastukh* in knee-high leather boots was studying the horizon through binoculars. 'I've lost two mares,' he said. 'Probably been rustled.' The next day, ambling down a track where clouds of white butterflies sucked at my boots, I was amazed to see a Bactrian camel standing beside a cottage. It looked happy, if somewhat perplexed, in this alpine setting. The owner told me he had brought the creature from Astrakhan, the dry steppe country by the mouth of the Volga. 'Just for the beauty of it,' he said.

At three thousand metres, a thick cornice overhung the lee side of the second pass and, through a cowl of cloud, white cumuli crashed like airships on a distant sunlit ridge. In good weather, Elbrus would have been visible. Now it was cut off from sight. The cloud closed in, cutting visibility. I scrambled down a fault in the cornice, my feet and hands skidding on its icy surface, then set my compass to east and began to move down, following a tiny stream capped with a crust of snow.

Below the cloud, huge droplets of water began to pound the earth. A tremendous clap of thunder broke directly overhead, and a bolt of lightning crashed across a screen of red crags to my left. I began to trot, feeling very exposed. Should I ditch my trekking pole? I wondered. Will it attract the lightning? No, no, I need it in case I get attacked by dogs. I moved jerkily downhill, my feet searching for grip on loose stones and wet grass. A hysterical laugh burst from my mouth. I'm on a bare mountainside in the middle of an electric storm with a four-foot rod of metal! As the rain sluiced over my back, I slipped off the wrist strap and held the pole horizontally. Another idea came to mind as I ran, the straps of my pack straining against my shoulders: Stop and sit on your rucksack. I had read once that the synthetic fabric can help insulate against a discharge of electricity. But now that advice seemed as stupid as playing dead in front of a bear. Just get off the mountain.

Little by little, the gradient eased, and a man and a dog came into view. I slowed to a walk, the fear receding. The man was hunched against the pelting rain. He had his back to me and was walking towards a farm a few hundred metres away, the bedraggled dog at his heel. I had reached Daut, an old Karachay hamlet that Anatoly had mentioned. Half a dozen stone cottages pegged the corners of meadows that slipped down to a river. Only a few people lived here now, in the summer months, Anatoly had said. Separating the fields were fences made of slender pines still covered in bark. The man with the dog looked startled when I called out. There was no time for pleasantries. I asked if there was a building where I could take shelter.

'I would take you home, but I have guests,' he cried above the downpour, recovering quickly from his shock. 'You can stay in that cowshed.' He pointed to the corner of a field. 'It's mine and it's empty.' I shouted my thanks and ran to the shed.

What a haven it was, in that moment of drenching. Straw packed the cavity under the roof and the walls were made of boulders sealed with dry manure. A sweet bovine odour met my nose. Against the wall stood two wheels from a truck, some bits of an engine, a tub of salt for cows and a shovel.

My waterproofs had soaked through, wetting the rest of my clothes. I stripped off, hung them on nails and pulled out underwear, trousers and a shirt from a sealed dry bag in my rucksack. The map that I kept in a plastic case inside my shirt had turned into a soggy pulp at one edge; fortunately a corner of territory that I would not be passing through.

CENTRAL

The rain was softening as dusk gathered. Over the waist-high door of the byre, the sky turned a cool grey, then mauve, then cerulean. Here and there by the fields were little circular patches of stones, the remains of long-abandoned homes that had collapsed into the grass.

Places like Daut, I knew, had a tragic history.

By the early 1920s, after the Bolshevik victory in the Russian civil war, the entire Caucasus was incorporated into the USSR. Integral to Lenin's new policy of korenizatsiya (indigenization or, literally, 'putting down roots') was the idea of giving ethnic groups a degree of control over their own territory. In the North Caucasus, a series of new republics were created. The Turkic Karachays were grouped with the Circassians in Karachay-Cherkessia, the republic I was now crossing, and the Balkars with the Kabardians, in what is today the next republic along, Kabardino-Balkaria.

Korenizatsiya meant promoting national elites, teaching native languages and institutionalizing ethnicity in the state apparatus. The idea was to differentiate the Soviet empire from the tsarist one by favouring non-Russians, in a kind of affirmative action. This, it was hoped, would inoculate them against more virulent forms of nationalism and dissuade them from seeking ties to troublemaking diasporas abroad. Yet in the end, the policy ran contrary to a greater Soviet desire: transforming an agrarian society into a workers' paradise, in which national characteristics should eventually be obliterated and traditional cultures consigned to an unjust past.

As Stalin moved to consolidate his rule in the 1930s, he decided rapid industrial growth was now the priority. Ethnic interests should be subordinated to economic efficiency. Korenizatsiya was reined in. The USSR had stepped down the road of terror;

purges began of national elites, and collectivization took hold. Karachays and other Caucasus peoples were especially incensed at the expropriation of horses, a symbol of their virility and martial prowess. Armed revolts ensued. Increasingly, the non-Russian peoples were viewed as dangerous and subversive; as sources of bourgeois nationalism. Such chauvinism was buoyed by patriotic sentiments at the outbreak of the Second World War, as well as by fears about potential fifth columnists for foreign powers. The scene was set for the deportations. In 1943 and 1944, the Karachays, the Balkars, the Ingush and the Chechens were all evicted from their homelands. Only much-depleted groups of survivors would be allowed to return home in the late 1950s, years after Stalin's death. Once-thriving settlements like Daut never regained their vigour.

Darkness was falling. Once, I thought, as I leaned on the door of the cowshed, the sights and sounds of village life would have filled this valley: shouting children, a clanking pail, perhaps the ring of a blacksmith's hammer as he beat the last horseshoe of the day. Now, only two lights glimmered across the fields.

I found some planks on which to lay my sleeping bag between the drips, and fell asleep to the sound of rats scampering in the roof.

Next day, I stashed my dry clothes in the pack and donned the clammy ones I had hung on the walls. It was an old SAS tip for jungle travel that I was trying to follow: always keep one outfit dry, never give in and get the spare set wet, otherwise you might get dangerously cold and weak.

The first half-hour in the damp outfit was unpleasant; after that, it became bearable, and then the sensation was forgotten as my body warmed. A loggers' track struck confidently uphill in a wood next to a stream which fed the Daut river. This was surely the way to the Karachay-Aush pass. I spent a happy hour climbing through the trees, glad to be making progress. Only then, with a sense of inevitability, did the track begin to fade. A few more steps, and it dissolved into the forest. I was too stubborn to retrace my steps. The alternative was a shortcut across a succession of steep gullies that were thick with saplings and rhododendron bushes. It was exhausting work. In a filthy mood, I gave up and headed straight up a gully, floundering through undergrowth. It didn't make sense to be getting so frustrated at these detours. I was not in a hurry. Yet I was concerned about burning energy, and perhaps a fear lurked: a fear of getting irretrievably lost, or tumbling through a crack in the rocks, never to be found again.

Above the tree line, it was clear I had taken the wrong route and veered a long way to the south. A chute of scree and ice severed the incline between me and the pass. I was venturing onto the scree when the stones began to slither uncontrollably under my feet. The chute was a vertiginous slope back to the Daut river, three hundred metres below. This is madness, I thought, and retreated as quickly as I could, stones clacking away from my heels. On your own, it was easy to lose concentration and blunder into such a moment without even thinking what you were doing. Sometimes, I wished I was not alone. A companion could ward against faulty decisions. I had expected to come across more people on foot in the mountains: down in the valleys, there was life, but higher up, I was meeting almost no one besides the occasional shepherd. A slip or a broken ankle here, especially off the beaten paths, could spell disaster. The fact I was walking unaccompanied had surprised several of the people I did encounter. Besides the potential danger, there was a cultural factor. Stopping alone at a Soviet campsite near Minsk in the 1980s, the writer

High Caucasus

Colin Thubron had been asked by a perplexed receptionist: 'Are you a group?' To travel without comrades was still considered odd.

Casting around, I found a way over rocky ground braided with snow above the scree. Across the valley, through a mile of thin air, a stream sprang straight from a cliff. In all, it took five hours to reach the saddle. Once again, Elbrus was not my reward. Low cloud blocked the view to the east.

With nothing left to drink, it was a thirsty descent across bare slopes until I found a rivulet in some mud and filled my canteen. I had decided to sterilize all my drinking water with iodine tablets after discovering the corpse of a sheep in a stream. The resulting cocktail reminded me of the taste in my mouth after swimming lessons at school, where our janitor lowered chlorine into the pool in a bucket on a piece of string.

Further down, horses grazed and two eagles revelled on a thermal. I sat on a rock for lunch, hanging my shirt on a thistle to dry. I was living off salami sausages and bread, a carrier bag full of peanuts and raisins, and occasional gifts of cheese from the shepherds. Two of the salamis I had bought three weeks earlier in Sochi were still in reserve in my pack. They required a daily ritual: scraping off a film of mould with my knife.

Far below, a depression made the shape of an elbow where one river met a larger one and the second flowed north, emboldened. At the confluence of the two torrents flashed the roofs of a village, named on my map as Uchkulan. To the east, I could see Khurzuk, another Karachay settlement, at the mouth of a gorge that led towards Elbrus, which was still concealed by cloud.

Uchkulan lay across a bridge at the foot of the hill. There was a dirt square with no one in it save for two old men in trilbies sitting on a bench in the lee of a house. They called out a greeting. One of them introduced himself as Seypul. He was swigging from a bottle of cheap port. 'Sit with us a while,' he said, pouring me a drink in a plastic cup that he produced from his pocket. I took a seat on the bench; the space between it and the house was knee deep in empty port bottles. 'We sit here every day,' said Seypul, by way of explanation. 'I'm a pensioner.'

We got talking about the deportations in 1943. When Seypul said he was seventy-three years old, I realized he was speaking from personal experience. 'Come and stay the night at mine,' he said. 'I'll tell you the whole story.'

It was not late in the day, and I could easily have pushed on. But these were the kind of meetings I craved, to help me peel back another layer of understanding. I accepted immediately.

On the way to Seypul's house, we dropped in at the local shop and I bought some chocolates as a gift for his family and a bottle of port for him. 'Maybe, um, maybe we'll just get a second one?' he enquired politely. 'Of course,' I said, and bought another.

Seypul puffed and wheezed as he led the way to his home. The roofs of the houses in his lane were crested with aluminium fretwork; his own was decorated with silhouettes of deer and eagles. Between the houses on the lane, facing onto the street, were little enclosures made from planks: for livestock, it seemed, although none was occupied. Each home had high gates with a yard behind. Two single-storey buildings stood in Seypul's yard: one for him, his wife and his younger, unmarried son; the other for his elder son and wife. There was a barn with a hayloft, a shed with a cow inside and a garage for his old Volga car, its bonnet coated in dust.

In the kitchen sat Seypul's wife, Asya, in the uniform of women her age: print dress and headscarf. She welcomed me but kept in the background, tending their latest grandchild, a baby boy wrapped in swaddling cloths. Two little girls, also grandchildren, flitted in and out, giggling.

High Caucasus

Evening had come. Asya served us soup and ayran, and Seypul switched on an old television. The end of a Michael Caine movie fuzzed the screen, the actor's Cockney strains rising occasionally above the hubbub of Russian translation. Seypul poured us glasses of the port, which tasted like alcoholic cough syrup. When the film was finished, he cleared his throat and said: 'The Germans came in the autumn of forty-two.' He had begun his story.

The Nazis, I knew, had invaded the Soviet Union in June 1941, and by August of the following year, they were already in the Caucasus. 'They didn't kill anyone, not a single Karachay,' said Seypul. 'They blew up the bridges when they left, but they didn't touch us. They billeted in the school, stood their guns together and got to work. They built roads. The officers were all Germans, but a lot of the ordinary soldiers were Romanians. They had harmonicas, which they played to us children. I was seven years old.'

To some highlanders, run ragged by Communist attempts to collectivize their precious livestock, the invading force had appeared to offer a different way of life. Seypul passed a hand across his ruddy face. 'My father was a carpenter,' he said. 'The Germans asked him to work for them, but Father refused. He was illiterate but he was a clever man. When an officer came looking for him, he made himself scarce for the day. He knew that Soviet power would be vengeful. He was right. When the Germans left in 1943 and the Soviets returned, they executed a lot of people. They killed an old man just for wearing a worn-out coat the Germans had given him out of pity.' Seypul wiped his mouth. 'Fucking bastards. An old man. For what?'

The sympathy of some Karachays towards the invading Germans had been, in Stalin's eyes, a treachery that tainted the entire nation. In November of 1943, a cohort of troops from the NKVD secret police arrived in Uchkulan. 'For three days, they sat around

157

their fires at night,' Seypul recalled. 'A group of them came to our home. My brother was away with the Red Army, fighting in Ukraine. The troops read a letter that he had sent home, and then they checked for weapons and took the sharp knives from the cupboard. They told us we were being deported.'

Soon, the villagers were ordered out of their houses and loaded into Studebaker trucks. These were American vehicles given to the Soviet Union under the US lend-lease programme to help fight the Nazis – now deployed in this vile act of domestic tyranny. Similar scenes were playing out across the mountains of Karachay: every family being wrenched from every home; seventy thousand people on the move.

'There were seven families in our truck,' Seypul went on. 'We left everything behind. I still remember the numbers: seventy-three goats, twenty-four sheep, two horses, one donkey. All the potatoes. Our house. They let my father take only his tools.'

Could he really recall such details? I felt sure these numbers were true, but most likely they had been passed down from parents to children. The deportation was a moment of immense trauma in the history of the Karachay people. For a tiny ethnic group like this, a droplet in Russia's ocean of 140 million citizens, the crusade against forgetting was one way of affirming nationhood.

At a train station, the Karachays from Uchkulan were loaded into cattle wagons. It was very cramped. They were given no food. People shared what little they had managed to take with them. 'We travelled for seventeen days in the carriages,' said Seypul. 'We passed through Stalingrad, in ruins. I saw Soviet soldiers with machine guns guarding captured Germans. It was very cold. The prisoners wore scarves around their heads. My sisters had dressed me in their extra clothes, several layers, so they didn't have to carry them.'

There were no toilets in the wagons, he said. Some of the men managed to punch holes through the floor so people could relieve themselves. A stench filled the trains. The old and infirm began to die. At occasional stops, the doors were thrown open and guards distributed meagre rations. The dead were removed and left by the tracks.

Finally, the train stopped and the Karachays got out. 'We didn't know where we were,' said Seypul. 'There were people every-where with faces like monkeys. Later, someone told us we were in Frunze, in Kyrgyzstan.'

Monkeys? Ah, he meant the Kyrgyz. I bit my lip.

Seypul's family was put together in one room: him, his parents, his three brothers and two sisters. 'It was very hard,' he said, topping up our glasses. 'There were many of us Karachays living in squalor. In the beginning, six or seven people died every day, from hunger, from disease. My father made their coffins. The Kyrgyz treated us as if we were cannibals. Things got a little better when we started to get some corn. Eventually, my father found work. He saved money and bought us an old cottage.'

The family's fate was repeated for thousands of others in the months to come. The Karachays were only the first to be deported. In February and March 1944, the Balkars, Ingush and Chechens would be sent away in the same fashion. There was no promise of when, if ever, they would be allowed back. They went into exile believing they might never see their homes again.

'It was Stalin, the serpent. He was to blame,' said Seypul. 'And Beria, the bastard. They scattered us like seeds all over Central Asia.

'Stalin wanted to create a greater Georgia. After we were deported, Svans and Georgians came over the mountains and occupied our homes. The Georgians kept pigs here. They burned down our mosque. They brought gravestones by aeroplane from

Georgia. Gravestones with Georgian inscriptions on them. They placed them over the graves of our ancestors. They wanted to pretend they had always been here. But they ran away when they heard we were returning.'

How much of this was true and how much embroidery, I didn't know, but the fact that Seypul felt fury was beyond doubt. He was shaking at the memory of it.

'My people were finally allowed back in 1957,' he said. 'I came home to Uchkulan in 1960 – to the village where I was born – after I finished my military service in Azerbaijan. Karachays had begun serving in the army again in 1955.'

'And your parents?' I was afraid to hear the answer.

'They came back, too.' He gave a smile. 'They made it home.'

I felt relief for these people I'd never known. And then?

'I found a job as an ambulance driver. I got married. Later, I worked for the local administration. All my life, I worked here in Uchkulan as a driver. Now I'm retired. I walk down the road. I sit on the bench. I drink a little. The port helps my high blood pressure.'

Besides the two sons, he and Asya had five daughters, all married. 'You are a great survivor and you've had a successful life,' I said.

'Yes,' said Seypul, rubbing the stubble on his cheek as if he had never contemplated the question. 'I suppose you are right.' And we opened the second bottle of port.

Seypul's story of the deportation got me thinking about what it would really be like to be pulled from your home – from your homeland – and transplanted to another, unfamiliar place, unsure if you could ever return. The human suffering was colossal, of course. But it was the abandonment of the livestock that came to mind as I lay down to sleep that night on a divan in Seypul's living room.

The fact his family remembered the exact number of animals they were made to leave behind was surely more than bean-counting. He and his relatives would have known every animal, every curl of a horn, every trembling flank and misshapen hoof.

That idea was something familiar to me.

My father, Rob, was born in Norfolk, in the same playground of damp fields and oozing ditches that was the scene of my own childhood. In the mid-1970s, he and my mother, Chrissie, helped organize the Barsham Fairs; hugely successful 'alternative living' fairs that were a mix of improvised theatre, music and medieval shtick. They were hippie fairs, really, but my father did not identify with that label. He came from a different mould to the weed-puffing longhairs who flocked to Barsham. His father was from a yeoman farming family who lived near Norwich. As a young man, Rob had become friendly with Adrian Bell, the Suffolk author who wrote vividly of his experiences running a smallholding near the Waveney after the First World War. At Low Tree Farm, the decaying old house where I grew up, my father set out to emulate Adrian, whose son, Martin Bell, became the BBC war reporter and MP famous for his white suits.

Sometimes I accompanied my father when he went shooting on the marshes. The first sign of mallards flying through the gloaming was the whistling of their wings. We would cock our ears and squint at the sky. There! And he would move the gun through a short, perfect arc to lock on the target. Once, in the winter, he shot a wigeon and it fell wounded in the Waveney. My father said we could not leave it that way. With a sharp intake of breath, he stepped out into the water. It swirled around his waist and he grabbed the bird and climbed out, breaking its neck with a swift movement. Ice tinkled in the folds of his jacket as we walked home down the loke. I felt excited and proud. It was not sport: we did not have much money, and everything that Rob shot, we cooked and ate, using the tips of our tongues to push the shotgun pellets out of our mouths and leaving them on the side of the plate.

My father was a schoolteacher, but his real passion was rare breeds of livestock. In an outbuilding at the edge of one of our meadows, he kept a Gloucester Old Spot sow, a Tamworth and one other pig. Three Red Poll cattle, the colour of rust, grazed behind the house, alongside a flock of thirty-odd sheep. Among these were a trio of Soays from the Scottish Highlands; agile creatures like wound springs that repeatedly leapt free across the dykes and fled with suicidal intent towards the buzzing traffic on the high road.

Rob is not a sentimental man. He named two of the pigs Pork and Bacon, and most of the animals would eventually go for a quick death at the local slaughterhouse, returning as sausages or chops for our freezer. But in their lifetimes, they were well looked after and cherished. We herded the Red Polls to our grassiest meadow like solicitous stewards guiding cars to the parking field at the Norfolk Show. When a couple of our haughty Teeswater sheep were afflicted by a skin complaint that made them shed their fleeces, my parents bought cardigans in a jumble sale and dressed them in those.

How would we have felt if we had been forced simply to let our animals loose, or – worse – leave them haltered in their barn, perhaps to die in agony of thirst and hunger? For the Karachays, herders and farmers to their bones, such an idea must have been unthinkable. The state was not only stripping them of a livelihood: it was compelling them to inflict suffering. They had no way of predicting the fate of their animals; how soon usurpers might come to adopt them. Without protection, the sheep would soon fall prey to wolves.

I tried to imagine that final day in Uchkulan in November 1943: the frantic collecting of a few, pitiful belongings, the restless huffing of cows in the byre, the bawling of babies as families trudged towards the Studebakers.

Perhaps the seven-year-old Seypul was excited at the hullabaloo, but he must also have felt the distress of his parents and older siblings as they gave up their home. I could see his father taking a last look into the stall of a much-loved horse; the animal's backward-eyeball glance, a wobble in its legs, sensing fear. What a terrible thing it must have been, that moment of departure.

At dawn came the sound of Seypul clearing his throat and hawking in the yard. He saw me off at the gate.

There is something delicious in early starts: the vapour on your breath, the silence, the feeling of lighting out for adventure while others are still snoring, witless, in their beds. As I sneaked out of Uchkulan, I remembered the opening to that wonderful book by Edith Durham, High Albania: 'It was Friday, May 8, 1908, and Scutari was asleep – even the dogs were still curled up tight in the gutters – when we started on foot and purposely oozed out of the town by the wrong road in the grey dawning.'

A fleece of cloud hung low in the valley. It was a five-mile march down an asphalt road to Khurzuk, but only one truck and one car came past. Khurzuk, with its traditional Karachay architecture, was the most unusual village I had come across. There were many barns and outhouses, crude affairs made from giant timbers. Each had a foot or two of earth on the roof, with a mane of grass on top. These buildings were in use – I could hear cows shifting inside and there was churned mud at their doors – but most had slumped under their own weight so they looked like galleons sinking into a swamp. The houses, too, had tree trunks built into their structure. They were sturdy and well kept, with brightly painted walls.

I saw no one – it was still early – and slipped down a path into the Ullukhurzuk gorge. Today, I hoped to finally catch a glimpse of Elbrus. It was less than twenty miles away now, and beginning to fill my mind. The pass I would have to cross to get around the mountain without a huge detour was the highest yet, and I wondered how thick the snow might be.

The path skipped back and forth on footbridges across the frothing Ullukhurzuk stream. Soon, I was veering right on the bank of a tributary, the Bitiktebe, down a green valley with conifers on the southern slope. A *pastukh* snoozed under a tree, his flock cropping the grass around him.

By lunchtime, the cloud had returned, and heavy rain had begun to fall. A shepherd's *kosh*, a log cabin, appeared by the side of the track. It was unlocked. Inside, there was a sleeping platform covered in loose hay, a bench and a window, but no sign of an occupant. The owner would forgive me in such weather, I thought. I stayed all day, glad of shelter, as the rain slashed the mud outside.

Towards evening, the downpour eased. Outside in the coolness, I thrust my hands into my pockets. There was no human or animal in sight. A rickety sheep pen stood by the *kosh*. Beyond it, perhaps a mile away, rents were appearing in the cloud that obscured the head of the valley. Through one, a bunched shoulder of rock and snow appeared, then – as if emerging from behind a tattered curtain – the whole colossus of a mountain, glaciers plunging from black crags below its double-headed peak.

High Caucasus

Elbrus! For scores of miles to the north, its white humps loomed across the plain; approaching through the mountains had denied me a glimpse until I was right at its feet. The plug of a long-extinct volcano, it stood proud of the big peaks at the centre of the Greater Caucasus chain. I was not to go to the summit, but the sight of the mountain made me gulp. Below its vast bulk, a farm building at the head of the valley with a smear of yellow flowers behind it was the tiniest of specks. The sun was setting, backlighting a last strip of cumulus into a corset of cabaret pink across the mountain's midriff, then burnishing the high slopes by the summit.

Next morning, I woke to the fragrance of my hay mattress, thinking myself for a moment back on the farm in Norfolk. I shouldered my pack. The kosh door creaked shut. Blue sky framed Elbrus, and all was silent. At the valley's end, a faint path struck up a spur covered in clumps of wiry grass; an earlier traveller had left tiny stone-men to mark the way. It was a long climb up that eroded hillside, across coverings of scree, to the shoulder of Elbrus. On the pass, a chill wind blew over chunks of granite edged with lichen and snow. At 3,700 metres, this was the highest point I would reach on the journey. What a relief: there was no cap of icy snow, nothing to stop me proceeding down the other side. I pulled on a hat and a fleece and stopped for a while to savour the view. Below, to the south and to the west, from where I had come, the Greater Caucasus chain reached to the horizon – hundreds of tops like choppy water frozen in motion, pin-sharp in the morning air. It was a ravishing sight. Here coated in snow, there of bare ground and rock, rank upon rank of mountains seemed to act in concert, flinging their sharpest peaks and ridges at downy puffs of cloud. Above me, to my right, hung the icefalls of Elbrus, its bowed head also tufted by cloud. The icefalls were coruscating in the sunlight, an unfathomable distance away – near, far, I could not tell – but hypnotic in their splendour. Wisps of cirrus occupied the sky above. Each detail seemed cut in glass. I wanted to stamp the scene in my mind. Would I see something so magnificent ever again? Was this Herzog's glimpse of the sublime, a moment that made all those before and after fade? I could do with such a paling of the past if the nightmare of the falling woman was to retreat altogether.

Well, that seemed fanciful, however fine the surroundings. I had not suddenly forgotten Beslan, nor did I believe my life would be all downhill from now on. But there was a feeling that the time in the mountains was beginning to take effect, blanching my harsher memories of the Caucasus by sheer force of light and warmth and beauty.

I was far from the only one to experience such rapture. In the 1860s, British climbers had become the first to desert the Alps in search of virgin summits in the Caucasus. Pre-eminent was Douglas William Freshfield, an Oxford graduate who, although only in his early twenties, had already bagged several first ascents in Italy and France. These mountaineers were attracted by the giant mountains between the Klukhor pass west of Elbrus and Mount Kazbek, another extinct volcano 140 miles to the east.

A tall young man with a broad upper lip that in later life would be colonized by a bushy white moustache, Freshfield found to his delight that the Caucasus was 'a range surpassing the Alps by two thousand feet in the average height of its peaks, abounding in noble scenery and picturesque inhabitants'. He was officially the first mountaineer to ascend Elbrus, with two other English-men, in 1868. (Freshfield scorned a Russian general's claim to have sent a Circassian guide to the top four decades earlier.) His party was accompanied by the famed Chamonix guide François

Joseph Devouassoud, a 'knight-errant of the glacier-cleaving blade', as Freshfield described him in a bad poem. For these experienced mountaineers, Elbrus proved relatively easy to scale, albeit in a tempest that left the group beating their fingers to preserve them from frostbite. Incredibly, two Balkar porters reached the eastern summit with the party, seemingly impervious to the cold in their sheepskin cloaks. The party's reward was something extraordinary. 'I never saw any group of mountains which bore so well being looked down on as the great peaks that stand over the sources of the Tcherek and Tchegem,' Freshfield wrote of the view towards Kazbek. 'The Pennines from Mont Blanc look puny in comparison with Koschtantau and his neighbours from Elbruz. The Caucasian groups are finer, and the peaks sharper, and there was a suggestion of unseen depth in the trenches separating them, that I have never noticed so forcibly in any Alpine view.'

Freshfield would return on two more expeditions, crossing the main chain eleven times in total by eight different routes. He was proud to have beaten a path for other climbers, taking, as he saw it, 'the first step towards converting the Prison of Prometheus into a new Playground for his descendants'.

More Britons followed, but there was a sad coda to this new era of mountaineering. In late August 1888, William Donkin, a chemistry lecturer and fine landscape photographer, set out with a young climber named Harry Fox and two Swiss guides to climb Koshtan-Tau, the fourth-highest summit in the range. The whole party disappeared without trace.

Freshfield and another climber named Clinton Dent led a search party the next year in an attempt to establish what had happened. They felt sure their friends had died in the snows, but rumours circulated that brigands had killed the climbers. A local man was said to have been found with a wound possibly inflicted by an ice axe. Fox's diary, recovered from base camp, suggested a villager had taken an exceptional interest in the climbers' planned route. There was also a cryptic reference to Donkin practising firing his pistol at 'imaginary enemies'.

Miraculously, Freshfield and his team found the expedition's last camp spot and, climbing to a pass above it, surmised that the group had likely perished as they crossed treacherous crags towards the summit: a conclusion that exonerated the locals.

The Caucasus seduced Freshfield and his followers with some of the same enchantments that seized Pushkin and Lermontov, among them the peacocky locals and a thrill of danger. Most of all, they found a sublime beauty that struck them as both pure and poignant; a vestige of a disappearing world and a place of solace in the face of relentless Progress. On the pass, Freshfield and his companions carefully pulled to pieces a small cairn to see if it held a note left by their climbing comrades. They found none, but inserted a memorandum of their own. Reflecting for a moment in the crystalline air on the pass, they looked down at the huge snow reservoirs and clustered peaks below them.

'Every detail was distinct as on a mapman's model, yet the whole was vast and vague, wonderful and strange, creating an impression of immeasurable shining space, of the Earth as it might first appear to a visitant from some other planet,' Freshfield later wrote.

> The splendour of nature on this day of days seemed not out of harmony with the sadness of our errand. It affected the mind as a solemn and sympathetic Music. While I gazed, four white butterflies circled round the little monument, and again fluttered off. An ancient Greek would have found a symbol in the incident.

*

High Caucasus

Below Elbrus, my heady thoughts were curtailed by reality. A moraine led down to the tongue of the Ulluchiran glacier, which I needed to cross. I had been on glaciers before, in the Rockies, some fifteen years earlier. Signposted, photographed, crawling with tourists, they had not seemed so ominous, despite solemn Canadian warnings about crevasses.

The Ulluchiran was cut by channels between yellow troughs of snow. With trepidation, I ventured onto its surface. On harder stretches, there was an unearthly creaking underfoot, and through fissures came the sound of water rushing deep below. Not for the first time, I recognized the inadequacy of my mountain experience. Was this dangerous? Was I a daft amateur, risking my life? Or was it nothing, a trifle, just what you should expect? I simply didn't know. As so often, there was not a soul in sight to ask. Within a couple of minutes, I had lost my nerve and was retreating to firm ground at the edge of the moraine.

Stinging with irritation, I took a detour up a bank of ice and stones, and then slalomed down a steep slope of scree to the stream that gave forth from the toe of the glacier. Looking back, that descent was probably riskier than the crossing I had embarked on and then abandoned.

In any case, there was a compensation: the Irakhiksyrt plateau, an airy roof skirting Elbrus, with a ridge to its north acting like a parapet. It was a pleasure to amble across the flat grass after days of careful foot-planting, my steps alerting ground squirrels that squeaked in alarm and fled to their burrows.

At dusk, a zigzag path dropped from the plateau past boulders and sods of earth that had detached themselves from the hillside. A gorge opened out where a bridge had been destroyed in a flood. Here was a collection of huts. It was Dzhily-Su, a makeshift 'people's resort' to which trippers came to drink from and bathe

CENTRAL

in springs of Narzan, a mineral water that was bottled and sold all over Russia. I took a bed in a dormitory where mice ran free and I was the only guest. Two Russian men were camping nearby. You could reach the springs by jeep, and they had travelled from Kislovodsk (Bitter Waters), the spa town on the plain to the north. There, you could sample water laced with sulphates and potassium that flowed from spigots in an elegant tasting gallery. Here, things were more rudimentary. By a waterfall blown sideways by wind, we drank aerated water with a whiff of rotten eggs using a mug fixed to the end of a pipe. A ramshackle latrine was a short sprint away in the event of sudden bowel movements. Fortunately, we had none. At another spring, fringed with orange deposits of iron and bubbling like a witch's cauldron, we sipped again.

The next morning, the Russians drained a bathing pool that was aerated by gas from a vent in the hillside. Once the pool was empty, we stood inside on a plank, fully clothed, as the gas puffed around our loins. 'This is the best way of all; it penetrates right to your bones,' one of the men said. 'Don't bend down. You'll pass out if you breathe it in.'

Rested after the stop at the springs, I climbed on through a hanging valley to a glen where horses ran in buttercups by an empty kosh and great rotted molars of rock jutted on the opposite ridge. Then, a pass where I floundered through waist-high snow. The reward was another vista of wild peaks. Descending past a spur scored with parallel tracks like contour lines, I saw a pastukh and his dog below me. They were trying to herd half a dozen horses and a flock of sheep across a stream that joined the river. Each time, the animals moved forward with purpose but peeled back on reaching the water's edge. Finally the dog forced them across.

High Caucasus

When I got down, the *pastukh* was sitting on a rock by the stream, his knees drawn up and his white feet planted on the warm stone. His socks and boots were drying nearby. 'A couple of the smaller lambs got swept away,' he declared. 'I had to run in and grab them. Come to my hut, we'll drink ayran and have some tea.' His name was Khamzat. He was a Balkar – I had crossed the invisible line that ran down through Elbrus, dividing the land of the Karachays from that of their Turkic brothers, the Balkars.

Khamzat called me 'Tomi', which sounded affectionate. He and his brother Khasan lived in a *vagonchik* next to a caravan-sized boulder further up the valley. On the side of the *vagonchik* were painted, in Russian, the words 'Upper Baksan General Headquarters', an image of a wolf and the twin peaks of Elbrus with stars and a crescent moon suspended above them.

Khasan came home, carrying a carbine. He had spent the day searching in vain for two missing ewes and a lamb, while keeping his eye out for a wolf he'd spotted. Khasan was a squatter version of the leggy Khamzat. Both looked tough and limber. The two brothers invited me to stay the night and I accepted readily. The inside of their *vagonchik* was hung with their possessions: a second rifle, a paraffin lamp, head-torches, a ladle, a knife. There was a sleeping platform, a stove, a small table, a calendar of Mecca and an Islamic wall-hanging in gold and green.

Khamzat said his elder brother had been born in Kazakhstan. 'After we were deported, the Kabardians stole our houses, our sheep, our knives. They started calling themselves highlanders, although they never lived here like us, they just grew maize on the plain.' The Jews, the gypsies and the Kabardians were cunning peoples, he said.

From an enamel bowl, we ate slabs of grey meat pulled from a boiled sheep's head and talked late into the night. Khamzat told a story I had trouble following, that I think was about Kabardians using ashes from stoves in abandoned Balkar homes to make soap.

The ski resort on the east side of Elbrus was not so far away, and the brothers had met tourists who passed by on day trips. Some had left behind telescopic walking sticks tipped with shock absorbers. Khamzat thought to entertain the visitors by digging a swimming hole by the river, but the excavator got stuck and had to be pulled out with a tractor. Still, he had several photographs and a flag of the republic of Mordovia that grateful trippers had sent him on returning home. One picture showed an attractive Russian woman in her forties. 'Fuckable, Tomi!' Khamzat declared, slamming the flat palm of his left hand down on top of the closed fist of his right, and grinning. I laughed and thought: All these Russian writers drooling over Caucasian maidens – and here's a Caucasian shepherd yearning for sexy Russian women.

Khamzat was keen to receive a keepsake from me, too. We swapped caps, but I hesitated at his request to give him my knife, a present from Masha, in exchange for his own, which had a faulty blade.

'Tell her you lost it or something,' he said.

'I don't lie to my girlfriend.'

'Quite right,' said Khasan.

'Well, tell her I really asked for it because it would be useful for cleaning sheepskins.'

It felt churlish to refuse. 'OK, she won't mind anyway,' I said. 'She got to like the Balkars and their hospitality when she was down here.'

I told them the story of how Masha, a sports correspondent, had been sent to Elbrus after visiting fans of Moscow's Spartak football club had got into trouble there before a match with a local team. A Spartak fan had been shot in the stomach at the ski resort on the mountain's lower slopes, and his fellow supporters were calling for justice. But Masha heard a different story from the Balkar hotel owners when she arrived. They said a large group of hooligans from the capital had got drunk, chanting xenophobic slogans, smashing up one establishment and attacking the owners, who were forced to defend themselves.

Khamzat was pleased with this uncovering of the truth, and the fact Masha had been well treated by the hotel owners. 'That is our way,' he said. 'If your Masha has any problems with those hooligans, Tomi, tell her we'll come to Moscow and cut them up.'

8

The Third Step

I had wanted to complete the main journey from the Black Sea to the Caspian in one long expedition, but now fate intervened.

Beyond Khamzat and Khasan's *vagonchik*, a good track led down to the Baksan valley, along which ran the main road to Elbrus. As phone reception reappeared, I received a text from Olga, my newspaper's office manager in Moscow: 'Can't prolong your visa and accreditation without you being here with your passport.' These were the papers that I had to get every year from the foreign ministry in order to stay in Russia and work as a correspondent. Naïvely, I had thought that Olga could pick them up on my behalf. It was not to be. I would have to go home and then come back here, to this exact spot, to resume the walk.

Angry at this blow to my plans, I took a bus to the city of Mineralnye Vody on the steppe, then flew back to Moscow. It was three frustrating weeks before I could return. The reunion with Masha was joyful, but I was desperate to continue my journey. I saw little of friends, sequestering myself at home in our flat by the river until the documents were finally ready.

On the flight back to Mineralnye Vody, a young man eyed my boots. 'Are you going hiking?' he said. He was Alim, a Circassian artist who had lived in Germany. 'No way!' he said, once I had explained. 'I'm taking a taxi to Prielbrusye near Elbrus to meet my parents. We'll drop you off on the way.'

In the car, Alim talked of *Xabze*, the code of conduct of the Circassian people; the way it governed all aspects of life, from marriages to blood feuds and treatment of the elderly. '*Xabze* demands honesty and courage and honour,' he said. 'You are not a Circassian, Tom, but you will need all of these to complete your journey.'

I wasn't so sure. By my own assessment, I had winged it so far with timidity, incompetence and the odd white lie.

It was now July, and the sky was incandescent. Alim and his driver left me at the place on the road to which I had descended from the trek around Elbrus. Traipsing north up the Baksan valley that afternoon, I came to Tyrnyauz, a small town with a ruined tungsten mine. My stop for the night was a children's holiday camp, where a cartoon of a toadstool and three girls' names decorated the door of my room. Groups of kids ran shrieking in the corridors and teenagers yakked half the night outside my window.

From Tyrnyauz, a track pushed east into the hills. I camped a night in shoulder-high grass and then reached a village with a loopholed stone defence tower, where a park ranger with a pistol in a holster put me up for the night in a half-built extension to his home. Nearby was a cluster of ancient tombs with octagonal roofs. Sheep squeezed into the tiny black aprons of shadow that they threw, escaping the heat, their sides heaving. A retired schoolteacher told me the tombs were said to be three hundred years old, coinciding with the coming of Islam to Balkaria. Personally, he believed they were older. 'People live long here,' he said. 'One man died recently, he was one hundred and fifteen. His father also lived beyond a hundred. Three centuries is not so many generations with such longevity. But our old people know nothing of who built them.'

It felt good to be on the move again. My legs had loosened in Moscow and the steeper ascents stole my breath.

One afternoon, I lay down for a rest on a slope covered in wild flowers, the hide of a dead horse stretched dry over its whitening bones. The grasses rising high on either side of my body were alive with insects: brilliant green aphids and grasshoppers and flies with iridescent eyes. Unhurried, the aphids trundled up stalks. I cast off my boots and socks, the socks drying stiff as boards as I dozed. When I woke, I thought again of Tolstoy's hero Olenin and the 'strange feeling of causeless joy and love for everything' that overcame him when he found the stag's lair by the Terek, myriad insects and lavish vegetation filling the forest, the sun pouring perpendicular rays on his head as he stepped through a glade. On that slope, baking among the flowers and grasses, I too experienced a moment of bliss, the heat a palliating force.

To my left, when I finally staggered to my feet, ran the cliffs of the Stony ridge, and on the next pass, a shepherd in a leather jerkin sat on a mare, watching his sheep below. His lambskin hat — how could he wear it in this temperature? — was chocolate brown and resembled the roofs of the tombs in the village. He said he was born in Kazakhstan in 1954. His father had fought from 1941 to the end of the war, almost reaching Berlin before getting injured. He returned home in 1946, knowing nothing of the forced removal of his people two years earlier. 'Father found his house in ashes and his family gone,' said the shepherd. 'He was told to make his own way to Kazakhstan.'

It must have been a common story. In a heat shimmer, a path descended into the village of Bezingi, squeezed tight in the

The Third Step

narrow Cherek valley. A few scraps of land between the houses were cultivated or dotted with haystacks. Donkin and Fox had stayed hereabouts before their fateful expedition in 1888, and a goat once startled the climber Albert Mummery from his sleep by leaping on top of his tent. My eyes stung with sweat and my hair was matted with dust. In the village grocery store, a woman said I could sleep the night in the 'house of culture' – the community hall – and led me there. Inside, a gallery of black-and-white portraits covered one wall: forty-eight men in flared papakha hats. They were villagers who had taken part in the Second World War: a large number for such a small place, I thought, fighting desperately for the motherland on faraway fronts while Stalin's NKVD deracinated their relatives and ravaged their homes, labelling the Balkars a traitor nation. (Later, I learned that two Balkar soldiers were put forward for the highest honour, Hero of the Soviet Union, and at least one added his name to the famous Red Army graffiti on the walls of the Reichstag, writing: 'I reached Berlin. Son of Balkaria, Magomet Osmanov.')

This obscenity, this uprooting of entire peoples – the very opposite of the idea of korenizatsiya trumpeted a few years earlier – was, of course, hushed up by the Soviet authorities. The Karachays and Balkars were not allowed home until after Khrushchev's Thaw, in 1957, by which time the news had crept out. When Christopher Brasher, the British mountaineer, passed by the old settlement of Bezingi on an expedition to the Caucasus a year later, he was told it had been devastated by a mud avalanche. Shrewdly, he noted there was no evidence of such a landslide, 'and it seemed far more likely that the village had been ransacked and destroyed when the inhabitants had been evicted under conditions of terrible hardship'. Brasher was surprised at the discrepancy between the flower-filled meadows he was seeing as he walked up to the Bezingi glacier and

CENTRAL

Freshfield's description of dull brown slopes in The Exploration of the Caucasus. Then he realized: the twenty thousand head of livestock that had once grazed the area had been replaced now by a few cows and one flock of sheep – all that the Balkars had been able to bring back from exile. 'For fourteen years the area had run riot without any mouths to feed,' Brasher concluded.

As I laid out my sleeping bag on the stage in the community hall, a painted board on top of a cabinet caught my eye. It depicted a stylized white bolt of lightning hitting a tree on a black background. The inscription read: '1944–1957. [ ] years since the day of the forced deportation of the Balkar nation.' The space had been left blank so that the number could be chalked up every 8 March – a yearly skirmish in the long battle against forgetting. Something about this reusable symbol of suffering struck me as ineffably sad.

Beyond the next pass, a dirt road hacked from the hillside descended past serrated spurs to the village of Verkhnyaya (Upper) Balkaria. At its upper edge, three men were cutting a sloping patch of field with scythes. They put down their tools to talk. Within moments, one, Kaisyn, was inviting me to stay the night. He pointed down a slope of shale to his house, where his brother Eldar met me.

Verkhnyaya Balkaria had more flat land than Bezingi. There were small fields of cabbages and potatoes, and some patches of orchard. Kaisyn and Eldar were farmers with a two-storey house that had lacquered floors and a flushable toilet, a welcome luxury. A small Czech tractor stood in the yard. I took a break and stayed two days with the brothers and their families. It was a marvel how willing people were to take in a stranger – moreover, a grimy foreigner of uncertain provenance. We sat and talked in the kitchen, or on animal skins under the eaves of an outbuilding. One afternoon, a herd of yaks rumbled down the street in a squall of dust, urged on by shouting men on horseback. They were kept up near the snowline, Eldar said, and brought down to the valley for meat.

Eldar had studied at an Islamic institute in Nalchik, the Circassian city down on the plain. He had been by bus on the hajj to Mecca. There was a mosque in the village, and he was leading prayers there while the imam was away. 'There are a lot of people interested in dissuading others from attending the mosque – those who sell vodka, those who control prostitution,' he said gravely. 'We upset their business. There's pressure on believers not to attend. I had trouble with the police when I wanted to get a passport. They wanted to know who was "sponsoring" me. I said: "What sponsorship? There is no sponsorship."'

Three years earlier, scores of Islamist gunmen had launched an extraordinary uprising in Nalchik, attacking police and FSB buildings and raiding a gun store. At least thirty-five police and security officers had been killed, but nearly one hundred militants died in the fighting and about sixty were captured. What had driven them to the desperate attack? There were insinuations about the involvement of foreign overlords. Eldar said the explanation was simpler: 'They rose up in response to persecution; to being prevented from practising their faith as they wished.' He meant harassment by the security services, whose monitoring of mosques and handling of conservative Muslims could tip them into violence even when they had not contemplated it previously. 'They were ordinary boys, believers,' Eldar said. 'But the siloviki harassed them, rounded them up. Men had crosses carved in their chests.'

After dark, Kaisyn joined us. 'The police are the most brutal, keep away from them,' he said. 'Sometimes they kill people, and when they realize they've made a mistake, they switch documents or move bodies to make it look like they were shot while putting up armed resistance. You shouldn't sleep in your tent in the forest. They don't think; they're stressed out – they shoot first and think later. They're more dangerous than the *boyeviki*.'

Eldar and Kaisyn were concerned about unbridled cruelty against conservative Muslims, whatever their nationality. But the ache of the deportations – and a concomitant fear of losing one's homeland – was never far away. On the fateful day of 8 March 1944, men in uniform had knocked on the door of every house across Balkaria. The inhabitants were given twenty minutes to pack. One survivor remembered old men stooping on their sticks to gather a few crumbs of native soil, not knowing if they would touch it again.

Recent disputes between Balkars and Kabardians – over pastures and commercial plots in the mountains – had stirred old fears. Walking down the street, I met a group of men swilling beer from plastic bottles and watching a friend render the front of his house. One of the men, drunk, harangued me with tales of how they would 'fuck' the Kabardians if they tried to encroach on Balkaria. 'All we have is what we grow and collect with our own hands,' he said, turning up his callused palms. 'But we are not complaining, we have all that we need. There's food on the table. Just don't try to push us off our land. This land is ours.'

It had become a familiar refrain: the Kabardian as usurper of culture and traditions; as stealer of stove ash and livestock. The Balkars believed their neighbours had oiled the wheels of the deportations. I suspected the truth was more complicated. If it was, that would not diminish the Balkars' dread of losing their homes and property.

Up the road on the other side of the river, I came to the mosque where Eldar worshipped. Outside was a stone tablet recording the fate of the inhabitants of this single valley during the Second World War: 418 people shot by the NKVD in 1942; 18 villages 'wiped from the face of the Earth' and 7,284 people deported two years later. Of the 975 locals who were away at the front serving in the Red Army, only 220 returned. More than 2,500 people from the valley died in exile before the Balkars were allowed home.

Yet the inscription was defiant. 'Our nation did not perish then,' it concluded. 'Let it live on for evermore.'

Two months had now passed since I had left the Black Sea coast at Sochi. As the crow flew, I was approaching the halfway mark to the Caspian. But a flying crow is not troubled by mountain passes or Russian rules.

During breakfast at the brothers' house, I examined my maps on the kitchen table. I could see there was no way of continuing the journey east through the mountains, because I would soon cross from Kabardino-Balkaria into the next republic, North Ossetia, where Beslan was situated. After the school siege, Russia had introduced security restrictions in North Ossetia, which meant foreigners were only allowed to travel to and fro between a few major towns on the plain, using designated roads. Walking along paths in the highlands, as I wanted to do, could get you detained and prosecuted. I thought about ignoring the ban and continuing east, but it was too much of a risk. I didn't want to get jailed or deported from Russia in the middle of the walk. There was no choice but to descend a road north through the foothills, from Verkhnyaya Balkaria to the city of Nalchik. Then I could turn right and head down one of the permitted routes that would lead through North Ossetia to Ingushetia and Chechnya.

Kaisyn had something else to say. He was looking over my shoulder at the map. 'Stay away from that main road down into

Nalchik,' he said, pointing it out. 'It goes through the forest, and the *boyeviki* sometimes waste policemen there. There are shoot-outs. And there are checkpoints along the way where you could get stopped. They're manned by cops from Krasnodar region. Nasty guys. Better to take the longer route here, through Aushiger, and stay safe.'

I said goodbye to the brothers and left Verkhnyaya Balkaria as mist floated over the boulder-strewn slopes that fell to the river in the centre of the village. To the north, the steep sides of the mountains receded in paling greys on either side of the valley, guiding the way to the steppe.

The road climbed through a gorge to a tunnel. I stayed outside, traversing the cliffside on a track blasted from the rock, and when it met the far end of the tunnel a security guard in a kiosk jumped out to greet me. Where was I from? Where was I going? Why was I alone? Where had I been staying? 'Good lad!' he said when I explained. 'So everyone says they only kill in the Caucasus, but in fact we are the warmest people, right?'

'Yes!' I said with feeling. 'Yes, you are!'

Further down, as the piedmont levelled into the plain, was a settlement the size of an English market town, where roadside billboards exhorted the population to vote for pro-Kremlin electoral candidates, and a young man shouted '*Allahu Akbar!*' at me three times as I passed, while his friend tried to quieten him down.

What had prompted this outburst? Was my appearance, with my rucksack and boots, a kind of affront — an overt demonstration of privilege and leisure? Was I, to this local man, a decadent Western intruder, marked out by my idiot smile? Or was it just fun to spook a tourist?

The houses here had steel gates and walled courtyards, and their owners had built little benches out front in the street, where they could linger and talk with neighbours. When I saw people sitting on them, I called out a greeting and they replied 'Good day,' lifting their bottoms slightly from the seats and leaning forward in a show of respect. On one bench were two beautiful young women and their rising gesture, sweet and simultaneous with knees together and hands lying in their laps, cheered me up after the shouting man.

Aushiger drew into view in late afternoon: the village was famous for the healing powers of its hot spring, and locals had partitioned their homes to rent them out to the stream of visitors as makeshift rooms and dormitories.

I spent forty minutes knocking on doors, looking in vain for somewhere to stay. The homeowners were brusque in a way that was a surprise after the hospitality of the mountains; I couldn't help feeling that the commerce offered by the spring had sharpened the people who lived here. Eventually, one house had a free space in a dorm; a cleared-out living room with iron beds lining the walls. I dumped my pack with relief. On one bed, a fat man in underpants lay asleep, snorting and snoring. On another sat an old man in a patterned shirt and a trilby made from perforated grey plastic. His name, he said, was Lyonya. He was a seventy-four-year-old Kabardian from the north of the republic who spoke only broken Russian. Lyonya had come to Aushiger for eight days of bathing, and was moaning about the expense; at another spring, he had paid thirty roubles a night for his bed, while here it was a hundred.

'I'm on a walking trip to the Caspian Sea,' I said, as we got talking. 'I'm from Britain.' Lyonya was a little forgetful and confused, skittering from subject to subject and making bold declarations while searching my face for signs that he had veered into silliness. 'Stalin and Hitler were the most evil men in the history of

mankind,' he said. 'Stalin was a Georgian, very cruel. And Hitler…
where was Hitler from?' He held a crooked finger to his lower lip
as he thought. 'Maybe' – he gave me look that was both sly and
questioning – 'maybe he was from your country?'

In the early evening, we decided to go to the spring, and
Lyonya led me there down a path of cracked earth between the
cottages with ice-cream wrappers in the grass on either side of it.

'Thanks for showing me the way,' I said.

'I've got nothing better to do,' said Lyonya, making a flicking
gesture in front of his trouser fly. 'He doesn't stand up anymore.'

'Is that why you came here to bathe?' I asked.

'My knees hurt – it's for my joints.'

We walked on. 'Do you have any children, Lyonya?' I asked.

He thought for moment. 'I can't remember,' he said.

The pool fed by the spring was a rectangular hole the size of
a five-a-side football pitch, with a grassy bank on one side and
concrete steps on the other, next to a car park and a shashlyk stall.
We changed in cubicles and slipped into the waist-high water. It
was deliciously warm. About 150 people were bathing: children
in marmalade-pot hats, elderly ladies in shifts and headscarves
becalmed in the shallows, teenage boys in bollock-nipping shorts,
skinny pot-bellied old fellows and bear-hairy musclemen in their
twenties and thirties.

Some of the bathers were scooping handfuls of green mud
from the bottom of the pool and slathering it on their arms.
Others crouched in the water like indolent frogs, only their eyes
and noses above the surface. Lyonya glided to and fro, a beatific
smile on his face, his irritation at the pricy dorm forgotten. Children doggy-paddled and threw balls. The teenagers yelled. Close
by, a fat woman in a two-piece swimsuit, her back mottled pink
with sunburn, was standing, hands on hips, next to a small grey-

haired man with a deep tan. Another woman, submerged to the neck, was saying to them: 'What I like is how you have managed to preserve your friendship. Fate brought you together and then pushed you apart. It happens.' The pair nodded glumly.

I poached in the water, letting the ache of the mountains fade from my limbs as I eavesdropped on the gossip around me.

At bedtime, Lyonya leered happily across the room and whispered: 'Good night, foreigner!'

The verge of the dual carriageway to Nalchik was strewn with rubbish: plastic bottles, broken glass, dumped tomatoes, a pile of rotting melons. It drizzled all day, and I ate fried mutton in a roadside café, where I steamed gently among the lorry drivers. By mid-afternoon, I was on the edge of the city. Another hour brought me to Hotel Russia, a typical Soviet-built establishment on Lenin Prospekt. My room had a stinking bathroom and a view onto a square with an ugly monument. Around the square were flags commemorating the previous year's 450th anniversary of Kabarda 'voluntarily adhering' to the tsardom of Russia during the rule of Ivan the Terrible.

The Kabardians are the eastern branch of the Circassians, the nation that was largely expelled from the northwest Caucasus. The idea they had agreed to join the tsardom in 1557 was a fiction – it was a temporary alliance. But over the centuries, some Kabardians had sided with Russia. In Nalchik, at least, they remained in the majority.

At the city's history museum next morning, I sought out its director, Betal Kerefov. The uprising in Nalchik which Eldar had described to me had taken place on 13 October 2005. It was the biggest outbreak of violence in Russia since the Beslan siege a year earlier. Among the scores of assailants attacking the FSB and other buildings was Betal's son Kazbulat, a lawyer. The attempt to seize control was a spectacular failure. Many of those who took part in the assault were not hardened guerrillas but educated local men who had been recruited shortly before the raid. Some were seen struggling to reload their weapons. One was a fifteen-year-old boy.

After the failed attack, a friend of mine, another Moscow correspondent, saw video footage of dozens of bodies of the dead gunmen, heaped on the floor of a refrigerated wagon, without clothes or dignity. 'A leg,' he wrote, 'a dark mound of pubic hair, a heavily burned head, a broad chest that must for years have seemed invulnerable.' A mother of one of the dead men had shown him the video, recorded on a mobile phone. 'It looks like something from Treblinka,' she said. Another clip appeared to have been recorded by a police officer; it showed one of the Nalchik attackers sprawled in a street after being hit in a firefight during the raid. The officer could be heard questioning the dying man in Kabardian. The man was pleading for water and gesturing agitatedly towards a wound in his shoulder. 'I've done nothing to regret,' he whispered.

Such a waste, I thought. Young men on both sides turned into a twisted mass of bodies. What had led to the futile revolt? I hoped Betal could help me understand. A handsome man in his fifties with clipped hair going grey at the temples, he led me to his office at the museum and offered me a seat.

Betal was an expert on the Samartians, an ancient civilization that flourished on the steppe of southern Russia, and one of his books on the subject lay on the desk between us. His son, he said, had trained at the city's police academy, winning several prizes. After a period as a serving officer, Kazbulat became disillusioned and requalified as a lawyer, studying at home for two years to pass the exam. He took on a client who was pursuing a complaint of physical abuse during the mass arrest of conservative Muslims in Kabardino-Balkaria in 2004. From there, it seemed, he was drawn into the rebel underground.

Betal believed his son had been tricked into participating in the raid. 'I think a lot of them didn't really understand what was going on until the moment the car boot was opened and they saw the weapons,' he said. 'After the events, Kazbulat was in hiding for a few days. I knew where he was, but I could not go to him because I was being watched, so I passed a message through an acquaintance. My son sent a message in reply, saying, "I was set up. How can I go on living when I let down my father, my mother, my brothers?" Three days later, he was killed. They say he lifted his weapon and shot in the air. He brought down fire on himself. He wanted to die.'

Betal sighed and leaned forward on the desk. He found it hard to comprehend how Kazbulat could have been so easily fooled. 'Why did this happen? I am an archaeologist. I dig things up, I sift evidence, I collate facts and draw conclusions.' He gestured towards his book. 'With these Samartian artefacts, I understand, I'm on familiar ground. But here, I'm lost for an explanation.'

I had a feeling that Betal, as a public figure in the city, could not say as much as he would have liked about why the men had taken up arms. It seemed implausible that they were all simply tricked. That afternoon, a Friday, I walked through rain by a railway track towards the suburbs, looking for the only mosque that was still allowed to operate, besides the main one associated with the authorities. At a food stall, a man gave me directions to the mosque and then offered me a shot of vodka: his own breath stank of it.

'Thanks, but probably best not, bearing in mind where I'm going,' I said.

He stared blankly at me and then, after I had gone a few steps, shouted: 'You won't be able to change any dollars there!'

The mosque was set in a yard between apartment blocks. It had a small minaret with a wonky tin roof. Crossing the threshold, I stumbled in my big walking boots and pitched forward. In the hallway were high racks for shoes with numerous shelves, and as I moved to talk to a group of men, my boot brushed the edge of the carpet. 'Don't touch the carpet!' said one of the men. 'What do you want?'

'Excuse me,' I said, stepping aside clumsily. 'I was hoping to speak to the imam.'

'Are you drunk?' cried another of the men. 'Get out of here!'

Another, less aggressive, said: 'What do you need?'

'I'm a writer. I'd like to talk to the imam about the Muslim community,' I said. After some confusion, I was allowed to take off my boots and shown to meet him, led there by a man who gently held my elbow, enquiring: 'Why can't you walk? Are you sober?'

'Yes, of course. I just tripped.'

The imam was pale and morose and guarded. He said he wouldn't give an interview and neither would anyone else visiting the mosque, but I was welcome to listen to the Friday prayers if I did not enter the main auditorium. I thanked him and took a seat on a bench in the foyer. Many men began to arrive and duck into an annexe where there were taps for ritual washing. Soon the auditorium was full and the spillover of men crowded the annexe in rows. At the end of prayers, they kneeled to perform *namaz* together, facing east.

As I left the mosque, I heard slapping footfalls from behind and flinched. 'I'm sorry,' said the young man who had caught me up, and introduced himself in English, before switching to Russian. 'I was praying at the mosque and I guessed who you were from my father's description.' He was Tembulat Kerefov, the second son of the museum director and the brother of the lawyer killed in the raid. 'I'll talk to you,' he said.

Tembulat had the thick arms and barrel chest of a gladiator and wore sandals, which only accentuated the likeness. His teeth were perfectly white, offset by several days' worth of dark stubble and a haircut that was not much longer. We walked back into the city together. He was a history student, he said, and worked with his father at the museum.

'My brother had a very acute sense of justice,' said Tembulat. 'When he became a police officer, he saw that things there were built on corruption and violence. There were two options – either to go along with it, or to leave. He wanted nothing to do with that, so he left. But it was hard as a lawyer, too. Judges are paid off, they have their connections.'

Tembulat said it was police persecution of conservative Muslims that had motivated many of the 2005 attackers. 'They beat people, they shaved crosses in their hair, they forced them to drink vodka,' he said. 'There were cases when people were raped in police custody. For a man in the Caucasus, that's the worst humiliation possible. For any man. After that, anyone would be ready to retaliate. To defend his dignity.'

But Tembulat, too, saw artifice in the way the raid had unfolded. When we got to the city centre in the fading heat of evening, he invited me to go with him to his family's apartment. His father was out, but his mother and his younger brother, home from studying in Syria, were in. Tembulat showed me his father's book-stuffed office with ornamental daggers hanging on the wall, and then we sat alone in the kitchen.

CENTRAL

'I think the police and the security services played out 13 October to a script,' he said. 'They had infiltrated the *jamaat* and knew that an attack was planned. They could have stopped it completely and arrested all those involved. But they let it go ahead as a means of destroying everyone, killing them.'

It was an extraordinary accusation, but one that I would hear many times over the next couple of days.

Tembulat, in his own way, had rejected the idea of solution by force. In the past, he had practised karate and boxing, only to find that the matches were fixed by bent officials. 'You knock someone out and then *they* are declared the winner,' he laughed. 'It was absurd. These days, I do yoga.'

Three years after my walk, I would come back to Nalchik to meet some more relatives of fighters who took part in the 2005 raid. One of them was Arsen Tukov, whose son, Anatoly, had died in an exchange of gunfire with police. Arsen, a composed, avuncular man with a long white beard, described himself as a Salafi, a follower of the pious strain of Islam. From 2001 to 2005, he was the imam of a mosque in the Nartan suburb of Nalchik.

As we sat drinking tea in a café called Salaam, Arsen described how during that period, police officers would cart off young men from his and other mosques for interrogation. Some came back with bruises and broken ribs. The police ignored all pleas to stop. Later, his mosque and several others considered hot spots of fundamentalism were closed and bulldozed.

Arsen didn't condone his son's actions, he added. Yet there was a reason Anatoly and his friends fought on that October day.

'In Islam, there are three steps one must take in the event of persecution,' said Arsen. 'The first step, if you live in a Christian state, is to apply to the authorities and request protection from harassment. Which they did: they wrote one hundred and sixty-two official complaints, all with no result.

'The second step is to ask to be resettled to a place where you can fulfil your religious obligations. Four hundred and eighty Muslims from here wrote an appeal to the federal authorities asking assistance to move to another land. The powers refused to help.'

Arsen paused for a moment to sip his tea. I noticed he smelled faintly and sweetly of incense. And the third step? I asked.

'The third step comes if all efforts are exhausted and the persecution continues,' he said, pushing away his cup. 'That is when you no longer have the right to sit at home, when you must come out and defend your religion.' Arsen lowered his voice and leaned forward.

'The third step,' he said, 'is jihad.'

By the road out of Nalchik, cobwebs glistened with dew in the grass. I followed a path shaded by trees, past fields where men and women were collecting the cucumber harvest. An old bus had been driven into one field to load up the cucumbers, which glutted the landscape, overflowing from crates and rotting in yellowing piles in ditches.

In a village, next to a water channel in front of their house, a family was taking a breather after a day of work in the fields. The matriarch had removed her shoes and, with gnarled hands, was slowly scrubbing the grime from her feet and ankles.

Did they know anywhere I could pay to stay the night, I asked. 'You can stay with us, but only for free,' said one of the two men with the old lady, wiping his hands on a cloth. The woman was their mother: she had learned some English in school in the

1960s, and when she found out where I was from, she looked up from her scrubbing and said brightly: 'Goodbye!'

Small with matted dark hair, the man who had invited me to stay was Aslim, and the other, bulkier, younger, was his brother Anzor. That night we sat in the dark on their veranda and ate a delicious lamb stew.

I asked about the harvest, and the brothers told me that labourers from neighbouring North Ossetia came to work the season, earning three hundred roubles per day: about six pounds.

Aslim had studied at veterinary school, but received poor marks because he could only afford to bribe the teacher with bottles of milk rather than cognac.

'So, we live by our produce, Tom,' said Aslim, smiling in the half-light. 'After all, in the past, your queen had a throne covered in fleeces. England grew wealthy on the wool trade. And we? We are rich in cucumbers.'

I was approaching Beslan in a tentative mood, unsure about how I might react when I got there. A bridge over the Terek river, sluggish and wide so far from the hills, offered an excuse to tarry. So did the sight of a circling hawk.

But there was no point in puttering to a halt. By the afternoon of the next day, the town came into view, and I reeled it in under my boots, reluctantly, steadily. In the centre, there was a guesthouse by a flower shop. I took a room, left my pack and went to visit the Beslan Mothers' Committee.

The mothers had an office on the ground floor of an apartment block on Oktyabrskaya street, a few hundred metres from what remained of the school.

The office was small and full of binders. I was greeted by Susanna Dudiyeva, the chairwoman, who had lost her thirteen-year-old son, Zaur, in the siege. The Mothers' Committee had been set up to lobby for an independent investigation that would answer troubling questions: why had the authorities not launched negotiations with the hostage-takers? What had caused the explosions? Why were tanks and flame-throwers used against the school when hundreds of survivors were still trapped inside?

Susanna was a no-nonsense woman in her late forties who had led a delegation of Beslan mothers to meet President Putin at the Kremlin in September 2005, a year after the siege; the only time he ever received any such group. On the eve of the meeting, Susanna had said publicly that she held Putin responsible for what had happened. A few weeks later, it emerged that Susanna and a group of mothers had travelled again to Moscow, this time to attend a gathering organized by a well-known psychic, who had promised he could resurrect their dead children. A video was said to exist in which Susanna took to the stage and expressed her belief in this promise. Some of the mothers who did not attend the psychic's session were convinced that Susanna had, naïvely, been tricked into association with a charlatan as a means of discrediting the group. The dissenting mothers broke away and formed a rival organization.

Susanna was unbowed. In the office, she said she had acquired intelligence memos from shortly before the Beslan siege. In them, police were warned that a terror attack was being planned, and security should be strengthened at schools and hospitals. 'Nothing was done,' she said. 'There should be the death penalty for these people; a demonstrative, public execution for all those in authority who are guilty of negligence.' The same went for those who had bungled the rescue operation at the gym, she said.

I had hoped – expected, even - that the horror of the events in Beslan would make its survivors recoil from the very thought of renewed violence; that it might even have turned them into pacifists. Susanna was no such convert. 'I'm in favour of harsh punishment,' she said, opening a packet of biscuits and laying them on a plate between us. 'If one can kill innocents, kill children, why can't you shoot the whole family that brought up the terrorist?'

Two more women entered the office. One, named Alla, with long, dark hair and deep-set eyes, had saved seventeen people, Susanna said, by hiding them in an unlit storage area behind the school boiler room as the militants stormed the building.

The other, named Svetlana, was birdlike and pale, in her late sixties. She had lost her nine-year-old granddaughter in the climax of the siege and walked every day for an hour to visit her grave outside the town – the field where I had watched the burials had been turned into a memorial cemetery with lines of red marble graves.

I was curious to know what the women made of the fact that many of the hostage-takers were not Chechens but men from the neighbouring Muslim republic of Ingushetia. The Ossetians and Ingush had an antagonistic relationship because of a brief but vicious conflict between the two nations in the early 1990s, in which hundreds died as the result of a territorial dispute.

'I never had any problem with them; we used to go shopping in their bazaar and my daughter and I both studied in Grozny,' said Svetlana, adjusting her headscarf. 'We had good relations with the Ingush and the Chechens.'

In the 1980s, she had got to know an Ingush mullah, she said. His family had adopted a son and they were poor. The mullah and his relatives had been sent to Siberia during the deportations. Svetlana's family had a shop and decided to help the mullah and his wife, taking them milk and meat and fish and vermicelli and butter. 'Everything!' she said.

The Third Step

The adopted son grew up and got married, and all was fine, Svetlana went on. 'But one day, the old man – he was a good man – he said: "Be careful. Maybe I won't be around anymore, but remember my words: every night here, they gather the young men in the mosque and stir up poison against you Ossetians, because they blame you for being sent to Siberia."'

Svetlana said that warning was the reason she was opposed to the planned restoration of Beslan's mosque, even though the town had a large Muslim minority. It could become an incubator of hate, she said. 'We can't have them gathering there and crying "*Allahu Akbar*". That's what the terrorists shouted over the bodies of our dead children.'

It was salutary to consider how the militants who seized School Number One had suppressed any feeling of empathy they might be expected to have for their intended victims.

Among the male fighters had been two women dressed in dark clothing and niqabs.

Their job on the first day was to take children from the gym to the toilets, and they did so in silence. Only their eyes were visible, but the women appeared to be in their twenties; the hostages noticed that one had carefully plucked eyebrows above the veil that screened her face.

Such women were already a familiar sight to Russians. There had been several among the militants who stormed the Nord-Ost theatre in Moscow two years earlier. The press called them Black Widows or *shakhidki* – a portmanteau of the Arab word for martyrs and a Russian feminine suffix. *Shakhidki* was the name given to female perpetrators of suicide bombings of both military and civilian targets, or to women who planned to commit such acts. They were said to be mostly Chechens driven to revenge by the loss of husbands, fathers and brothers who had been killed by Russian forces. The women at Nord-Ost had been gassed before they could detonate the explosives at their waist, but in several other terrorist attacks in the early 2000s, female martyrs had killed scores of people.

At School Number One, the shakhidki were so wraith-like and disturbing that survivors' recollections of their appearance, recorded later, are contradictory. Some hostages remembered the women as wearing black clothes, some as grey. At least one person reported having seen three shakhidki in the gym at the same time, not two. In video footage shot by the militants that was released after the events, the camera zooms in on a shakhidka standing motionless in a doorway at the far end of the gym, melting into shadow. She has a belt of explosives around her waist and she holds a Makarov pistol vertically by her head, the side of the barrel resting against her temple.

On the first night of the siege, the day before I arrived in Beslan, there was an altercation between the shakhidki and one or more of the male militants in a classroom that was off a corridor linking the gym with the rest of the school. An explosion tore through the room, killing one of the women and fatally injuring the second. At least one gunman died and several male hostages positioned nearby were injured, some fatally.

Only months afterwards would a Russian prosecutor announce the identity of the Black Widows at Beslan as two friends from Chechnya, Roza and Maryam. The women, it transpired from the diligent investigations of Russian reporters, had worked as traders at the main bazaar in Grozny, the Chechen capital. I knew it myself: a depressing place, full of potholes and dirty puddles. Roza had first moved to an apartment in one of the semi-destroyed buildings on the fringe of the bazaar with her older sister Aminat, with whom she ran a stall selling children's clothing. Two other traders, Maryam and Satsita, then joined them to share the thirty-dollars-a-month rent. The women tacked plastic sheeting over the smashed windows and rose early, working from 7 a.m. until 7 p.m. in the market. In the evenings, tired, they would make food and watch television together.

Roza, at twenty-nine years old, was divorced, while Aminat was unmarried. In the only picture of the sisters made public, the taller Roza wears an orange Nike T-shirt and cocks her head slightly, her eyebrows fine and arched. Aminat, full-lipped with dark hair spreading across her shoulders, is smiling and has linked arms with her sister, drawing her close.

Every month or so, the four women would travel via Dagestan to Azerbaijan to bring back supplies to sell at the bazaar in Grozny. On 22 August 2004, they told their relatives they were setting out as usual for the bus journey to Baku, with a plan to acquire briefcases, uniforms and the white ribbons that girls across Russia would wear in their hair on the first day of the school term. But the traders never came home. On 24 August, the Russian passenger jets that had departed Moscow's Domodedovo airport were blown up, killing ninety people. Aminat was quickly identified as the bomber who had brought down Flight 1303 to Volgograd. The *shakhidka* on the other plane, flying to Sochi, was Satsita. Within a few days, Roza and Maryam were storming School Number One.

In just over a week, four female friends from Chechnya had chosen to give up their lives in the name of terrorism. Why? Relatives claim they displayed no signs of radicalization. The women did not have a record of being in trouble with the police. But in the case of the two sisters, there *was* a potential motive. In the early 2000s, *zachistki* had begun in Roza and Aminat's home village in the hills of southeast Chechnya; indiscriminate 'cleansing operations' conducted by federal forces that were designed to flush out real or potential rebel fighters. In April 2001, men in uniform had kidnapped Roza and Aminat's brother Uvays from a friend's house in the village. The soldiers took him and the friend to the local cemetery, forced them to lie down among the gravestones and opened fire. The friend was killed instantly, but Uvays played dead and survived. Injured, he made his way home. Soldiers returned a few days later and took him again. A mediator for the family later found out that Uvays had been tortured into confessing to unspecified crimes, and then murdered. His body was blown up; a common tactic to destroy evidence.

Had Roza experienced a change of heart at Beslan?

We do not know exactly why she and Maryam died. Either one of them blew herself up after quarrelling with the Colonel, it is thought, or he detonated the explosives at her waist remotely, leading to both women's deaths.

Several hostages believed the *shakhidki* had been misled about the terrorists' target, and may have refused to kill a boy hostage. One captive recalled hearing the sound of an argument between a man and a woman in Russian, with the latter raising her voice to say: 'I'm not going to! You said it was a police station!' Another hostage, a nurse who had been ordered to bandage two wounded fighters in the corridor, said the militants were taken by surprise by the explosion in the classroom, thinking it was an attack by the forces outside the school. That suggested one of the women detonated it herself.

I had wondered about Shamil Basayev's motives in launching terror attacks like Beslan. In fact, it was not such a mystery. In interviews from his mountain hideouts, he had spoken openly of the reasons. He wanted, he said, to visit the same horror on Russians as they had perpetrated against his own people: the annihilation of villages, of children and of the elderly. A couple of weeks before he launched the hospital siege in Budyonnovsk in 1995, Russian bombers had killed eleven or twelve members of Basayev's own family – mostly women and children – in a raid on the Chechen hill village of Vedeno. In Beslan, having lost her brother three years earlier and knowing her sister had just ended her life on the plane to Volgograd, the *shakhidka* Roza had similar cause for vengeance. But maybe something she saw at School Number One made her balk at what she was doing. Instants of recognition and longing can throw a mind into doubt. Did the play of sunlight on a girl's hair remind Roza of one of her nieces? Did the scurry of a boy through the yard as he was herded into the gym make her think of her brother Uvays in childhood, rushing down an alley between the stone houses, the mountains of the Greater Caucasus piled on the horizon?

Perhaps Roza decided that enough was enough.

School Number One was a few minutes' walk from the Beslan Mothers' Committee office. The shell of the building had been left as a memorial. There was nobody around, and I walked alone through the wrecked classrooms, debris crunching under my boots. Pictures and other objects still hung from the walls: a portrait of Pushkin, a string of plastic leaves, a cut-out of a wily fox from a fairy tale carrying a stolen chicken under its arm.

The corridor linking the classrooms was a delicate shade of blue, blotched with dark craters of gunfire, like the pattern on guillemot eggs. On the floor of the gym stood dozens of bottles of water: offerings to the departed hostages, who were given nothing to drink by their captors. Below the gaping window frames on either side, lengths of charred timber were propped behind a rail; the same timber that had fallen from the burning roof onto the hostages.

The walls of the gym were still sooty and flaky to the touch. Along them, between the windows, hung placards with photographs — hundreds of photographs. They were portraits of the pupils, parents and teachers who had died — head-and-shoulders shots with their names and dates of birth. Below the pictures, wreaths of plastic flowers had faded in the sunlight.

At the centre of what had been the basketball court, a lacquered Orthodox cross held out its arms as if pleading for mercy. A breeze feathered through the windows, stirring a smell of ash and the faintest tinge of burned flesh. I stopped for a while by the cross and crabbed my hands on top of my head and pushed my fingers through my hair until the nails bit into the skin, and I wanted to scream but I couldn't.

During the siege, the hostages' relatives at the perimeter around the school had been tortured by their inability to act, and I didn't know how to comfort them.

What *can* you say to a parent whose child lies in mortal danger? To a parent who can do nothing to remove that child from the danger? Who can exert no power, no influence? Who can only wait for the unfolding of events?

Something like the hostage-taking at Beslan leaves those of us who have never been subjected to such depravity searching for parallels, however inadequate. Not so long ago, my mother spoke to me about when she split up with her first husband and lost custody of my two half-brothers at the hands of a misogynistic court. It was the early 1970s and, against my mother's will, my brothers' father took them away to Africa in a converted Mercedes van, on a shoestring budget with no planned return date. For a long time – more than two years – it was difficult, if not impossible, for my mother to stay in touch with her boys, then seven and eight. They were constantly on the move. Most of the time, she had no idea where they were or when, if ever, she would see them again. Her ex-husband was a white man who had grown up in Africa, and there was every possibility he could decide to settle there. 'Those were years of terror for me,' my mother said in our recent conversation. I had not heard her use that word before to describe the experience, and the nakedness of it was chilling. Terror, I thought: yes, that is true terror, to know your child is somewhere alive but you cannot get them back.

At the time – and for a long time afterwards – my mother would have a recurring nightmare. She would be running, panic-stricken, through a dilapidated building with long corridors, bursting into empty rooms, knowing that she was looking for children in distress, unable to find them. Finally, she would fling open a door and make out a figure lying on a cot. But before she could discern their face, she would wake with a start.

During this period, she tried to stay sane by performing a daily ritual. She would go to 'a kind of inner sanctum in my head', where she would imagine reaching out to my brothers to reassure them she had not forgotten them. 'It was sort of agonizing but also helpful,' she told me. 'It was a magical way of embracing them, a sense of protecting them.' Later, when they did finally return to live with her, my mother learned that during the journey, my brothers' father had run out of money and the boys had to eat rotting bread doused in vinegar and siphon petrol from cars to keep the van going.

It seems trivial, perhaps, to compare my mother's experience to that of a parent whose child is kidnapped by terrorists. But that is the point: most of us don't have the tools to measure such anguish. How would *we* behave? How much could *we* withstand?

Now I have a three-year-old son, and I wonder about my response if he had been in the school at Beslan, without his father or his mother with him, as was the case for some of the children.

My colleague Julius had been right: the siege could have stretched on for weeks. Would I, a coward in most other things, have had the courage to hold on for day after day, just in case a moment would come when I might be able to help?

The instinct, of course, is to cling to hope, to the belief in a chance to act, however desperate the circumstances. Who, after all, could abandon their child at a time when they might need you most?

But night after sleepless night, would a temptation grow to end the torment? Perhaps I would be the one to show weakness. Perhaps I would be the one to put the razor blade to my wrist; to climb to a high roof and step out of the pain, into oblivion.

From the school, I walked beyond the railway tracks to the little house that I had visited after the siege, once the funerals began.

Natasha Rudenok's mother, Olga, was not at home, but I found her washing the windows of a nearby building. She remembered me and said, 'Thank you for coming,' and we went back to the house. Olga made tea and brought some sweets in foil wrappers, and we took chairs in the living room where we had sat around Natasha's body.

Survivors had recalled that inside the gym Natasha kept up their spirits, encouraging her pupils to drink their urine, saying it wasn't so bad, really, just close your eyes and imagine it's Coca-Cola. She died from gunshot wounds that she received as she tried to help children escape the building.

The Third Step

In the living room, Olga had placed a portrait of Natasha on a shelf, alongside a soft toy. 'My daughter was a very cheerful person,' she said. 'She made us all happy. We can't have fun like we used to, without her.'

Olga had dark patches under her eyes. She couldn't sleep, she said. The authorities had given other victims of the siege an apartment as compensation, she told me, but she didn't want one herself. 'I felt it was wrong. I didn't want to earn something on Natasha's blood.'

What she desired most of all was to talk to her daughter again. 'They say time heals,' she said. 'For me, it only gets worse. Year after year.'

The next day, I got up early and hiked out of Beslan past fields of maize. I was glad I had gone there, but also glad to be leaving.

Below the right verge of the road, the Terek appeared alongside me again, and the mountains were a smudge on the southern horizon. Vladikavkaz announced itself quietly: petrol stations and tyre-repair shops gave way to a scattering of low-rise apartment blocks. North Ossetia's capital was popular with journalists and foreign aid workers for its attractive central streets, its easy attitude and relative security. On fine mornings, the gleaming cone of Mount Kazbek stood proud on the horizon. The city had a grand but fading old hotel called the Imperial, where the two house prostitutes sometimes sat behind reception, their beads clacking on the desk as they checked the register for potential clients. In the evenings, they would ring you in your room with purring voices to offer their services. 'Really, you are not interested in girls? Can there be such a man?'

Vladikavkaz was a good staging post for the rest of the North Caucasus. During the day, you drove out to report on despicable things, and in the evening you came back to a steak and a soft bed at the Imperial. But the Imperial was full, and so was the Vladikavkaz, a Communist-era hulk just across the river. Someone gave me the address of a small hotel on the outskirts, by a sports arena. My room – and everyone else's, it seemed – was made from plastic panels that were so thin as to be translucent, neighbours' lights casting glowing orbs on the walls, their conversations clearly audible. I turned on the news and sank onto my bed. A bulletin was showing tracer fire streaking into a night sky, and the crash and crump of artillery strikes.

Somewhere in Africa, I thought, lazily.

But no. Overnight, the newsreader was saying, Georgia had launched an attack to reclaim its breakaway republic of South Ossetia, on the other side of the Caucasus mountains. Ossetian irregulars from the Russian North Caucasus were already gathering where I now was, in Vladikavkaz, to travel into the conflict zone and help their brothers defend themselves.

For a moment, I lay uncomprehending. Then the thought formed: I've walked into a war.

9

Interlude: War

I had wanted to cut loose from news reporting, to rid myself of its constraints. Now I was to be dragged back in against my will. In my hotel room in Vladikavkaz, I received a call from an editor in London. 'Can you step in and cover?' she said. 'We've got no one on the ground and you're right there.' I hesitated. But it was hard to refuse an old acquaintance. I agreed to take a break from the walk.

It was a fortnight since I had resumed the journey in the Baksan valley. Sun- and wind-burned from long days outside, I was suddenly surrounded by 'the hack pack': my colleagues from Moscow. They arrived in Vladikavkaz that day and the next: in freshly laundered clothes, smelling nice, wisecracking and wearing dark glasses. It was at once strange and pleasant to be back among them. We went out to interview refugees who had fled north from South Ossetia. Cossack volunteers were also arriving in the city from across the North Caucasus to travel south and join the fight against the Georgians.

The road into South Ossetia was controlled by Moscow, and passed through a two-mile tunnel under the mountains. Russian tanks were being sent through it to support the Ossetians against

Georgian government forces, who had launched an all-out attempt to retake Tskhinval, the South Ossetian capital. It was a few days before we were allowed to follow. By then, the Georgians were largely defeated. We drove in a bus, with official chaperones from the Russian ministry of defence. The bus went through the tunnel in the morning, cowled in exhaust fumes. Halfway to Tskhinval, they transferred us to armoured personnel carriers (APCs) with no windows, supposedly because of the danger of sniper fire. On later trips, we travelled all the way to Tskhinval in the bus, and could see that hundreds of houses in a Georgian enclave north of the city had been set ablaze by Ossetian militia. 'These homes were abandoned and electrical faults have caused the fires,' the chaperone lied. He was a slick PR type who liked to invite us for evening drinks on the terrace of the Vladikavkaz.

For me, the war was an aberration. Despite the week of walking across the plain, I was still intoxicated by the memory of the high peaks, the far views and the nostril-filling scent of the sheepskins in a shepherd's kosh. Now I clumped around the conflict zone in my walking boots, feeling out of place and out of kilter.

The Russians were keen for us to see the destruction wrought by the Georgian advance. At a hospital, we spoke to patients who had cowered in a basement as bombs fell. Mortar fire could still be heard in the city. Some reporters stopped to take pictures of themselves grinning in front of the twisted wreckage of a Georgian tank at a Tskhinval crossroads. The idea of posing for a snap on the spot where young men had died in agony only a few days earlier filled me with anger, but I stayed quiet.

The press trips were tightly controlled. Only once did my friend Andrew and I manage to slip away. We heard a rumour that Georgian troops had abducted several young women from a South Ossetian village called Khetagurovo. Female underwear had

Interlude: War

supposedly been found in an abandoned armoured car. When we got to the village, no one knew anything about it. Instead, we met a pensioner in front of her sheet-metal fence, which gunfire had turned into a sieve. Her husband had died on their doorstep, a few steps from safety in the cellar, she said. He was caught in the back of the head by shrapnel. Inside the house, we ran our fingers over a splintered hole in the back of a wardrobe left by a passing bullet.

Shuddering though potholes on the way back to Tskhinval, our driver casually lifted the lid of a box between the front seats. Half a dozen grenades were jiggling against each other; the smooth ones that look fragile as eggs. 'Found them by chance,' he said. 'The Georgians left them behind. Thought I'd take them home as a souvenir.'

I did not have my laptop with me, and was reduced to writing from internet cafés in Vladikavkaz or phoning in my reports to copytakers in London. Andrew could not find a hotel and took the second bed in my plastic room. At night, we lay sleepless as a medley of sounds filtered through the walls: drunken men arguing to the left; an energetic bout of sex followed by post-coital chitchat from the ceiling.

In Abkhazia, the de facto government had used the fighting in South Ossetia as cover for an assault on the Georgian end of the Kodori gorge, my destination before I ran into the partisan. At our evening gatherings in Vladikavkaz, my Moscow friends were alive with talk of geopolitics. The war had ignited debate about Russia's tactic of using separatists to prevent neighbouring former Soviet states drifting towards the West. My mind was crowded instead with the images of recent days: the blank gaze of the widow in Khetagurovo, the flames licking across the roof of a house, a trembling Georgian man held hostage in Tskhinval as a pawn for a prisoner swap. Although our mood was blackly cheerful when we were in a group, on my own, it felt almost dangerous to be sinking again in such a sea of misery so soon after revising Belsan.

Mercifully, the hostilities came to a close. In Vladikavkaz, I had befriended a South Ossetian family who had travelled north to seek shelter from the fighting. One night, they invited me to dinner in the apartment where they were staying, to say goodbye as they prepared to return home. A power cut hit the neighbour-hood, and we sat and talked by the light of candles in glass jars. This is the abiding memory of those days, the one my mind has preserved most acutely in order to suppress the others. My diary entries faltered during the war. The words that were spoken have gone; so have the names of the refugees. But there is a low babel of voices, a giving of thanks, an orange glimmer on faces flushed by wine. Toasts are murmured to the Almighty, to the holy places, to the trees and the stones. We are safe in the darkness.

On our minibus rides through the mountains to the war zone in South Ossetia, we had passed a uniquely graceless statue fixed to a cliff, as if bursting from the stone; a giant metal figure on a boxy horse that had, I learned, been carried there by helicopter in the 1990s. 'Oh, that's Uastyrdzhi, our version of St George,' explained the receptionist at my hotel. Uastyrdzhi, I discovered, was the most revered from a pantheon of gods who had returned with new force after the fall of Communism.

One day in the city, a long green tent was pitched down the edge of a street. An army field kitchen? But no, it was a wedding party, the guests sitting inside at benches. By the entrance, men were boiling meat in cauldrons, and three triangular cheese pies lay on top of each other on a table: pagan symbols in honour of God, the Sun and the Earth. 'This is nothing,' snorted one of the cauldron-stirrers, wiping a greasy hand on a rag, when I stopped to chat. A few weeks earlier, he said, tens of thousands of Osse-tians had decamped to a sacred grove in the republic's Alagir district, there to slaughter bullocks and sheep in an annual event that was part ritual, part shindig, with dancing and booze and tearful pleas for divine intervention in wasted lives.

I wanted to know more. At the city museum, two skulls, elon-gated into cylinders by some means of compression during their owners' childhood, sat in a smudged glass cabinet. They belonged to ancient Alans, progenitors of the Ossetians, the label said. The museum staff invited a historian to meet me, and he kindly appeared, a tall man with a bald head and a neat moustache.

We sat in the courtyard of the museum, a little oasis where a grapevine spread above our heads. It was a folly, the historian said, when looking at the history of the Caucasus, to perceive black-and-white divisions between Russian occupiers and ethnic highlanders, for there were always many examples of syncretism and overlap – in clothing, in attitudes, in identity, in religion. For hundreds of years before Russia's final conquest of the Caucasus in 1864, the area where Russia's southern fringe met steppe nomads and highlanders was a typical frontier zone in which identities were tangled and complex, and outside influence ebbed and flowed.

The Russians, the historian went on, saw their missions to spread civilization and Christianity as two prongs of the same pitchfork. At best, their efforts at conversion were patchy. The Ossetians were descendants of the Alans; themselves an offshoot of the Scythians, a warrior people who roamed the steppe in the first millennium BC, living in wagons and riding horses decorated with griffins and antlers. Settled at the centre of the predomi-nantly Sunni Muslim North Caucasus, the Ossetians speak an Eastern Iranian language. Today, their ancestral pagan traditions remained vital and relevant – as the three pies I had seen, ubiquitous at any celebration, confirmed.

'So when did the Ossetians become Christians?' I asked.

'The first encounters with Christian practice came in the tenth century AD, under Byzantine influence,' the historian said. Christianity, however, gained little ground, and old beliefs reasserted themselves in the fourteenth and fifteenth centuries as ties were severed by the Mongol invasions. But in the centuries that followed, a so-called 're-Christianization' took place through the activity of Georgian and Russian missionaries. Traditional Ossetian deities and rituals, the historian said, were assimilated to Christian saints. (A significant minority of the people also came under the sway of Islam.) The Christian archangels Michael and Gabriel were conflated into Mikaelgabyrta, a single character associated with both fertility and the underworld.

How wonderful, I thought, as the historian burbled pleasantly on: to think of this process of gods of wolves and thunder – so tangible for highland pastoralists! – shaping the intruding faith instead of retreating into the shadows. I raised an imaginary glass to Uastyrdzhi and his kind.

Yet despite the continuing ambiguity of their beliefs, I knew the Ossetians had served for centuries as an anchor for Russia at the centre of the North Caucasus. With their formal conversion to Christianity after the empire absorbed the northern part of Ossetia in 1774, they acquired privileges and became important allies of tsarist power. The Ossetians had not resisted the Russian empire in the nineteenth-century Caucasian War, as most of their Muslim neighbours did.

Today, the Ossetians remain the North Caucasus's only indigenous nation that is predominantly Orthodox. This historical loyalty to Russia is one reason they received Kremlin support in

School Number One, Beslan.

Some of the 314 hostages who died in the siege.

Cossack ancestors of a Russian woman living in Ingushetia.

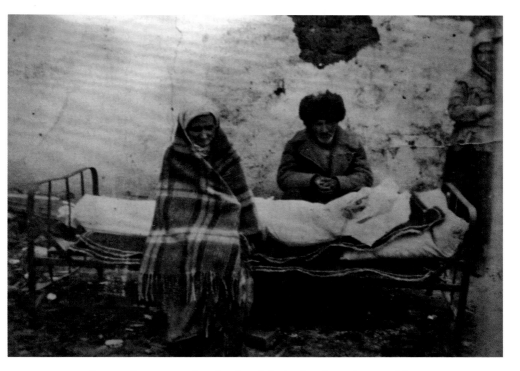

An Ingush couple mourn the death of their daughter in Kazakhstan, 1946.

Ingush family photographs.

An Ingush survivor of the deportations.

Leo Tolstoy in 1854, the year he finished military service in the North Caucasus.

Grozny, the Chechen capital, in February 2000, after weeks of Russian bombardment.

Masara Murtayeva (Babushka) prays at a memorial to the victims of the
Stalin-era deportation.

A boy collects scrap metal
in Chechnya.

Police guard a statue of Kadyrov Senior
in central Grozny.

Imam Shamil
photographed in
Saint Petersburg
after his surrender
in 1859.

The 'martyrs' cemetery'
in Gimry, Dagestan.

Gunib village, 'a massive soufflé of rock' and the scene of
Imam Shamil's capitulation.

'Dagestani types', an early twentieth-century image by
Russian photographer Sergei Prokudin-Gorsky.

Suleyman, my walking companion in Dagestan.

The mausoleum at Kala-Koreysh.

Interlude: War

perhaps the most bitter inter-ethnic conflict on Russian territory in the post-Soviet era, between the Ossetians and the Ingush.

I had hoped that I would be able to continue my walk without delay, but now there was a new problem.

It was no more than a day's hike from Vladikavkaz to Nazran, the biggest town in Ingushetia, and from there only about twenty miles across the tiny republic to the border with Chechnya.

Chechnya at the time was designated a permanent 'zone of counterterrorist operations', requiring foreign journalists to acquire a government-issued pass in order to travel there. Once inside the republic, you were supposed to stay in a designated guesthouse or at an army base.

Despite several attempts, I had not managed to receive the pass – an ID card valid for three months. There was no choice but to fly home to Moscow again and try to get it. If I was successful, I could return to Vladikavkaz and set off again from where I had left off. If not, I would have to consider giving up.

I gathered my meagre belongings, said goodbye to Andrew and got on a flight home.

Masha met me at the airport, took one look at my lean and sunburned face, laughed and said: 'Mozhet, khvatit?' *Maybe enough already?* Masha had been sceptical about the walk from the beginning, considering it a hazardous whimsy. She didn't hide her feelings, but, to her credit, she never tried to prevent me from doing what I wanted to do.

It was strange to be home once more. Friends were surprised to see me, but preferred jawing about the global financial crisis to hearing about what I had seen. It was the end of August, and the leaves of the lime trees in the yard flashed and turned in the summer breeze. I caught flu, as if my body had lowered its defences after weeks of operating under stress, and wallowed for a couple of days in bed. Then, one morning, I woke with a clear head and a sense of purpose, and called Yevgeny.

Yevgeny was an urbane career diplomat who had a small office behind the Russian ministry of foreign affairs: a Gotham-like tower on the inner ring road, its fawn-coloured stone blackened by fumes.

Tall and slim, with neatly parted fair hair, Yevgeny looked in his late fifties and had worked in Mozambique. He was unfailingly polite and agreed to meet me at a café on Stary Arbat, the pedestrianized street of artists and souvenir shops that is Moscow's equivalent of Covent Garden or Montmartre.

Yevgeny was the man responsible for issuing the Chechnya permits, and two years earlier, in 2006, he had accompanied me as my government escort on a visit to Grozny. That trip had been the result of months of negotiation after I requested an interview with Chechnya's heir apparent, Ramzan Kadyrov. In his late twenties, Ramzan Kadyrov was the son of the former president of the republic, Akhmad Kadyrov, who had been assassinated by militants at a Victory Day parade in a sports stadium a few months before the Beslan siege.

In the café, Yevgeny ordered black tea and placed his briefcase carefully on a chair. He had told me once that the day he earned enough money to buy his first Soviet briefcase had been a landmark in his diplomatic career, conveying a status and privilege to which he had long aspired.

It was hot, and Yevgeny was wearing the summer uniform of the Russian bureaucrat: a short-sleeved shirt, cream slacks and beige loafers with ventilation holes that made them look like cheese graters. My reportage from the Chechnya visit two years

Interlude: War

earlier had been unforgiving. The Kremlin, I concluded, had the same attitude to Kadyrov as Franklin D. Roosevelt supposedly did to the Nicaraguan dictator Anastasio Somoza García: 'He may be a sonofabitch, but he's our sonofabitch.' So the fact that Yevgeny was prepared to meet me at all was positive. But the news was not encouraging.

'I still have no answer from above, Tom,' he said in good English, sipping his tea. 'We will have to wait.'

Through the window, tourists were trying on fur hats at a stall on Stary Arbat. 'Yevgeny,' I said, 'don't you think that if I walked across Chechnya and all went well, then that would look favourable for the Russian government?'

'Yes, of course, but what if all doesn't go well? That might not appear so good. And we have to think of your safety. Bad things still happen down there. The boyeviki are weakened but attacks are possible.'

'What if I walked with a chaperone or a bodyguard?'

'I don't feel like going myself,' he smiled. 'And for Kadyrov's people, this is a headache – several days. Chechens don't enjoy to go by foot.'

Yevgeny promised to get back to me once he got a response on my permit application. Over the next ten days, I phoned him several times. The answer was always the same: nothing yet.

A flicker of doubt passed through my mind. I had got used to being with Masha again. At night, my body curled around hers, I lay awake and wondered if I really needed to resume the journey. After all, I had walked all the way from Sochi through the high valleys, circumnavigated Elbrus, crossed the steppe and passed into a war zone. That was a decent achievement. And the republics that lay ahead – Ingushetia, Chechnya and Dagestan – were the most dangerous yet.

CENTRAL

One day, I bumped into a friend with whom I had reported on the war, when we travelled via the tunnel under the mountains. With exceptional bravery, Dario had managed to evade our Russian government handlers at the end of one such trip and stay on for several days alone inside South Ossetia, reporting on how local militia plundered and torched Georgian villages.

'Oh, I thought you were still in the Caucasus on your journey,' said Dario, surprised.

That smarted a little. And there was something else: I had begun to miss the hypnotic rhythm of walking, the heat and the dust of the plain, the gulps of ozone on rocky ridges. It was late August, and the mountains could soon start to turn cold.

There was no point in phoning Yevgeny again.

I flew back to North Ossetia.

EAST

10

The Cauldron

AUGUST

In the cool of morning, I crossed the bridge over the Terek, the pink-orange glow of the Mukhtarov mosque to my right, and headed north out of Vladikavkaz past a sprawling factory and heaps of red slag.

Within half an hour of shouldering my pack, familiar niggles returned like old friends: a tingling at the top of my left thigh, the occasional sound of rearranging gristle from my right knee, an ache between my shoulders.

Pacing once more on asphalt, I hankered to get back into the hills. There was no choice but to stay in the low country for now. Here in North Ossetia, you had to follow a designated road to leave the republic; in Ingushetia and Chechnya, it would be impractical and risky to trek up into the peaks, where militants skirmished with the security forces. I comforted myself with the promise of a highland climax to my journey in Dagestan.

The road to Ingushetia passed through an Ingush-dominated village, with its characteristic large houses and walled gardens made from smooth Kuban bricks. Beyond was the Chermen checkpoint between the two republics, manned by soldiers and armed policemen.

EAST

The Caucasus checkpoint – or *blokpost* – can be an intimidating place. Once, a few years earlier, I had been stopped at one as I drove with two Chechens back to Grozny from the lowlands. It was dark, and a suspicious Russian officer kept us for an hour of questioning in a damp cinderblock room where draughts ruffled torn posters of wanted women – potential *shakhidki*.

At Chermen, Misha was waiting for me on the North Ossetian side, having gone through document checks in order to enter from Ingushetia: a filter to try to identify incoming terrorists. Four years before, the Beslan hostage-takers had gathered at a militant camp in the woods of Ingushetia before attacking the school, and several of them were Ingush, inflaming an already-fraught relationship with the Ossetians. The Chermen checkpoint was a symbol of the divide between the two nations. To cross in either direction required a certain chutzpah.

Misha, with the ropy arms and flat stomach of an amateur sportsman, had spread his handkerchief on the kerb and sat on it gingerly to avoid dusting the seat of his trousers. We had never met: he was an in-law of a friend, and had agreed to walk with me across Ingushetia.

I had decided that in the three remaining republics – Ingushetia, Chechnya and Dagestan – a local companion would be essential. Islamist violence was more common here at the eastern end of the North Caucasus, and the army and security services more suspicious of outsiders. Under the wing of a local, I would be less likely to get into trouble.

In each of the three republics, I would pay the men who accompanied me. Each of them was also desperate I should get a different squint on the region, so often maligned in Moscow. 'We are always the guilty ones, Tom,' said Misha with a smile. 'But that can't be right, can it?'

The Cauldron

On the Ingush side of the *blokpost*, there was a kerfuffle: officers were digging in the boot of a saloon at the head of a queue of cars. I was expecting questions. Instead, we walked past without even a request to show our papers. 'Going in this direction can be a lot easier,' said Misha as we moved swiftly away.

To the left of the road, agricultural land graded towards the steppe; to the right stretched a belt of low trees. My hip belt had resumed its familiar squeak. It was getting warm, the air soupy, stirred by only the barest whisper of wind. I had always worn trousers out of respect for local custom, but on days like this, I longed to exchange them for shorts.

One of Misha's nephews, a tall, jolly man in a tracksuit with 'Russia' on the back, stopped his car to enquire what tragedy had forced us to walk. He grinned and shook his head when he found out, gesturing at his Moskvitch. 'Well, it's up to you. The iron camel is here if you need it.'

As Misha and I walked on towards Nazran, he told me he had not been afraid of crossing into North Ossetia, as some Ingush were, especially after Beslan. 'I grew up in Vladikavkaz,' he said. 'I know it well.' Misha was my age, born in the early 1970s to parents who had returned from exile in Central Asia after the deportation.

The road was tremoring. A small convoy of tanks and armoured cars growled past, heading back to Chechnya or Dagestan in the wake of the war. On the edge of Nazran, an APC bumped onto the opposite pavement and soldiers got out to stop cars and check drivers' documents. The Chechen refugee camps dotted around the town had gone, but Nazran seemed to have changed little since my first visit six years earlier: the same potholed streets, the same sheep cropping on scorched verges, the same Ladas driving by with blacked-out windows. Above an intersection strewn with litter, a billboard read: 'Nazran: City of Peace, Goodness and Hope.'

A halt for a drink in the near-darkness of an air-conditioned café was an icy delight after the heat outside. Each table was illuminated by a feeble lamp, and men in black winklepickers squinted through the gloom at my outsized walking boots. Misha's house was a couple of miles out of the town on the far side, in a neighbourhood of recently built houses on a bare slope, divided by dirt streets. It had a five-metre-high metal gate and brick walls surrounding the garden.

Misha introduced me to his wife, Liza, his mother, Leyla, who gave me a firm hug and a kiss, and his daughters, eleven-month-old Adiliya and two-year-old Lina. That afternoon, we ate in the sunshine in the garden, and Lina hurtled about, grinning and singing, her blond hair a halo in the sun. Misha was obviously besotted with his family. He called Lina *khuliganka* (the hooligan) and pinched the nape of her neck as the wide-eyed Adiliya pitched and rolled on a blanket, giggling.

At night, I woke to the chatter of automatic gunfire; not close, but near enough to give me a start.

'Could be criminals, could be *boyeviki*,' said Misha over breakfast in the garden. 'Sometimes they shoot up alcohol stores or torch them. Sometimes they murder faith healers and people who don't pay them protection money.' This was the reality of life in Ingushetia.

The evening before, Misha had received a phone call to let him know that an uncle had died after an illness. After a talk with his mother, it was decided that Leyla would go to the funeral in a hill village to represent the family.

'Won't they be offended if you don't go as well?' I asked Misha.

'On the contrary, they'd be very angry if they found out I had a guest and failed to stay with him,' he said.

The Cauldron

Leyla nodded. 'This is true,' she said. She had put on a black dress with polka dots and a black headscarf, and with a sudden twinge, I thought of the Beslan mothers, and of all the mourning women of the Caucasus, forever stooping at coffins. She said goodbye as she headed to catch a minibus taxi to the mountains.

The talk of relatives sent Misha inside. He came out with a scroll of thick, cream paper. 'This is my family tree,' he said, spreading the chart on the table. 'A lot of people know it in their heads; it's our tradition that you should know seven generations back.'

One node near the centre was Misha's great-grandfather Berd, a formidable toughie who had lived from 1846 to 1956, he said, surviving the deportation to Kazakhstan at ninety-seven years old. At the top of the chart, ancestors receded towards the moment when Misha's clan had split into two strands. Misha spread his fingers and ran them down through the generations, as if raking through sand. At the bottom, he pointed out some distant relatives descended from Berd's brother. 'This one, Khasbulat, got killed in 2006, he was a boyevik. His brother, Dzhambulat, is in prison. This one's in the army. This one's only nineteen – no children yet, there's still time.' It seemed a characteristic spread of experience: the Ingush had fought on both sides in the Caucasian War and stayed out of Chechnya's post-Soviet bids for independence, although some were drawn to the guerrillas.

Ingush family rituals were numerous and intricate and often performative, Misha explained. Many were deeply sustaining; others were a drag. Handing over money at funerals and weddings could add up, as could the expense of handkerchiefs given to every visitor as a gift at the end of Ramadan. 'One year, we men even stitched up our pockets, but the women just stuffed the handkerchiefs down our shirts,' said Misha.

The contrast between this rich inner life and the Islamist war intrigued me. How did you swing between the peace of the family yard and the gunshots of the street? Misha worked for an international relief group running a project in Nazran. He invited me to stay for a while before we set out for Chechnya, and I agreed readily, keen to learn more.

The next morning, I walked into the town with Misha to visit my friends at Memorial, the human rights group, in their little office at 46 Mutaliyeva Street. I had been there many times in the six years since I had first visited the North Caucasus, and was filled with happiness to see them again. Katya had moved on, but there was Albert, the humorous, rubbery-faced man who was Misha's brother-in-law; Akhmed, the handsome young Ingush who had shown me around the Chechen refugee camps; Israil, the man-mountain driver; and Timur, the even-tempered and keenly intelligent head of the office.

We sat in the kitchen, sipping tea and eating sweets, the loose tiles on the floor slipping under our feet. 'If anything, things have got worse since you last came,' said Timur. 'Ingushetia has become a kind of cauldron of terror. It's out of control.'

Timur, steel-haired, calm, gave a succinct briefing. President Zyazikov's security forces were proceeding with a campaign of extrajudicial killings of about forty per year against suspected militants. In one recent case, a six-year-old boy had died in a special operation that destroyed his family home. 'A six-year-old boy,' said Timur, looking up for emphasis. The security forces, he went on, continued to beat or torture suspects, often innocent of anything but a deep belief in conservative Islam. They employed electric shocks or pins pushed under their nails. Meanwhile, Timur said, in the first seven months, the militants had assassinated dozens

The Cauldron

of policemen and officials, injuring scores of others. They had also executed a series of ethnic Russian and other non-Ingush civilians in their homes. This was all in a republic of no more than 500,000 people, the size of Essex – one tiny patch of Russia, a supposedly peaceful European state. 'You should take care, Tom,' said Timur. 'You don't want to get caught up in this somehow.'

'Thanks, you're right,' I replied. Although getting caught up was kind of the point.

In the North Caucasus, as in many places, however, everything is fine until the moment it isn't. Much of the violence came in spasms, cordoned off or conducted in darkness, short and quickly curtailed. In between, people went to work and raised families and did their shopping, just as they did anywhere else in Russia. Unsettled by Timur's briefing, all I could think to do was the same. After an hour or two, Misha and I said goodbye to the Memorial staff and walked in the sun to the bazaar to get some kurdyuk, the fatty tail of a fat-tailed sheep.

Young men on the streets wore velvet skullcaps, while older men sported trilbies with their suits; young women were in blouses and denim skirts to below the knee, their mothers and aunts in long, printed dresses. Near the butchers' stalls, a gypsy girl with colourful skirts and a David Beckham T-shirt was chasing her friends and laughing. Sides of lamb hung on hooks above stacks of kurdyuk and beef tongues. Congealed and distended, the kurdyuk looked faintly obscene. 'Like half a human backside,' said Misha, laughing, as he pointed at a reddened lump. 'Let's take that smoked one. They're the tastiest.'

The stallholder was cheered by my presence. 'Our old people assure us that one day the English will come to rule in the Caucasus and all will be well,' he said as he wrapped the kurdyuk. 'Maybe you are their herald?'

'I can't be certain,' I replied, smiling, as I took the package. I'd heard this myth of English influence before; there were even rumours of shared heritage. London, an Ossetian beekeeper had told me near Elbrus, was given its name by conquering Alans, the warrior race who were his people's ancestors. Lon meant quiet or calm in Ossetian, and don meant water, he said. Wasn't the Thames a peaceful river? The traveller Stephen Graham had noted in 1911 that the Ingush – or Ingoosh, as he called them – were 'said to be descended from Englishmen, hence the name'. Crusaders heading to the Holy Land over the Pass of the Cross, so the theory went, had dallied and converted to Islam. It was far-fetched stuff, but I was secretly pleased at this thought of Anglo-Caucasian kinship.

On the way home, we bumped into a man whom Misha knew. He had worked at the town hospital as a security guard, but had recently left the job. 'They started saying we should guard the morgue as well as the hospital,' he explained. 'They bring the dead boyeviki there all the time; there's blood everywhere, it's a mess. And the boyeviki don't give up their own: they come at night to collect the dead. The police said it was only their responsibility to bring us the bodies, then it was our duty to guard them. But I didn't even have a weapon. Was I going to stand in the way of an armed boyevik for four thousand roubles a month?'

'Actually, it's a good thing you didn't have a weapon,' said Misha. 'That could have turned out much worse. Best just to stand aside and let them through.'

I asked: 'Why don't the security forces lie in wait for the boyeviki at the morgue?'

'They do sometimes,' the man replied. 'But the boyeviki have their spies. They don't show up just like that.' He had left the job at the hospital and started a new one lifting fifty-kilogram boxes at the post office for a third of the money, he said. 'I don't know how long my back will hold out, but at least I won't get shot.'

Ingush pain was rooted in the deportation during the Second World War, but there were more recent causes.

Misha and I were becoming friends. In the evening, after dinner, we drank tea with spoonfuls of apricot jam in the kitchen, and he began to tell me his story.

He had grown up in Vladikavkaz in North Ossetia, after his parents came back from the Ingush exile in Central Asia. His father found work in the city as a policeman, and the family lived in a modest apartment. As a teenager in the twilight of the Soviet Union, Misha had become one of the leaders of a gang of young toughs in his neighbourhood. They gathered after school, playing football and working out in the yard. Misha was a keen athlete who earned the Soviet designation of Master of Sport in freestyle wrestling. The gang extorted what they could get from vulnerable locals: clothes, cash, sometimes a Japanese tape recorder. 'We were bandits,' said Misha.

'Petty ones,' I said.

Misha shrugged. 'Still bandits,' he said.

At the time, relations between Ossetians and Ingush were already fractious. On their return to the Caucasus in the late 1950s, the Ingush had been treated as traitors. Part of their republic had been handed to North Ossetia, and many Ingush found their homes inhabited by new occupants. Disputes over ownership continued for decades.

Nevertheless, Misha grew up in Vladikavkaz with almost exclusively Ossetian friends. The best of them was a curly-haired schoolmate named Marat, who was three years younger. The two of them were together all the time. Marat was energetic, cheerful and loyal. He was a junior member of the gang. Misha was also close to Marat's twin sister, Albina, whom he remembered by the affectionate nickname Albinka.

One night in December 1989, a rival gang tried to rob two of Misha's friends as they bought food and drinks for his seventeenth birthday party. In the ensuing melee, one of the muggers cut Marat in the face with a knife made from a sharpened slide gauge. Enraged, Misha wrenched the knife away and stabbed the assailant nine times. The gang fled, but under police questioning, one of the members gave his friends away.

It was touch and go who would be the accused: the mugger had survived, and he had struck first. In the end, Misha and his friends went to trial. 'All our criminal buddies flooded the courtroom and made a commotion,' he said. 'In revenge, the judge gave Marat and two of our guys five years, and I got seven.' His parents paid to get all the sentences reduced by two years. Misha was sent to a *zona*, a penal colony for minors at the other end of the North Caucasus, in Adygea. The inmates slept in barracks, and for the first few weeks he was forced every night to fight a group of a dozen other prisoners. They beat him savagely, but he hurt enough of them to earn respect.

'I was such a disappointment to my father,' Misha said. 'He was a high-ranking policeman; he knew all the KGB chiefs in the republic. And his son was a crook.'

Behind the scenes, Misha's mother contacted an influential relative, a veteran of the Soviet-Afghan War, who wrote to the deputy minister of defence requesting a pardon. The request went to Boris Yeltsin, the new president of Russia. Yeltsin issued an order to reduce Misha's sentence further, to three years. Eventually, he was released early for good behaviour, in June 1992.

It was time to rebuild his life: to go straight, to find a job. But

The Cauldron

something was looming, a national catastrophe that would affect tens of thousands of Ingush. Misha's world was to about to turn upside down once more.

The days in Nazran passed with excursions on foot, and the evenings with long talks in the garden or the kitchen.

One morning, Misha took me to meet a well-known filmmaker who lived on the other side of town. As we approached the neighbourhood, there was a rapid pop-popping. I stopped, alarmed, and cocked an ear. Could it be gunfire? Yes. Yes, it was. My first notion was to turn tail and run. 'Special operation?' I asked Misha.

He squinted in the direction of the popping, put his hands on his hips and then said: 'More likely a wedding. Let's go on.'

The film-maker lived in an area of dirt roads that had obviously been a quagmire in winter, but in the heat of summer had solidified into ruts and crests. Something in the distance was bucking towards us along one of the tracks. Pop-pop, came the noise, amid a fainter sound of shouting. I stiffened a little. What to do? This could be dangerous.

The object moved closer and resolved into a pristine blue Rolls-Royce Phantom with a man sitting on the passenger window and firing a Kalashnikov into the air. There were cries of joy from inside the car as the bullets ripped into the sky. Misha and I watched dumbly as the Rolls cavorted past and down the track. It was a vision of such absurdity that it might have been a Hispano-Suiza coming down the loke on my childhood farm in Norfolk.

The film-maker chuckled. 'One of our boxers won gold at the Olympics, and he just got home to celebrate with his family,' he said.

I was tired, and the film-maker talked for hours in a sonorous voice about his career and the perfidy of the Stalinist deportations.

All the while, we could hear the sounds of music, wild revelry and gunfire coming from the boxer's family compound not far away.

With hindsight, I cannot understand why I did not simply excuse myself and walk down the track with Misha to offer congratulations to the boxer and join the party. In a list of missed opportunities that I carry around in my head, this moment is marked down as one of the silliest in my life.

Misha and I sat in his kitchen, talking again, as Liza served us soup and rissoles. Liza rarely ate with us: it was a frustration to me on my walk that opportunities to engage women in conversation were few because of social constraints. Looking back, I regret that I did not try harder. The one time I asked Liza to tell me about her life, she smiled and said: 'Work, work, work,' and rushed off to the next chore.

Once Liza was gone, Misha began to talk me through a timeline of modern history; dates that were scorched in every Ingush mind.

The Ingush and the Chechens are brother Muslim nations of the Vainakh group, he said, with similar languages and customs. The district where his father was born, Prigorodny, had originally been part of the joint Checheno-Ingush autonomous republic, itself a component of the Russian republic inside the Soviet Union that had existed since 1934.

With Stalin's deportation of the Chechens and Ingush to Central Asia in 1944 on suspicion of siding with the Nazis, the Checheno-Ingush republic was dissolved and – in the planting of yet another territorial timebomb – Prigorodny district was handed to North Ossetia. When the Ingush and Chechens were allowed home from exile in 1957, their joint republic was reinstated, but Prigorodny, which abutted Vladikavkaz, stayed inside

The Cauldron

North Ossetia. Although discouraged from repatriating to Prigo-rodny, many Ingush managed to do so, returning in the face of threats and discrimination to the land where tens of thousands of them had once lived, forming ninety per cent of its population.

'The Russians and the Ossetians saw us as enemies of the people who had been allowed to return,' said Misha. 'We had no rights. Ossetians had occupied our homes. Some gave them up; many refused.'

Decades later, when the Soviet Union began to implode, an overexcited Yeltsin urged the regions to 'take as much sovereignty as you can swallow'. In 1990, Chechnya broke away and launched a bid for independence. The Ingush stayed out of the fight and Ingushetia remained part of Russia, but there were increasing calls for the return of Prigorodny.

One evening at the end of October 1992, four months after his release from the *zona* and now almost nineteen years old, Misha was sitting in a pavilion in a communal yard with friends in Vladikavkaz. He had been reunited with Marat, the knife wound on his cheek healed into an impressive scar, and their other Ossetian friends.

'We were playing cards,' Misha recalled. 'One of the boys went away for a while and then came back and said: "Lads, war has broken out with the Ingush in Prigorodny."' And we were like: "Are you crazy, what war?" And we went quiet for a while, and then we started to hear – far, far away – gunshots. And not just single ones, but volleys of automatic fire. And everybody started saying: "Yes, it's war."'

Misha hurried home, and for three days, he and his parents and his younger sister stayed in their flat, flinching as the gunshots got louder. On the fourth day, the Ossetian militia came and broke down the door. 'They said, "You're Ingush, right? You are going to be exchanged for Ossetians taken hostage by Ingush forces." I said: "What's that got to do with us? We're not on the warring side. We live here in the city." They said it made no difference.'

The family were pushed into a car and taken to a half-finished garage outside Vladikavkaz where scores of other Ingush hostages were being gathered. At the entrance, Misha's mother and sister were released. He and his father were taken inside, the older man leaning on his son because a stroke had affected his gait. A crowd of Ossetians formed at the entrance to the garage. 'They wanted to kill us. I remember a guard firing over their heads from the door, and turning to us to say, "Because of you animals, I have to shoot at my brothers."'

As Misha and I talked in the kitchen, Leyla returned from the mountains. Greeting us, she poured fresh tea and brought a plateful of apricot jam. She sat down quietly as Misha continued the story.

More Ingush men were pushed into the garage, he said; some bloodied. (One, a badly beaten policeman, was later found dead.) The newcomers explained what had happened: following months of tension, armed clashes had broken out in four Prigorodny villages after a thirteen-year-old Ingush girl was crushed by an Ossetian armoured personnel carrier. Hundreds of people were being held captive, mostly Ingush. Ossetian militia were said to be killing civilians and looting while federal troops failed to inter-vene; Christian Ossetia's historical fidelity to Russia was paying dividends.

On the fourth day, Russian soldiers transferred the hostages in the garage to a bomb shelter on the edge of Vladikavkaz. Misha and other young men, along with two ten-year-old orphans from a children's home, occupied a room, where they smoked and broke up old desks for planks to sleep on the floor. They were fed bread and water, and sometimes the elders got boiled meat. Rumours circulated that the women and girls had not been released but sent to another holding centre, from which few escaped alive. 'I fell into a depression thinking about my sister; she was like a daughter to me,' said Misha.

One afternoon, as he spoke to a guard who had agreed to buy him some cigarettes, Misha missed the visit of a Russian military commission checking on the hostages. The visitors recorded each person speaking their name and address into a dictaphone. Misha's father spoke but did not mention his son, thinking he had been recorded in the other room.

In the kitchen, Leyla raised a hand. 'Let me tell my part, son,' she said. Misha nodded.

'My daughter and I were not taken to another centre,' said Leyla. 'We were released and came by a roundabout route to my sister's, here in Nazran. Our people were being killed in Prigorodny and the bodies were brought here to a square. I went there to look for my son and husband every day.'

Recordings of Ingush hostages speaking into dictaphones at various holding centres were played over a loudspeaker in the square. One morning, Leyla heard her husband talking, but not her son. 'I decided that Misha was dead, that they had murdered him,' she said. She began to search again among the corpses. Then she saw a wooden crate that had been fastened shut. Next to it stood an Ingush with an automatic. 'I went up to him and said, "Give me that crate. That's my son. I know it's him." He refused and gave me a telling-off, and I lost my temper. I was shouting at him: "If you're a real man, then why don't you go and fight rather than standing here guarding corpses?"'

Flushed, the man called over an official who tried to calm Leyla down. 'He said I would put a curse on my son if I carried on like that. He said my son was surely alive, that he'd just been missed for some reason. I said: "OK, but promise you will tell me where you bury that crate. If I don't find my son, I will know where to go to visit his grave.""

Misha said: 'Mama thought it was me in the crate. Probably it was the remains of someone burned in their home in Prigorodny.'

Misha and his father spent several more days in the underground bunker until they were released with about forty other men. They were driven by military truck out of North Ossetia and into Ingushetia via the Chermen checkpoint, the one Misha and I would cross on foot sixteen years later. The truck dumped the men in the middle of Nazran on a snowy day in early November. Father and son hobbled to the flat of Misha's maternal aunt on the third floor of a five-storey block, struggling to remember the address. Leyla, Misha's two sisters and his aunt cried with relief when they opened the door. His uncle gave Misha a hug and went into another room to return with a gift of a silver signet ring to celebrate his safe return.

The family had escaped, but they had lost their home. There was no going back to Vladikavkaz. To live among Ossetians was impossible now that such enmity had been stirred. Travel between the two republics became fraught, if not impossible. Misha got a job as a cameraman with a local television station in Nazran. Over the next few years, he and his family would move seven times from flat to flat in Ingushetia. It was not until 1996, four years after the conflict, that he dared pick up the phone and call Marat, his old friend in Vladikavkaz.

'I said: "It's me, Misha, your brother Misha." He was angry and said: "What Misha? Get lost." He thought someone was playing a joke on him. I told him a couple of things that only we could know, about our friends. Then he realized it was me and started crying and shouting: "Why did you disappear, you bastard? Why didn't you write? I couldn't find where you were. I will come! I will come to Nazran."'

The very next day, the friends met at the Chermen checkpoint. There was no public transport from Nazran, so Misha walked there. Marat came with three other friends and his sister, Albinka, from Vladikavkaz. 'We sat down on the grass right by the round-about and had a picnic in front of the Russians and Ossetians. And we ate pies and drank *araka* and we cursed the mother of whoever it was who started the war.'

At the picnic, Marat scolded Misha again for not getting in touch. During the conflict, he had been away on a business trip in northern Russia, selling vodka. He told how when he got back, he went straight to Misha's family apartment, only to find some South Ossetians had moved in among their possessions. They refused Marat's request to leave, but at least allowed him to take the family photo albums – which he handed over to Misha at Chermen.

After the meeting at the checkpoint, Misha was at work at the television studio in Nazran one day when the security guard came in and said: 'There's someone to see you. An Ossetian with a frightened face.'

Misha went outside to find Marat, with his tousled hair, waiting with two surprised Ingush policemen, who had shown him the way to the studio. The two friends embraced. 'Do you know this man?' asked one of the cops.

'Yes, he's my friend,' said Misha.

'OK, he's your responsibility now,' came the policeman's reply.

Misha laughed as he told the story. 'Marat was with several friends. It was obvious they weren't Ingush or Chechens. I mean,

Albinka was there; she was basically wearing a miniskirt. Our women don't dress like that. We went back to my house. Imagine them getting out of the car and all my neighbours just STARING.'

'What did the neighbours think?' I asked.

'They were surprised that Ossetians would come here, just like that. And maybe they despised me a little for going around with them.'

I asked: 'And did you keep up contact with each other? What about now?'

Misha paused for a moment and looked bereft, and then said: 'Marat died.'

'Oh no! What happened?'

'The drink killed him. You know, every family there makes *araka*. Everyone drinks it: men and women. And with him, it got to the point where he became an alcoholic. He couldn't settle in a job. He sold vodka: that didn't work. He manufactured plastic bags: that didn't work. Albinka told me later that he had problems with his girlfriend. He was in and out of hospital with the drinking. And you know what, he always used to say on the phone: "Misha, if you were home in Vladikavkaz, everything would be different."'

It was a devastating thought: that by separating two friends, the conflict had seized another victim, years later.

'And you?' I asked. 'Do you think that's true?'

Misha was silent again, laying his hands in his lap. 'I'm not sure,' he said. 'I didn't use alcohol much at all. And when I lived there, Marat and I were always together. We had common interests, common enemies. So yes, I don't think he would have drunk like that if I was around. And that means I could have saved him. If I hadn't been forced to move away.'

The Cauldron

Misha and I set out for the border with Chechnya past a bank of low, rolling hills.

It was hot and the asphalt was tacky. Misha wore his handkerchief on his head like an Englishman in a seaside postcard, with the corners knotted.

Over the years, the story of what happened in Prigorodny had festered in the minds of the Ingush, to the point where real and imaginary depravity were inextricably mixed. As we walked, Misha told me that Ingush men in captivity had strangled their own sisters rather than let them fall prey to the Ossetians. 'Moreover, at the girls' request,' he claimed.

In all, about six hundred people were killed. While there were atrocities on both sides, the Ingush casualties were greater. Tens of thousands of people were driven from their homes – an enormous number for these tiny nations.

'When the hostages were being held at the school in Beslan, the Ingush didn't act gleeful because they were Ossetians,' said Misha, pulling the handkerchief forward to mop sweat from his brow. 'One person is a viper, another is a best friend. No nation is all bad. But we do wonder why nobody cries in the same way over our dead women and children.'

For many Ingush, the deportation during the Second World War, the loss of lives and homes in Prigorodny in the 1990s and the current chaos in the republic were links in the same chain. All of them seemed to flow from Moscow's contempt. The boyeviki were hateful fanatics, but the Kremlin's own terror campaign had boosted their number.

That night, we stayed with Misha's uncle and aunt in a small town on the way to the Chechen border. Behind the house, Misha's uncle kept three bullocks in a pen in a yard; in another were a pair of grey-brown heifers from Astrakhan. The yard was dominated by a stack of hay bales covered in tarp. After dinner, Misha caught a ride home for the night and left me with his relatives. We sat outside in the smell of hay and the dark and were joined by a handful of neighbours. Someone produced a bottle of *araka*. One of the visitors was a teacher who had fled on foot into the Ingush mountains with her husband and children during the Prigorodny conflict.

Four of us men stayed up talking, a weak bulb burning on the side of the house. The topic of conversation was: 'When will the Ingush be free of suffering?' Sometime in the early hours, one of the neighbours turned on music on his mobile phone. Misha's uncle leapt to his feet to dance a *lezginka*. Dimly illuminated, he threw out his limbs in graceful arcs and thrusts, spinning in the dirt, the stamp of his shoes raising little puffs of dust, his lips pursed with effort, his head thrown back, his eyelids trembling as they closed in ecstasy.

11

Land of the Boy King

I woke with a nasty hangover and a dry mouth, lying diagonally on a sofa bed in the living room. Misha's car engine was revving outside. He had returned from Nazran to walk with me from his uncle and aunt's house to the border with Chechnya. After a hasty breakfast and a last fondle of the calves' ears in the hay-scented yard, we left.

All my attempts to get the security pass from Yevgeny for Chechnya had failed. There was nothing to do but risk it. A new Chechen friend called Musa who ran a small business in Grozny making illuminated signs had agreed to be my next companion. He had been born in exile in Kazakhstan after his family was deported there and only returned 'home' to Chechnya as a four-year-old in 1972. We had met in a hotel restaurant in Vladikavkaz a few weeks earlier in the aftermath of the war, where Musa was working as a photographer.

Musa and I were to rendezvous near the Ingush side of the border and then, if I could get across, we would walk on together through Chechnya. He was, I knew, not really cut out for a hike. At forty, with a fleshy, clean-shaven face and a swelling stomach, Musa was the antithesis of the pinched-waist Chechen brave of popular fantasy. That did not matter. I needed a dependable companion for this tricky part of the journey, not a warrior. And there he was, waiting at a crossroads on the edge of Sleptsovskaya, where minibuses were disgorging passengers into the dust.

Misha greeted Musa, then said goodbye and went to catch a minibus back to his aunt's. I was sorry to see him go: the story of his lost friendship with Marat had touched me deeply, and I was impressed that he had managed to transcend his past to become a caring father to his girls.

The question now was how to get into Chechnya. 'There's a road to the north we could take from here,' said Musa. 'The blokpost there is much smaller than the Kavkaz one and should be lightly manned.'

'OK,' I said. 'Let's try that.' I knew from experience that normal practice at these checkpoints was for people to drive their cars slowly up to a chicane of concrete barriers and then offer their documents. At night, you had to switch on the interior light in your car and approach even more slowly or risk being shot. The procedure for pedestrians was less clear.

We set off. After twenty minutes, the blokpost came into view: two guardhouses made from cinderblocks and several tents under camouflage netting by the side of the road. Too late, I considered our appearance. Musa, in his best get-up for outdoor exercise, was wearing a yellow and blue shell-suit jacket, a T-shirt, a fake Dolce & Gabbana belt and brown deck shoes. On his back was a minuscule rucksack, and he was carrying a spade handle he had found by the roadside that struck him as a potential staff despite being far too short. I had left my red hiking pack and boots behind in Nazran, and walked on from there in shoes and a pair of jeans, with a small black daysack. The idea was to appear less like a foreigner, but now I thought that our little rucksacks looked worryingly metrosexual in the Caucasus, where no self-respecting man would be seen with such a thing.

So this was the moment I had been agonizing about for weeks. If we were turned back here, my plan to walk every step of the way to the Caspian would be in shreds. Even a casual question could reveal my accent and give me away. And then what? Arrest, perhaps; interrogation. A long wait and a humiliating journey back to Moscow.

By one of the guardhouses, a single Russian soldier was leaning down and parting the dry grass. It was not clear why. Was he cleaning something from his hands? Observing a snake? Concealing an object among the yellowed stalks?

As he turned towards us, Musa said cheerily: 'So, what are we hiding?'

The soldier laughed and exclaimed: 'A bomb!'

Musa shot back: 'In that case, we'll be on our way!' And in this pocket of levity, we marched on down the road into Chechnya, without the soldier giving us a second glance.

Before us was a flat landscape of cropped pasture and cultivated fields, then a small town with a mosque, where Musa showed me rough-ended blocks of stone stacked on top of each other to make the foundations of a bridge: Chechen gravestones put to use by the Soviets after the deportation, he said. Under lowering skies, a deserted road of crumbling asphalt led on across the steppe. Occasionally, there were unfinished brick houses to the left and right, as if abandoned during construction. Dotting the horizon stood clusters of cypresses.

This, I reminded myself, was a landscape shaped by war. The wedge of Chechen plain into which Musa and I were now advancing, between the Terek river to the north and the Sunzha river to the south (meandering, they would converge beyond Grozny), had been dominated by forest as late as the 1830s. As Cossack settlement intensified, more and more trees were chopped down, for firewood and to build forts and homes. Then, in the 1840s, forest clearance increasingly became a military tactic; a means of pushing the Chechens out of the fertile lowlands into the hills of the Greater Caucasus. Leo Tolstoy described one such expedition in his early story 'The Wood-Felling'. It tells of a column of tsarist troops coming under Tatar cannon and rifle fire as they chop down two square miles of forest, creating a vast clearing through which they could advance. (Muslim or Turkic-speaking highlanders in the North Caucasus were often referred to collectively as Tatars.) Woodland, after all, was a place of refuge. Imam Shamil was said to have sent ten thousand men to defend the forest by the Sunzha to no avail. He was forced to withdraw to the highland villages of Chechnya and Dagestan: those were easier to hold but less opportune as bases for attack. 'In the long run it was by the axe and not by the sword' that Russian victory was achieved in the war, concluded John Baddeley in *The Russian Conquest of the Caucasus* (1908). When Chechen rebels retreated from Grozny a century and a half later, in the 1990s, they headed for the remaining forest belt to the south, in the foothills of the main range. Now, when the few hundred militants who were left released videos calling for vengeance and jihad on the Russians, they did so from woodland camps with leafy backdrops and an audio accompaniment of birdsong and gurgling streams.

Musa had announced gaily that it would take us 'two days, no more' to cross the seventy-odd miles from one end of Chechnya to the other. Within two hours, he was sinking to the verge to examine his blistered feet. We slowed to crawling pace. 'I haven't gone this far on foot for twenty years or so,' he admitted.

Land of the Boy King

Musa's ambition was not to walk, but to fly. Since childhood, he had nursed a fascination for light aircraft, he told me. A television programme about gyrocopters, the small craft that use an unpowered rotor to generate lift, had prompted instant obsession. 'I want one,' he said. 'I want to fly around the world in it. It will cost about one hundred thousand euros.' He had already planned a route, starting in Grozny and heading first to Karaganda in Kazakhstan, where his grandparents had died in exile. From there, he would go via Siberia to Alaska, Canada, Greenland, Iceland, Britain and Europe, and then home to Grozny through European Russia. All he needed was sponsorship. 'Imagine what a PR victory it would be for Chechnya!' he said, stopping to lean on a pole he had found to replace the spade handle, his belly protruding. 'Imagine the air traffic controllers – "God, what is it, a Chechen suicide bomber? No! It's Musa the peace envoy, going round the globe!"'

We both giggled.

The sky had cleared a little. To our left, clouds were casting shadows on the low, tawny swell of the Sunzha ridge, a crease in the landscape guiding us eastwards. We passed a cow by the roadside and reached the village of Samashki.

During the early months of 1995, the Russian army sought to take control of western Chechnya. The people of the prosperous village of Samashki – with their homes and byres and vine-wreathed yards – were in a difficult spot. Self-defence groups of local men attacked several Russian military vehicles that entered the village, but larger units of *boyeviki* with a more aggressive stance sometimes appeared from the forest – a surviving patch on Samashki's southern edge – to take on the federal troops, who responded by sending helicopters to strafe the streets, killing civilians.

Elders of the village pleaded for calm on both sides, to no avail. On 6 April 1995, interior ministry troops surrounding Samashki issued an ultimatum: to hand over, by the next morning, 264 automatics, two machine guns and an APC, and let troops into the village. The elders responded that there was no such quantity of weapons, but that they would tell the self-defence units not to attack the incoming soldiers.

Overnight, well before the deadline, the edges of the village came under artillery bombardment. Then, the next afternoon, after a new bout of shelling, about 350 Russian troops advanced into Samashki. A Russian lieutenant general later claimed Shamil Basayev was there, putting up a fierce battle with his unit of Abkhazia veterans – the ones who had supposedly kicked heads around the stadium in Gagra three years earlier. Locals and members of the self-defence force told Memorial that that was nonsense: a few dozen local men knocked out one Russian tank and gave patchy resistance before withdrawing.

That evening and the next morning came the true horror: the *zachistka*, the mopping-up. Soldiers moved through the village, going into homes; killing some occupants, detaining others. One group of unarmed men was pushed into a garage inspection pit and shot. Soldiers carried hay into houses and set them alight; they killed cows in their pens with their Kalashnikovs, pushed over water butts to prevent anyone dousing the flames, and then sat across the street laughing, eating looted jam and nuts. They beat teenage boys and forced men to strip. They carried off televisions and carpets to their trucks and APCs, and pulled up onions. An elderly man recalled cowering alone in a basement, where he had put a small bed to rest on during bombardments. A soldier threw in a grenade; miraculously, it exploded under the bed and caused him no harm. The old man emerged and managed to slink away as two soldiers tried to smash open his safebox in the yard; a third was shooting his chickens. His house was ablaze.

Samashki was Chechnya's My Lai: a village massacre that exceeded even the terrors of Grozny. According to Memorial's exhaustive report, at least 112 residents were killed, including twelve women and seven people under eighteen years of age. The large majority were civilians. Two teenage boys died when they were hit by a mortar shell as they drove a group of calves home from their pasture. Twenty-three of the victims were over sixty years old. One man was murdered after having clumps of hair torn from his head; another as he tried to pull his disabled brother from a burning home; a third as he hung a white flag on his fence. The troops poured petrol on corpses and set them on fire.

Musa led me through streets of brick houses with corrugated roofs and blue and green metal fences. Samashki was once again the bucolic place it had been on the eve of war. We went to the home of a family that Musa knew. 'For tea,' he said, wincing, but I knew that he needed a rest. The family were delighted to see him. Wherever we went over the next few days, Musa elicited affection. A stool was brought to relieve his throbbing feet. We sat in the living room, talking. Where had we come from, what was I doing? Soup and salads and sweets appeared.

I wanted to know about 1995. Had the family been there, I wondered. What was it like? But as I looked around, at the matriarch in her red rayon housecoat, at the eager young son chatting to Musa, at the older daughter, smiling shyly as she brought more cups of piping-hot black tea, I didn't have the heart to ask. What would it give us, on this September afternoon, to bring up the past?

Sometimes it felt like the best way to extinguish the horror was to steal its oxygen.

*

Musa's feet had swollen up. From Samashki, it took us four hours to hobble the seven miles to the next village, Zakan-Yurt. The remains of trenches and bomb craters scored the landscape, and dry seed pods rattled in acacia trees.

That night, the parents of a friend of Musa put us up in Zakan-Yurt. Their yard was large, with a vegetable patch and a covered area draped in vines that hung down at the edges, their leaves crisped by the summer sun. The couple had had four sons, but only the youngest was still alive. The first brother had died in a car accident; the second was killed at a roadblock by Russian soldiers. In 2002, security forces had tied up the rest of the family and abducted the third. He had reappeared at the local police station, was released and abducted again, then seen no more.

The father was welcoming, but his eyes were guarded. He did not have the power of forgetting. How could he? How could anyone, for more than a fleeting moment?

Afraid that he might soon be unable to walk at all, Musa called a friend and asked him to pick up his son Adam's bicycle and bring it to us in the man's car.

We turned south, crossing the Sunzha river and the main road that led from the Kavkaz checkpoint to Grozny. It was warm but overcast. Flocks of turkeys and goats skittered by the roadside. Unoiled, the bicycle squeaked and chafed as Musa pressed his feet gingerly against the pedals, stopping every fifty metres for me to catch up. This was not how I had imagined crossing Chechnya.

A dirt track led through fields dotted with teasels to the west bank of the Valerik river, little more than a stream, fringed by trees, undergrowth and tall reeds that whooshed in a breeze. It was hereabouts, on the banks, that the writer Mikhail Lermontov had fought hand-to-hand in 1840 as the Russian army met a force of highlanders led by Imam Shamil's *naib*, Akhberdil Mukhammed. Lermontov had been exiled to the Caucasus for the second time the previous month; his first spell in 1837 was the result of him blaming Tsar Nicholas's court for the death of Alexander Pushkin in a duel.

We stopped on the grass for a rest. Musa stretched out on his back, exhaled deeply and lay still, stroking his paunch. 'Ekh ty, capitalist, come here to torture a poor Chechen terrorist!' he said.

I laughed and reached into the front pocket of my rucksack. Lermontov had written a poem, 'Valerik', about the battle here by the river. Knowing we would pass this way, I had printed a copy. Now I took out the crumpled pages and read aloud a few lines in Russian:

> You would have hardly
> Ever seen from close at hand
> How people die. God grant
> You never will . . .

Much of the Russian writing about the Caucasus in the early nineteenth century was lurid orientalia: tales of savage infidels and dusky maidens in a thrillingly wild and dangerous landscape. Pushkin, whose narrative poem *The Prisoner of the Caucasus* was published in 1822, took a more nuanced view – but not much. He gave the highlanders a seductive appeal while still endorsing their conquest. Alexei Yermolov, the new Russian commander-in-chief in the Caucasus, had declared his desire that 'the terror of my name shall guard our frontiers more potently than chains or fortresses'. Pushkin wrote triumphantly in the poem's epilogue: 'Bow down your snowy head, submit, O Caucasus, Yermolov comes.' ('I am sorry that Pushkin bloodied the last lines of his tale,' wrote one horrified critic in a letter to a friend. 'Poetry is not the ally of butchers.')

Lermontov was far more ambivalent than Pushkin. After all, he had been there – here – in the thick of the battle, not skulking far to the rear in the Russian town of Pyatigorsk. In 'Valerik', the opposing sides slaughter each other methodically, 'like beasts'. As the poet and his comrades grappled with the enemy in the shallows of the river, the gore of the dead spoiled the water. While the baggage of romanticism remained with him, Lermontov's poem was an indictment of the idea that you can civilize a people by subjecting them to genocidal war.

Musa huffed. 'A good writer, of course,' he said. 'But he came here to fight my compatriots.'

I could not argue with that.

We walked on and took off our shoes and socks to ford a brook that joined the Valerik, the wheels of Adam's bicycle grinding the pebbles as Musa pushed it across. At the edge of a field, three shepherd boys were tending a herd of cattle and eating a sticky mess of ice cream from a wrapper laid on the ground. In the village beyond, I bought some grapes from a stall and we stopped on a butcher's forecourt to look at his wares. A side of beef was dripping blood onto the concrete; a bullock's head had been propped on its nose and its pointed horns, its windpipe protruding from the red pulp of its severed neck.

We reached Grozny after dark, stumbling over unlit, unmade pavements and down footpaths next to the road, blinded by oncoming cars, until finally we were lifting Adam's bicycle across the railway track by the Minutka roundabout in pouring rain.

Land of the Boy King

Musa had moved to the city from a village to the north only a few weeks earlier. He lived in a rented flat in a block not far beyond Minutka, with Adam, thirteen, and Musa's mother, who was seventy-eight.

The flat was small and poorly furnished. There was no hot water and the cold water ran black with dirt. But it was home. A female neighbour who knew we were due to arrive had come round and left us some lamb soup on the gas burner in the kitchen. We put mattresses down in the living room – Musa did not have a bed. He fell asleep immediately, fully clothed. I splashed myself in water from a plastic tub in the bathroom, then drifted off to the sound of his snoring, and the never-ending tinkle of the toilet cistern across the corridor.

Grozny, which means 'Threatening' in Russian, began its life in 1818 as one of the chain of forts that Yermolov built to intimidate the highlanders and strengthen the North Caucasus Line. (Other forts were named Vnezapnaya, or 'Sudden', and Burnaya, or 'Stormy'.) Lying towards the southern edge of the plain on a squiggle in the Sunzha river, it expanded in the twentieth century into a centre of oil refining and a sizeable city; many inhabitants fondly recalled its late Soviet incarnation as a place of flower beds and parks and relative prosperity.

The city was now under the control of Ramzan Kadyrov, a thick-armed former Chechen rebel who, in exchange for loyalty to the Kremlin, had got the nod to run the republic as his personal fiefdom. Kadyrov had vowed to rebuild Chechnya after the devastation of the First and Second Chechen Wars, which left it looking like Berlin or Stalingrad.

As Musa dozed in the morning, I stepped out for a walk. The streets were full of young people, mostly men, many of them slight but strong-looking, with neat, black clothes and the Beatles haircuts that had come into fashion in the North Caucasus (a photograph of the Fab Four standing on the steps of an aircraft had recently circulated as an internet meme with the caption 'Dagestani Airlines').

In the centre of the city, high-rises were sprouting, and workmen laid paths around a new mosque that stood opposite a statue of Kadyrov Snr holding some prayer beads. The statue was protected by two armed policemen. Then came Victory Avenue, where more workers swarmed and a machine was tearing up the surface of the road. Dozens of hydraulic cherry pickers lined the avenue. Men were leaning from their buckets to repair the walls on either side, applying cladding, painting facades and decorating pillars. As welding lamps flashed, other workers on their knees hammered new paving stones into place with rubber mallets.

'Why the rush?' I asked one of them.

'We've got to finish everything by Ramzan's birthday next month,' he said, without raising his head.

Two years earlier, I had flown to Grozny with Yevgeny, the foreign ministry chaperone, and a British photographer, to interview Kadyrov. At that time, the apartment blocks like Musa's near Minutka were still in ruins. We spent three days shadowing Kadyrov. He was then the prime minister and heir apparent to the presidency. At our first meeting, in a chintzy living room at his residence in the town of Gudermes, we had given Kadyrov two gifts: a portrait that Simon, the photographer, had made of Mike Tyson (Kadyrov was an amateur boxer and had recently welcomed Tyson to Chechnya for a visit), and a large, thick book full of glossy photographs of animals for his children. An aide stood, legs akimbo, riffling the pages in the book to make sure an explosive device had not been inserted in a cut-out.

Land of the Boy King

Kadyrov's entourage was growing. A pretty Russian PR girl called Tanya had been drafted in from Moscow to help polish his image. 'It's all down to Ramzan,' she had breathed, as she teetered through the mud in stilettos, showing off refurbished apartment blocks. Another aide paddled at the Chechen leader's head with a hairbrush as soon as the camera heaved into sight.

One night, Kadyrov had invited us to his home in his family's ancestral village of Tsenteroi. From a doorway shining on the far side of the yard came a rhythmic hubbub, and a figure cast in shadow beckoned us forward.

Inside, ten big men with beards and skullcaps sat on their knees in a circle on a carpet, swaying in unison and crashing their hands together in thudding claps. One was leading the ceremony with cries of prayer; the others responded in chorus, their chant rising and falling. Beyond the circle, an elder jumped gleefully from one leg to the other, striking a beat on the floor. To his side, a thickset young man also pounded his feet. He was dressed all in black and his face was coated in sweat. It was Kadyrov. I stood by the doorway, transfixed.

We were watching a zikr, a Sufi ritual; probably the only Westerners to witness such a scene at Kadyrov's home, before or since. Just as they appeared on the point of entering a trance, the clapping men rose and began to gallop in a circle around the room, faster and faster, continuing the chant, each man's hand resting on the back of the man in front, each face wrought with ecstasy. The whirl of noise reached a crescendo and the men slowed to a halt, slipping into murmured prayers and taking their places once more, kneeling on the floor. Looking on in silence, Yevgeny appeared like a creature from another planet. As an official of the Russian federal government, of which Chechnya was a subject, he was, in theory, a representative of the highest authority in the room. But it was clear his writ did not run here.

Towards the end of the night, Kadyrov paraded for us the squad of fifty men who guarded his home – they bellowed 'Allahu Akbar' in unison at his command – and brought out two animals from his menagerie: a lion cub and a young tiger, which he spat on and goaded as it strained against a frayed length of twine.

In effect, Kadyrov had won. A few months after our interview, having reached the requisite age of thirty, he would be appointed president. Tranches of federal money began to be funnelled to Grozny, with little oversight. Kadyrov's bodyguards changed their silver Ladas for Porsche Cayennes.

Now, walking through Grozny, I could see his personality cult had only burgeoned. Portraits and billboards of him were everywhere – on roundabouts, by the road, above a bathroom-fittings shop: 'Hero of heroes, proud son of the Chechen people!' A portrait of Akhmad Kadyrov: 'You are alive in our hearts!' A picture of Ramzan with a Chechen Olympic champion: 'Better death than coming second!'

A mantle of calm had fallen over the city; shops were open, there were cafés and beauty parlours. But I knew that blood seeped from its edges.

The guerrillas, much weakened since the 1990s, still presented a deadly threat. In an attempt to stamp them out, Kadyrov's militiamen – the *kadyrovtsy* – had turned to wholesale terror.

At the end of Victory Avenue was the Soviet statue of three revolutionaries, known to all in the city as *Tri Duraka*, or 'Three Idiots', their blunt heads and shoulders rising into a cloudy sky from one block of stone. I turned right and came to Memorial's office on the ground floor of an unprepossessing building. I had been here numerous times in the past to sit with Shamil and

Land of the Boy King

Natasha in the kitchen, eating biscuits and poppy-seed cake: smiling Shamil with his dignified bearing, Natasha with her latest tale of depravity, never hardened to cruelty, ever incredulous, ever shocked. 'How can this be?'

At the entrance, the lacquered front door stuck in the frame in the same old way. I entered the main room, where a couple of employees sat at computers squeezed between shelves of reports and lever-arch files.

In these reports and on these computers were page upon page of witness statements recording the transgressions of Russian forces and their allies, the *kadyrovtsy*: a son shot dead at home by masked men in uniform, a nephew detained and tortured, a family made homeless after security forces burned their house to the ground.

There was no need to sympathize with the militants (their hate-filled crimes were clear) in order to think that these methods of fighting the insurgency were wrong and counterproductive.

The Memorial team were phlegmatic. They worked on. One of the women at the desks welcomed me in. Shamil was away, she said, and Natasha had been sent abroad for a while. She made it clear this was for Natasha's safety.

I could not know, as I stood in the office just down from the Three Idiots, that I would never see Natasha again.

At Musa's flat, we slipped for a couple of days into the rhythms of family life.

Adam was a polite, sandy-haired boy, who went off to school in the afternoons with pasted-down fringe and smart black-and-white clothes. It was September and, watching him leave, I thought again of the children in Beslan four years earlier – first-graders serious and sweetly trusting, teenagers chatting and telling jokes — as they headed to their first class of the school year. In the portraits of the dead in the burned-out gym, they wore the same monochrome uniforms as Adam.

Musa's mother spent her days sitting on a divan, watching videos of men performing zikrs, circling, clapping and swaying in gloomy rooms. We all called her Babushka – Adam, for whom she was really 'Grandma', Musa and I, the visiting friend.

A heavy woman who moved with difficulty, Babushka rarely left the room with the divan. She wore a headscarf, woollen socks and voluminous brown skirts that spooled around her. As the youngest of five siblings, it had fallen to Musa to look after his mother in her declining years, and he did so with unfailing kindness and warmth. If we went out for a while, he would always tease her on our return. 'Babushka, were you here or did you sneak out and go drinking in bars with your friends again?' Babushka would open her mouth to reveal the stump of a single yellow tooth and wheeze with laughter. She and Musa conversed in Chechen; she spoke only broken Russian.

Babushka had survived the deportations as a fourteen-year-old girl. One day, when I stayed alone with her in the flat, she suddenly turned to me with tears in her eyes and said: 'Such hunger. We collect frozen potatoes from field. Thrown out potatoes, stuck to the ground.' She stretched out a cupped hand as if holding the meagre food. 'It was so cold. Mother no shoes. She fell down. I thought dead.'

In the kitchen that night, when Babushka and Adam were asleep, Musa said: 'That's how they stayed alive in the beginning in Kazakhstan, collecting rotting food, peelings. That was a particular incident she told you about. Babushka's mother had only an old pair of slippers that were falling apart. She was practically barefoot in winter. They heard about these dumped potatoes and went a long way to find them. Babushka's mother, my grandmother, collapsed on the way back. She was ill for months. Another of her daughters, Babushka's sister, died when she was four. She had been begging for something to eat. Babushka remembers her mother carrying the body to be buried, and some Russian women saw them and took pity and gave them salted tomatoes. And they were starving, so my grandmother carried on walking, holding her daughter's body with one hand and eating salted tomatoes with the other.'

A few months after my walk, Musa would take a portrait of Babushka among the broken gravestones that made up the monument to the victims of the 1944 deportation in central Grozny, near the Sunzha.

In the picture, Babushka is holding out her palms in prayer, her face twisted in anguish. Snow is falling, settling on the tops of the shattered gravestones and Babushka's shoulders. The image became well known; an icon of Chechen suffering.

Kadyrov had wanted the deportation monument removed from the city, but Natasha and others protested. In a compromise, it was shut off behind three-metre-high walls.

Later, Kadyrov would move the official day of mourning from the anniversary of the deportation, 23 February, to early May, combining it with annual events to commemorate his father's assassination. A Chechen activist who criticized the decision was abruptly found by police to be 'carrying heroin' and spent three years in prison.

Musa had a lover, Vera, a Russian woman in her early twenties. She was one of the few Russians who remained in Chechnya: the population was now ninety-five per cent Chechen, the most mono-ethnic place in the country. In the 1970s, a third of the population had been Russian; many fled at the outbreak of the post-Soviet wars, or were killed in the fighting.

Vera was slender and pale-skinned and impishly intelligent. She and Musa brought each other joy. One afternoon, I turned up at Musa's shop to meet him and, finding it locked, banged on the door. He took a long time to come out, and when he did there was a sheen on his forehead. Vera was there too, pink-cheeked and smiling, adjusting the collar of her shirt.

Finding intimacy in Chechnya was not always easy. One morning, Musa said that a young woman from a family we had seen on the way into Grozny was coming to the city for the day, and had offered to show me around.

Her name was Anita and she was in her thirties. She was wearing high heels, a pencil skirt, a fashionable white jacket and a silken headscarf with the word 'Chanel' printed on it many times, her black fringe escaping at the front above a sculpted face. She had arrived with her younger sister, a student who was dressed all in black, and had kohl around her eyes. I felt ashamed to be stepping out with them in my stained hiking trousers and walking boots.

On Kadyrov Avenue, nearing the mosque, Anita's heels squeaked on the newly laid pavements. I asked her what she thought about Kadyrov. She said she was a care worker and, like all state employees, she had a percentage of her pay docked and sent to a murky charity that supposedly did good works in the name of Kadyrov's assassinated father. 'It's not legal, but they do it openly,' she said. 'A lot of people at work are not happy about it. I don't like it much, either. But there is a kind of result. There's a lot of rebuilding and Chechnya is mostly peaceful. In the beginning, I couldn't stand his illiteracy – he can't speak Chechen well, let alone Russian. Now I think maybe he's done some positive things for the republic.'

We looked for somewhere to eat among the chaos on Victory Avenue, and found a tiny café in the back of the House of Fashion, a department store. I had innocently thought I was to be given a tour of the city, but the promenade had begun to look uncomfortably like a date. 'It's so lucky that we met,' said Anita. 'I hope you will help me learn English. I came especially to see you today.'

Soon we were joined by Anita's middle sister, a bank teller. If anything, she was even more striking than her siblings, and more direct. I pointedly mentioned my girlfriend, Masha, and said that we lived together in Moscow. The middle sister tossed her head. 'So you have a Russian girl? Surely I'm just as beautiful? Maybe more so?' She and Anita teased me about staying to live in Chechnya and having several wives, while the younger sister stayed silent, emitting an occasional giggle. The three of them had lit up the grey little café. A man alone at the next table was looking amused. 'Imagine, you could be sitting here with these three and they'd all be yours,' he said. Polygamy was illegal in Russia but common here, unofficially.

We left the café and walked on together. 'So, you're thirty-five?' the middle sister was saying. 'That's not old. I'm twenty-seven, that's not so young, either.' She and Anita continued to tease me, jousting with each other for my attention, although Anita was less forthright. They did not seem to resent each other's advances.

'We could be happy together,' said the middle sister, looking me directly in the eye. 'You know we're joking, but in every joke there's a little truth, isn't there? Some women are happy to share a husband. I'd rather have him – you – all to myself, of course. I wouldn't be good at sharing.'

I had never been the focus of such naked female attention, and it was an unusual feeling as someone who was all but married, and happily so, albeit thrilling as well. I struggled to imagine myself such as a catch.

It was time for the middle sister to go home: it was Ramadan, and she had begun to get hungry. The three women had taken only a few sips of water as they watched me eat a salad in the café. We put the middle sister on a minibus taxi back to her village. 'When will you be coming again?' she asked as she said goodbye, her eyes flashing. 'I'll be waiting.'

Anita and the younger sister escorted me back to Musa's. The sky had become a slaty frown over the city, and drops of rain spotted Anita's silken headscarf. 'Can I call you?' she said. I could see that it wasn't a joke. In my stupid, English way of politeness, which brings only misunderstanding and false hope, I said yes and we exchanged numbers. A minibus drew up. Careful not to smudge their tights on the muddy doorframe, the two sisters climbed inside. It pulled away fast.

When I told Musa about the afternoon, he laughed, but then he said: 'You know, I don't blame our girls for wanting to get married and to be close with men. A lot of them were robbed of sex and intimacy because so many men were killed in the wars: there just aren't enough males to go around. And it's frowned upon for a woman to have a relationship outside of marriage – it can spoil her reputation, but not a man's.'

Weeks later, when I was back in Moscow, Anita would call me a dozen times. Like a coward, I didn't answer. Looking back, I feel wretched about that. Her sister may have been joking, but I don't think Anita was. She had taken a risk to express an interest in me. I wish I had had the courage to pick up the phone and talk to her;

to make it clear that I was flattered, but nothing could happen between us. It would have been so simple.

Musa's feet were still swollen, so the day we left Grozny, he got in his car and drove next to me on the road.

That first morning beyond the capital, heading east across the plain, I walked alongside a freshly laid dual carriageway. Now and then, Musa would motor ahead a little, never out of sight, and stop and wait for me to catch up. By the road, in the dust, an old man in a patched brown suit jacket and a velvet green skullcap was collecting scrap metal with a boy, no more than eight years old. The boy was pulling a little trolley with wooden wheels that was full of bits of broken piston and other objects. 'We'll get four roubles per kilogram if we can find twenty-five kilograms,' said the old man. That would be two pounds sterling, all told. We gave the old man some money and he took it with dignity; grateful but not effusive.

In Argun, there were huge portraits of Kadyrov, and beyond the town a billboard loomed over the road, showing him wearing his Hero of Russia medal and standing with a group of boys and girls: 'Children's smiles are the best reward for a Hero!' By late afternoon, Gudermes had appeared, a stronghold of Kadyrov's family, where 'Allahu Akbar' was marked on a hillside in large white letters. Two relatives of Musa, big taciturn brothers, devout and serious, put us up for the night. One of them sat slightly apart, murmuring and flicking his thumb along a prayer counter, a string of beads with a silk tassel at the end.

On the second day, Musa said he was fed up with driving the car and borrowed another bicycle from his relatives, an old fold-up one that threatened to buckle beneath him. After a few miles, he stopped and got off and said, 'It's here.' We left the road and climbed a track that rose lazily up slopes below a low ridge to a dip where there were three half-finished buildings like small bungalows with green roofs. Nearby, hot water poured from an open tap that jutted from the ground, and ran through shallow pools between grassy banks and bushes dotted with litter – bottles, cake wrappers, teabags, the detritus of the 'people's resort'. To let the muddy water cool, little dams of earth had been set up. Between them, it flowed through a channel towards a rusty tin hut in the shape of a yurt.

'These springs are very good for the sexual organs – the water kills all infections,' Musa announced, uncorking a pipe that had been plugged with a spade handle, sending another scorching arc into the top pool, where steam looped off the surface. He had pushed a handful of wild herbs into two plastic cups, and now we filled them from the pipe and waited a while before drinking. Then we took off our shoes and socks, stripped to our underpants and descended to the next pool. It was no more than eighteen inches deep and as hot as a hot bath. Mud oozed between our toes. We lay down in the water. The delicious, liquid heat enveloped my shoulders and lapped at my throat. Around us, a handful of other men had also come to take the waters. Slathered head to toe in mud, a teenage boy was lying as motionless as a lizard on a rock, drying in the sun.

Back at the top pool, two upturned orange crates were planted in the shallowest part. Lowering ourselves onto the slats, we placed our feet on the dried mud at the edge of the pool, our nether regions positioned over the water like dumplings in a bamboo steamer. 'This is the best of all; it helped my prostate,' said Musa, shifting on the crate.

Land of the Boy King

Did Tolstoy seek similar relief during his stay in Chechnya, I wondered with amusement as sweat prickled my forehead. He had arrived in 1851 and first lived with his soldier brother in Starogladovskaya, a Cossack settlement on the left bank of the Terek. Later, he moved closer to Grozny, to Goryachevodsk, a village famous for its springs. In July that year, he wrote to his aunt:

> It is an enormous mountain of rocks lying one upon the other, some of which have become detached, forming a sort of grotto, others remain suspended at a great height. They are all intersected by torrents of warm water, which in some places fall with much noise, and, especially in the morning, cover all the elevated part of the mountain with a white vapour which is continually rising from this boiling water. The water is so hot they can boil eggs hard in it in three minutes.

Bathing there, said Tolstoy, had eased his rheumatism and the pain in his feet. 'I have seldom felt so well as now,' he enthused.

Tolstoy's diary of the time, as it would for much of his life, swings queasily between exultation and guilt. He is often disgusted with his own behaviour: with his losses at cards, his drinking and his sexual exploits with Cossack girls. It was not hard to picture him hunched on an old artillery box over a bubbling pool, steaming off his latest bout of the clap.

Like many aristocratic young men of his time, Tolstoy came to the Caucasus to kill his ennui in a splendid arena, but his early stories announced a revolt against the romanticized accounts of his predecessors.

In The Cossacks, the 1863 novel he based on his stay in Chechnya, Tolstoy perfectly skewered the daydreams of his Russian protagonist, Olenin, who imagines himself living in an isolated hut with a submissive oriental maiden, while spending his days 'killing and subduing an untold multitude of tribesmen'. While in the Caucasus, Tolstoy had noted his own such aspirations in ironic fashion. 'To the best of my ability,' he had written in a letter to his brother Sergei as he anticipated his part in a raid on a Muslim village, 'I will facilitate with the aid of a cannon the extermination of *treacherous predators and unruly Asiatics.*' (His italics.)

Sometimes, I wondered if I had sunk into my own reverie about the Caucasus. Repulsive as they were, the modern-day bloodletting and abductions had their own seductive power. To set oneself up as a witness to these horrors was to adopt a look of inviolable seriousness and import. Once or twice, I had caught myself in this pose: the grave emissary of odious things, the noble observer who could shock you with a tale of torture – before hastening back to Moscow and the latest party. Was the Caucasus my own playground, a mere provider of thrills? The promenade with the three sisters in Grozny had provided the necessary frisson of sexual promise.

I hope it wasn't that. The Caucasus did have its siren calls. The terrain was throat-tighteningly awesome. And clandestine trips could be exciting. But it was the sheer grandeur of humanity that captivated most of all. When you saw a woman in the Caucasus leaning over the body of a dead man, running her hand over his paling brow, you imagined how she might feel if she was your mother, leaning over your father's corpse, or your brother's. Or yours.

12

To a Rebel Village

Darkness was falling by the time we arrived at the border with Dagestan. I cursed myself for allowing us to linger at the hot springs and still be on the road after sunset. The checkpoint ahead of us was known as a target for night-time attacks by the guerrillas. I felt my mouth go dry with nerves. Would the policemen be jumpy?

Musa's fold-up bicycle squeaked on through the twilight towards the little roadside building and the pool of light. I had a momentary vision of the bicycle lying on its side in the gutter, its wheels spinning vainly after some catastrophic unfolding of the next few moments. But there was no shout, no burst of gunfire. Our exit from Chechnya was as underwhelming as our entrance. A simple check would have revealed my lack of permit. Instead, two officers were leaning into a driver's window, their automatics pushed round onto their backs. Another, through a yellow square of window, peered at something on his desk. No one paid us the slightest heed.

Beyond the checkpoint, cars barrelled past through the inky night until, a couple of weary hours later, the road arrived in Khasavyurt, the first city in Dagestan. Under a street lamp by a deserted market, Musa and I said our goodbyes. He had arranged a taxi to bring my pack from Nazran; we pulled it out of the boot and replaced it with his bicycle. From the dashboard heater inside the car came a whiff of warm dust and oil. I had scorned car interiors in favour of the unsullied air of the mountains, but now I felt a pang of longing at the familiar smell. It reminded me of rides home late at night in Moscow: of flagging down a Lada in the bite of cold outside a bar, of the comforting fug inside as you slid though the suburbs, the car's windscreen spectacularly cracked, the driver easing forward the clear-resin gear knob encasing a flower. I imagined Masha laying her head on my shoulder, the note of her perfume mingling with the scents of the car.

Musa gave me a hug and climbed into the passenger seat. Within an hour, he would be home in Grozny, glancing round Adam's bedroom door and saying goodnight to Babushka. The cistern would be tinkling in the bathroom.

I was now about three-quarters of the way between the two seas, although mileage was about to become meaningless again. When you walk in rough terrain, gains and losses in altitude mean much more than horizontal distance.

For weeks, since leaving the peaks of the central Caucasus, I had walked on the steppe. For the final stretch, I would head to the highlands again, to the mountains that covered southern Dagestan, up to the crest of the Greater Caucasus, and the frontier with Georgia and Azerbaijan. Here, over millennia, fast-flowing rivers cutting down from the heights had carved a plateau that sloped back from the main range into gorges and precipitous cliffs. The rivers' ice-cold water was a diamond tip, slicing through earth and stone to produce a landscape of head-spinning drama.

To a Rebel Village

I had started my journey in the lush, forested hills of the western Caucasus, deserted and redolent with loss. Below the gigantic peaks around Elbrus, only the occasional shepherd had invited me into his hut. Upland Dagestan was different. A severe landscape, short on rainfall and vegetation, it was nonetheless bursting with people.

Makhachkala, the unlovely capital down on the coastal plain, was the only place I had visited in Dagestan, and I had no desire to return to its concrete sprawl, choked with traffic. What drew me were the mountains and the people who lived there. I knew that hundreds of villages dotted the highlands, often stacked on rocky outcrops – for defence, and to avoid using up precious cultivable land. Once, the roofs of the oblong houses had been flat, of rolled earth, with the roof of one forming the forecourt of the one above. Now, they were mostly of pitched tin and asbestos. But the villages still recalled the staircased settlements of Tibet or Kurdistan more than the chalets of Switzerland and Austria.

On that reporting trip to Makhachkala a few years earlier, I had met a Dagestani anthropologist. It was late one evening and he was tipsy after a wedding, but he had tried to convey to me something of the wonder of the highlands. In this lofty backwater, he explained, natural barriers had shaped speech and identity. Settlements that were physically close but separated by rivers and passes bunged with snow might have their own distinct language and traditions. A bone-juddering seven-hour ride by *marshrutka* from Makhachkala lay Tsumadinsky district, on the border with Chechnya. There, said the anthropologist, some ethnic groups occupied a single village, speaking a language that was unintelligible to the inhabitants of the next canyon across. In many places, dirt tracks and horse trails were the only lifeline. Hospitality towards guests was sacrosanct.

263

EAST

Under Kadyrov, the Kremlin satrap, Chechnya had become a mono-cultural dictatorship, its free spirit extinguished. Dagestan was the opposite. With more than thirty ethnic groups, its plurality lent itself to cliché: a mosaic, a melting pot, a patchwork. A 'mountain of tongues', as the Arabs had called it in the Middle Ages. The corollary was a great clamour of regional crime bosses and politicians, each with his own saloons and mansion and hired thugs. Kidnappings and car bombings were common. Dagestan could be a place of casual brutality. Women were mostly subservient and burdened with physical labour. A village where a man had once lowered himself to the task of milking a cow had become known, inevitably, as The Village Where A Man Once Milked A Cow. Poverty was typical. But for years, the very tumult of ethnicities had mitigated against larger-scale conflict, forcing a kind of consensus. When Shamil Basayev and a group of Islamists invaded Dagestan from Chechnya in 1999 in an attempt to carve out a sharia enclave, they were resisted by armed locals and eventually forced to accept defeat. There was little support for a Chechen-style break with Moscow.

Nonetheless, almost a decade later, bloodshed was on the rise. Islam ran deep in Dagestan, having first taken root in the eighth century. With its revival after the fall of the Soviet Union, an increasing number of young men had travelled to study in the Middle East. Many came back yearning for a return to earlier Muslim ways, and for a purge of the rituals and superstition that freighted Sufism, the dominant practice in Dagestan. Some adopted violence.

Russia's government viewed the Islamists as instruments of global extremism, receiving cash from abroad to keep up their insurgency (in part, this was true, although the main animus was local grievances). A visiting foreigner like me – rarely seen

– might easily be taken by the security services for an emissary, come to lend support to the fanatics.

In Moscow, before entering Chechnya, I had spoken to the anthropologist again, by phone. What did he think – would it be safe to cross Dagestan?

'Oh, of course,' he said. 'At least – what colour is your ruck-sack? Red? That's good. The most important thing is that they don't think you're a combatant moving from one hideout to another. It's very important they don't make that mistake.'

Outside a café by the market in Khasavyurt, a sinewy man with mahogany skin approached. He was wearing a baggy black tracksuit and an orange rucksack and carrying a ski pole. His head bobbed as he walked, and with every step, his right foot made a little sweep-ing movement just above the ground like a metal detector. 'A rock fell on my head when I was a child,' he explained, after we had shaken hands. 'I was in a coma for three months. When I woke up, I couldn't lift my foot properly – the nerves had been damaged.' He pulled up the right leg of his tracksuit bottoms and rapped his knuckles on his shin. The leg was withered but looked hard as a skittle. 'Don't worry, it's strong,' he said. 'And I play volleyball on the beach in Makhachkala every morning, so I'm fit.'

Thinking a local might protect me from suspicious officials, I had called ahead to Makhachkala and asked Dagestan's minis-ter of tourism to recommend a walking companion. The minister suggested Suleyman, a former arbitration court judge in his early fifties who had climbed several minor peaks in the Greater Caucasus.

Suleyman had accepted the assignment and travelled up from Makhachkala by *marshrutka*. 'It's more the chance to see the repub-lic than the money,' he said, after we agreed a rate. Over tea in the café, we discussed our plan to spend three weeks or so looping south and then east through the highlands. If we got that far, we would end our – and my – journey in Derbent, the fortress city on the Caspian coast, south of the capital. In the villages, there would be no hotels or guesthouses, and the tourism minister had proudly advised me to dispense with my tent. 'Everywhere you go, just ask to see the head of the village or the school director,' he had said. 'They will take you in.'

I was doubtful; Suleyman was not: 'He's right. Anyone who does not agree to have us is not a Dagestani.'

As a first objective, I was desperate to reach Gimry, the most famous of all Dagestan's mountain settlements. Gimry was the birthplace of Shamil, the imam who united resistance against Russia's advance in the 1800s, holding off the might of the imperial army for a quarter of a century. Set in a dramatic highland landscape, Gimry was now a centre of defiance again. Russian helicopter gunships pounded militants' dugouts on nearby slopes and, the winter before my walk, boyeviki had shot dead a prominent MP in the village. In response, the authorities declared an antiterrorist zone, dispatching seven hundred policemen and special forces units to lock down the village of 4,500 people. 'It's almost certain we'll be refused entry,' said Suleyman. 'We can only try.'

Rain had begun to fall as we set out from Khasavyurt. On the edge of the town, there were car repair workshops and grilled-chicken kiosks, and then a village where men were building houses of adobe, which Suleyman called saman. I thought affectionately of our equivalent in Norfolk, the wattle and daub of which Low Tree Farm was made.

It was pleasing to be reunited with my usual rucksack. Coming down the road, a damp torrent of sheep parted around us like water running past a rock, shepherds in green rubber capes driving them on. It was late September, and the tide of transhumance that had been rising in the mountains before Elbrus in June was now receding. Breaking through, the sun dried the scorched, yellow grass of summer, and a wild pear tree standing alone in a field offered a place to lay out a picnic of cheese and tomatoes. Further on, skirting a wooded spur where barberry and hawthorn stood among the beeches, the road led to a drawn-out village.

The school director's name was Apandi and he was, he said, filled with joy at our arrival. A small, stocky man possessed of enormous energy, his luxuriant moustache resembled a Skye terrier crouched on his upper lip. 'You are walkers!' he declared, as we sat in his office. 'I am a walker too. I have walked all over the republic in the footsteps of Imam Shamil!'

This was Avar country and Apandi was an Avar, like Imam Shamil. He immediately invited us home and introduced us to his wife and adult son. In their living room, his wife served piles of buttery chudu, flat pies stuffed with meat and cabbage, and urbech, a sweet and gritty paste made from ground flax, walnut and pumpkin seeds that stuck to our tongues. Displayed on the walls of the room hung a cherkeska, a nineteenth-century sabre and several Caucasian daggers. One, inscribed on the blade with the name 'Magomed' in green lettering, had belonged to Apandi's great-great-grandfather.

Apandi told several stories about Shamil and his exploits, and then talked animatedly about the different temperaments of Dagestan's national groups. 'A drunk Dargin is like a sober Avar,' he said, his moustache doing new gymnastics. 'We Avars are emotional, impulsive, foolish. The Laks are a cunning lot – where there are Laks, the Jews can do nothing. The Lezgins are cultured people with writing skills.' Suleyman, a Dargin, nodded agreement.

We ended the night by attempting some Avar tongue-twisters. One of them translated as 'Seven hundred and seventy-seven thousand frogs croaking under a bridge'. Apandi guffawed at my efforts. He was delighted at the idea of us going to Gimry, and promised to call ahead to friends who might help us along the way.

Apandi had set a tone for the last leg of the journey. Sated and entertained, Suleyman and I snored late into the next morning. I woke thinking that if the militants didn't do for us, then the hospitality might.

Austere, with a flowing beard and long, humourless face, Imam Shamil enthralled me. His feats of bravery during the long war with Russia were beyond doubt, his resilience recognized far beyond Dagestan. But before he reached middle age, he was already wrapped in legend: not just a warrior but a clairvoyant and a superman. Tales of his upbringing and exploits resembled those about the Prophet Muhammad. He was rumoured to have grown up an orphan, scrabbling a living by going from village to village selling dried peaches or working as a shepherd (in fact, he was born into minor nobility in Gimry in 1797). He had seen his first visions, it was said, in the solitude of mountain pastures.

During my winter of reading before the walk, I had absorbed more of the myths: as a boy, Shamil spent hours perching on a boulder that others feared to touch because the Simurgh, the giant bird of Solomon, was thought to have nested there; walking to another village, he confronted a rock so steep and smooth that no one else could climb it, only to fling himself up, 'engraving his footprint on its surface'. In time, Shamil would become leader of the Naqshbandi Sufi order, from whose structure and ideology the anti-colonial resistance in Dagestan and Chechnya was

To a Rebel Village

born. The miracles of his younger life were an affirmation of his special destiny.

Long after his death, the Soviets – atheists and Communists as they were – hardly knew what to do with Shamil. Over the twentieth century, his image oscillated between hero and degenerate. One moment he was a ferocious opponent of tsarist tyranny, the next a British spy or a backward religionist. Dagestan's best-known poet derided him, and then recanted. Only after the Soviet collapse in 1991 did Shamil gain his rightful status. Now he was an idol in Dagestan, claimed by both the authorities and the militants, the former seeing a patriot, the latter a forebear of the renewed battle to throw off Russia's yoke. But I had no interest in one-sided heroes. I liked to think more of the real, flawed Shamil and of the dilemmas he was forced to face. I liked, too, to imagine the sights and smells of his surroundings.

In his time, homes in the high villages – known as *sakli* – were embedded in the landscape, with their lower storey, kept for livestock, often carved from the mountainside. Inside the dimly lit upper room, copper trays hung from walls made of clay and chopped straw next to glinting knives and pistols, and over the fire dangled lumps of kurdyuk, their odour mixing with the funk of goatskins and the stable below. Stepping outside, the highlander would see tiers of crenellated cliff and scrubby slopes receding into the distance; unforgiving terrain that supported only flocks of animals and the odd terrace of crops. From such a place, Shamil rose to meet the advance of the Russians. Like the houses, he too was born of rock and orange dust.

'Russia had two great tsars – Peter the Great and Stalin,' the *krayeved* declared. 'Both tried to build the country up.'

'What about the gulag?'

'Pah, anyone who ended up there had only themselves to blame.'

We were sitting in the home of our next host, a few hours after saying goodbye to Apandi. Apandi had called a friend and his wife to ask them to take us in. The friend was a *krayeved*, that charming Russian term meaning a 'localist', or a human repository of local lore and history. At a font that ran into a stone trough in his village, a group of headscarfed women filling ewers had not replied and turned their backs when Suleyman and I – two unknown men – asked them the way to his house. The *krayeved* and his wife arrived in a car to receive us: they had returned especially from a visit to a sick relative in Khasavyurt. Soon, we were talking to the sound of an Italian pump, sucking and thumping water into their kitchen.

The *krayeved* had been director of the village school, he said, but was ousted by the head of the district in favour of a crony. 'In Soviet times, there was a collective farm here. Everybody worked. It was a crime not to. Fuel was practically free. Now fuel is twenty-three roubles a litre and fertilizer costs seven hundred a bag. Who can afford to farm on their own now? No one. No one has the machinery. People just keep animals and grow a little maize for themselves. The government is absolutely no help. It's sunk in corruption. The police only look out for themselves. Some men in camouflage and masks pulled me out of my car and beat me. They said nothing – I had no idea who they were. No explanation, no apology. Everything is falling apart. The young people are leaving. Tradition is dying out.'

His wife had brought in some *chudu* and caught the last phrase. She said: 'The young boys no longer get off their horses in the village as they should, as a sign of respect.'

To a Rebel Village

The *krayeved* nodded. 'All you see on television is killing, rape, smoking, drinking. Our youngsters take it as an example. Many can't get jobs. The injustice eats them up inside and they go to the forest.' That was the euphemism used across the North Caucasus for joining the insurgents, although the bare hills of Dagestan offered little forest to hide in.

The *krayeved* had no sympathy for neighbouring Chechnya. 'The Chechens are born in blood and warfare,' he said with a dismissive wave. 'They will cut off your head at the first opportunity. They should have been pushed into the Caspian, just as Beria wanted. Did you know they prepared a white stallion for Hitler during the war?' (This was a hoary myth that was frequently cited to justify the deportations.)

It was the further past in which the *krayeved* sought solace. Here lay Shamil, the invulnerable hero. 'For me, Shamil is the archetype of a real highlander, who loved his motherland and his people. A man to be emulated,' he said. 'True, at the end he began to understand the scale of what he was facing; that there was no point in going on. On his journey into exile in Kaluga, he asked where he was – weeks had gone by – and was amazed when he was told he was still in Russia. And he said: "If I had known Russia was such a big country I would never have fought so long."' The *krayeved* stopped and raised his right index finger. 'But just imagine what it took to do what he did: to battle for twenty-five years, never pitying himself, never showing mercy to himself or others. Never sleeping a proper night's sleep, or eating a proper meal.'

There it was, the cult of the spartan strongman, I thought, as Suleyman and I lay down to sleep on divans in the *krayeved*'s living room. Little wonder that he was such an admirer of Stalinist times. The popular images of Shamil and the Soviet dictator had something in common: necessarily ruthless, ascetic and self-sacrificing.

I remembered the young soldier's words at Stalin's dacha on the cliff in Abkhazia: 'I saw myself on TV what he left behind when he died. Fifteen cups, one of them chipped. Nothing!'

It was perhaps inevitable that Suleyman and I should provoke some suspicion in a region where only rebels and soldiers carried rucksacks, red or not, but I had not expected it to come quite so early.

A long, gradual climb had led to a pass through rain and cold, past prayer rooms and simple block houses. There was a steep drop next to the road and a feeling of space, but wet, tingling mist filled the valley like a trough. Soon the mist was around us too, thickening at twenty paces. Two shepherds loomed out of the whiteness to ask us for cigarettes, and then a pair of policemen in a car, who got out reluctantly to check our documents. Chilled and damp, we ate bread and *kolbasa* (sausage) in a crumbling bus stop, and took a turn down to the left to the village of Danukh. On the descent, a jeep coming towards us slowed to walking pace, its window open.

'Excuse me, could you tell us how to find the school director?'

'That's me,' the driver replied cheerily.

'Oh! Do you know anywhere we could stay the night and get some food, please? We're naturally very happy to pay for it.'

'Of course. You can stay at my home. And you will certainly not pay.'

It was a dialogue that would be repeated numerous times over the coming weeks. The school director was going out to visit relatives, so told us the way to his house. As the mist lifted, Danukh revealed itself as a cluster of homes cheek by jowl on top of a little hill girded by rock, many of them retaining the traditional flat roof. The school director's house was one of these, its lower storey supported by huge timber beams.

'You are very welcome,' said Yusup, one of his sons, helping us remove our sodden rucksacks. 'We are about seventy families in Danukh. It's not easy here. The road was blocked for a month and a half last winter. There's a danger of avalanches. It's not warm enough for fruit. We plough small areas with donkeys and grow potatoes, carrots and maize. We keep cows and sheep. Sometimes we shoot the wild boar that upset the potato patches – we got six recently. I wanted to sell them to the road-builders, but they were too heavy to drag. No, we can't eat them ourselves, we are Muslims.' He paused. 'A lot of land here is not cultivated. Many people have gone down to live in the lower village.'

This was the talk I enjoyed most: of animals and crops, of livelihoods and families and work and things that mattered. The pairing of an upper village with a lower one on the plain was interesting, and I was about to ask Yusup more about it when the policeman arrived.

Slight and serious, with a muscle twitching in his jaw, he was the local officer. He was wearing civilian clothes and a tyubeteyka. 'Show me your documents, please,' he said. Yusup and his brother regarded the policeman evenly – they knew him, of course – but they did not protest at his question. We proffered our passports. The policeman inspected them, lingering over mine.

'You will have to come with me to the station for an extra check,' he said. 'It's not far, about thirteen kilometres.'

'But why? We've done nothing wrong.'

'It's necessary for security reasons.'

'I don't want to go. Can't your bosses come here if they want to talk to us?'

'You will have to go with me.'

273

Suleyman sighed and spoke to the policeman. 'Listen, you can't do this. I'm a judge, I have some friends in the MVD. Let me give them a call.'

The village officer stiffened almost imperceptibly. The MVD was the interior ministry, which controlled the police.

Suleyman stepped outside for a few minutes, then came back in chuckling and said: 'Here he is,' handing the officer his mobile.

The officer took it and listened, then said quietly: 'I understand you,' and handed the phone back. Within ten minutes, we were sitting on the living-room floor of his house and drinking tea and eating spoons of honey.

I felt bad for him. Despite the heinous deeds of the police and security services in the North Caucasus, local officers were often innocent men who were only doing a job. But he looked relieved rather than humiliated – the phone call from above had absolved him of responsibility, and he was glad to entertain us.

'We don't get many foreigners around here,' he said, pouring more tea. 'There was a Czech a few years ago.'

'How did he get on?'

'Someone shot him and stole his car. They found his body in the river down by Chirkata.'

The day began auspiciously. Yusup and his brother Salim were straight-backed, clear-talking men in their twenties whom I liked a great deal. Without eating anything themselves, they served us a gargantuan breakfast of Avar *khinkali*, mutton, smoked sheep's tail, walnuts in honey and tea made from wild thyme. Going to visit the outdoor loo at 4 a.m., the night still starry, Suleyman had spotted the brothers already preparing our meal. It was the last days of Ramadan and they were observing the rules of the fast, from dawn to dusk (wayfarers like us could abstain). As Suleyman and I steadied our packs before heaving them on, Yusup gave me a brilliant white singlet wrapped in cellophane – one of the gifts he had got ready to distribute to friends when Ramadan ended.

We had hoped to strike across open mountainside to reach Chirkata directly; we could not avoid the place if we wanted to reach Gimry, whatever the fate of the poor Czech, and it seemed wrong to judge it for that single incident. But the mist had come down again and we were doubtful we could navigate through it. There was little choice but to labour back to the road and, feeling overfed and unwieldy, take the roundabout route.

Morning passed with ups and downs to the village of Argvani, where a few dozen houses were embedded in parallel outcrops of rock: one a striated slab like a fibrous cut of beef, the other a crustaceous ridge like the flexed tail of a snake. Some of the homes had crumbled; others, painted white and blue, offered long rows of windows behind verandas held up by timber props. Above the village were steep slopes and gullies. Here, in 1839, Shamil's murids had fought a desperate battle with the tsar's army, its grim tally remembered on a plaque by the road: ten thousand soldiers against 1,750 highlanders, it said, of whom sixty-four survived.

The weather was clearing again, and below us lay Novy Argvani on a shelf – New Argvani, the lower, more prosperous partner of the upper village, its streets hung with fruit trees. Skirting around it, the road hairpinned down into a gorge flanked by soft, grey-brown cliffs studded with stones. We had arrived in the valley of the Andi Koysu river. Only occasional splashes of brilliant green – young apricot trees on patches of flat ground by the water – relieved the earthy walls. The scale and grandeur of the landscape sent a rush of excitement through my body. This was the great valley at the heart of Shamil's Dagestan that would lead us on towards Gimry. Near the tops of the surrounding mountains stretched a tier of sedimentary rock like a waistband, skirts of smooth little ridges flaring below it.

The fecundity beside the river contrasted with the bare slopes and cliffs rearing on either side. Irrigation channels slaked the thirst of mulberry trees whose fruit had fallen on the road and been crushed by occasional passing cars, the sweet smell filling our noses.

'You must understand how difficult life is in these mountains, Tom,' said Suleyman. 'The climate is good but the irrigation systems are inadequate and the slopes are dry. Water runs quickly down them and disappears. So it's hard to grow anything unless you're close to a good stream.'

We had walked more than twenty miles and were beginning to tire. On the edge of Chirkata, a man in his fifties was standing by a plot of apricots. 'I came to check on my trees,' he said. He had cauliflower ears – a sign of prestige in wrestling-mad Dagestan (in Makhachkala, you could pay to have your ears split to acquire the battered look of a champion without going through the sweat of the sport). The man's name was Abdulmazhid. 'Come to my house,' he said. 'I'm a poor person, you can see from my clothes, but I will share all I have.' He was, in fact, immaculate in a black tracksuit, a cap and Puma trainers.

Abdulmazhid's home was in the centre of Chirkata, surrounded by vines and figs – he was not far from the valley's life-giving torrent. Like most of the houses in which we stayed in Dagestan, it had no running water or gas, but was warm and comfortable nonetheless, its living room adorned with two tapestries of Mecca. 'This is a very religious village,' said Abdulmazhid. 'I myself have been six times on the hajj.'

Abdulmazhid ran a wrestling school just down the street. He was so kind and solicitous that I balked at asking him about the

Czech found dead in the river. Later, as we sat on the floor eating the fast-breaking, after-sunset meal of iftar, he told a story of how two surgeons had come to Chirkata, offering money in exchange for human organs, which they suggested removing by operation.

'How awful. What happened?'

'They were captured. The centre of the village was sealed off, the police were kept out and they were set alight.'

'You mean, killed?'

Abdulmazhid shrugged. 'It was the only way. If they'd been handed over to justice, they'd have been set free.'

I was beginning to understand that mountain Dagestan lived by its own rules.

After the highlanders' defeat at Argvani in 1839, the people of Chirkata abandoned the village and destroyed the bridge to the other side of the Andi Koysu in order to slow the advance of the Russians towards Imam Shamil's stronghold of Akhulgo, just downstream on the right bank.

The Russian troops were less exposed in the barren mountains of Dagestan than the forests of Chechnya. An advance party tramped upstream to another crossing, came back down the right bank, and rebuilt the bridge at Chirkata using timbers pulled from its homes and bound together with vines, allowing the main force to cross and take up position.

Shamil was now holed up with about four thousand people at Akhulgo, two fists of labyrinthine crags joined by a precarious walkway and enclosed on three sides by a meander in the Andi Koysu. The ensemble was overlooked by a defensive tower on a nearby height.

This much I had read, but how did the battle – one of the key episodes in the Caucasian War and the myth of Shamil – sit in the landscape? In the morning, keen to help me understand, Abdulmazhid asked his former schoolteacher to accompany us to Akhulgo, which had become a kind of shrine.

Suleyman and I walked down the road on the right bank while Abdulmazhid collected the old man in his car and brought him to us. The steps to the top of the side-by-side bluffs named Akhulgo began by a modern tunnel through the mountainside, and the banister traversing the face of the cliff was tied with prayer scarves, flicking in the breeze.

The old man had recently had a heart attack and was too infirm to climb. Eyes milky and feet unsteady, he propped himself against a wall in the shade at the foot of the steps and told the story of the battle in 1839.

'For two years,' he said, his voice muffled, 'Shamil had been fortifying Akhulgo, preparing for war, building houses, dragging apricot trunks by donkey for beams. He even had two cannons made from apricot wood – it's hard as iron. At least half the people were women and children. Then the Russians began to bomb this mountain with forty-six cannons.'

He pointed up the steps with his inlaid walking stick, and then, reaching for his pocket, smuggled a pair of false teeth into his mouth. 'The ground was shaking. The highlanders fought off attack after attack with daggers and sabres.' His speech had become clearer, but was now accompanied by the soft clacking of dentures. 'Every night, they had to evade the Russians and get down to the river to fetch water and haul it back up. Soon there was nothing left to eat. Eighteen grains of maize per person per day was the ration. The women fought too. The cliffs were red with the Russians' blood!'

The old man had gone into a kind of trance, imagining the fight, his head thrown back. 'Look at that saddle of rock there, that slope. One murid had lost his right hand and was hanging on to a clump of grass with the left. He had no food. But he carried on pushing down stones with his feet on the Russians below.' Now the old man was sobbing with emotion, his own hand grasping an imaginary tussock. 'It was a war among the rocks and caves,' he said. 'For eighty days, every murid did his utmost.'

Eventually, the Russians had scaled the corpse-crowded heights and taken control, the teacher said. But, unseen, Shamil and thirty followers managed to descend the cliff by the Andi Koysu and hide in a ravine, where they stayed for two nights. Making a raft with straw-filled dummies aboard, they launched it down the river, distracting the tsarist snipers and fleeing by a hazardous path towards Gimry. During the escape, Shamil declined food, in favour of his companions. 'He gave a whole pocketful of roasted maize to a man from my village, Chirkata, and told him to share it out,' said the teacher, shifting his back against the wall and miming the imam trickling the corn through his fist into the palm of his comrade. 'Shamil said he'd had his portion, but he hadn't taken a grain. He was very honest. That's why he was loved and respected. Marx and Engels said he was a democrat!'

Abdulmazhid had followed the story intently, interjecting the odd detail when his teacher faltered, tipping his head in concentration. Now he nodded and said: 'Yes, that's right, everyone received the same in Shamil's time; the leaders and the simple people.'

Vivid as it was, the old man's account neglected one of the most important episodes of the clash at Akhulgo. When he had finished telling the story, Suleyman and I pumped his and Abdulmazhid's hands in thanks and climbed the steps up the western crag. At the top, green satin flags snapped in sunlight and a crude portrait of Shamil painted on a board was propped on a slope against scrubby tussocks of yellow grass. No one else was around. We studied the almost vertical falls to the river and a vista of dry mountains beyond, their midriffs crinkled by bands of rock like the edge of a cake fresh out of a baking case. Black shadows silted ravines, and a pair of eagles were rising to our left on a thermal.

As the circumstances for his murids became ever more perilous, Shamil was obliged to hand over his nine-year-old son, Jamal al-Din, to the Russians. It was a token of his willingness to compromise, but the tsarist forces insisted on complete surrender and did not give back their captive.

This was the Shamil who interested me, not the zealous imam or the performer of superhuman leaps, but the sentient father. How had that felt, to abandon his son, a small boy? To touch his shoulder for the last time, to watch his little back disappearing towards the enemy troops? The parents of hostages in the school in Beslan had at least that – they did not give up their own. The terrible fact of their children's captivity was out of their hands. Here, at Akhulgo, a parent had instigated the horror himself, albeit under threat. Only the Beslan mother confronted by the dilemma over her two children – who should stay, who should walk free – had endured a similar torture: the torture of choice.

Handing over *amanaty*, or hostages, as a surety was a common demand in the nineteenth-century Caucasus; it was mostly a Russian practice but Shamil himself had forced it upon his own rivals. I doubted that assuaged his pain. He resisted surrendering Jamal al-Din until the last, only giving in when he realized his murids were too weak to continue fighting.

According to his personal chronicler, al-Qarakhi, in the final days of the siege, an exhausted Shamil had sat down in a conspicuous place in view of the Russians, placed his second son, Ghazi Muhammad, on his knee, and declared: 'O Lord, this child is the dearest spirit in the world to me. If my death comes from a bullet in the middle of my forehead, then let it come in the same way for my child.'

When he eventually fled, Shamil's third son, Said, aged two, and the boy's mother, Jawhara – one of the imam's several wives – were left behind in the melee and died on the battlefield. The imam had a dream in which he saw Said crawling over her injured body. Shamil's uncle was also killed, and his sister would soon draw her veil over her face and fling herself into the gorge as the Russians advanced.

On top of the crags, I imagined the imam stumbling away from Akhulgo after the dangerous descent down the cliff. He was carrying Ghazi Muhammad on his back as they moved up dried creek beds and over ridges, his emaciated body shaking with hunger and fatigue, his feet searching for purchase among the stones.

What was going through his head in those desperate moments? He had lost four members of his family and his boy was in captivity. His forces were in disarray, his enemy rampant.

After days of hard walking, Shamil and his followers reached a village where they could finally draw breath. He 'stayed there', wrote al-Qarakhi, 'like a discarded rag'. He would not see his son Jamal al-Din for sixteen years.

Beyond the tunnel, in the direction in which Shamil had fled, the river widened and was joined by another flowing from the south. We turned upstream, into a canyon. A cold wind was blowing but the sun was warm. Men were laying nets from a boat in the river, and a flat boulder provided a table for a lunch of bread, cheese and spicy adjika.

In the distance, smudges of green came into view by the river. Only when we got closer did we see they were canvas tents – military tents – pitched in a line on the far bank below a strip of apricot and persimmon trees. Beyond the trees, dozens of houses with gently pitched roofs packed a series of low rises and crests. The whole was enclosed on all sides by a natural amphitheatre ascending to the sky in subtly varying shades, from sandy-brown slopes to rusty-yellow cliffs and, at the very top, a band of shark-toothed rock, pink and grey. It was a wild and impressive scene. Suleyman looked at the tents at the foot of the village and shook his head, saying, 'Just like the nineteenth century, under siege.' A hundred metres away across the river, a couple of soldiers cast rods into the water and watched us balefully. We had reached Gimry.

At a bridge to the village, Dagestani police let us through, and I was saying 'pretty easy' to Suleyman when a shout came from a blokpost that we hadn't spotted. In a moment, a dozen men in uniform were in our faces, jostling and shouting for us to open our rucksacks and show our passports. They were Russians. One of them, stinking of vodka, gripped the neck of Suleyman's T-shirt and wrenched it to one side, saying: 'Let's have a look.' (Only later did I realize he was checking for the bruising that a fired rifle can leave on the chest by the armpit.) Finding nothing, he ordered Suleyman to raise his arms and lean against a wall, legs akimbo, then began to search him.

'We are just travellers,' I said feebly. 'I have a letter from the minister of tourism.'

Suleyman was enraged. 'I'll strip off naked and show you all I've got if necessary, but I don't want you pawing me,' he said loudly to the soldier. 'You should give some respect. I'm a free citizen of Dagestan. I worked fifteen years as a judge!'

To a Rebel Village

The soldiers were unmoved. We would have to go to the regional police headquarters for our identities to be established, they said. There was no choice in the matter.

There were times on the walk when I was exasperated, times when I was alarmed, and times when I was exultant and grateful. Occasionally, all these emotions converged around one incident. This was one of those.

To be detained again made the back of my head ache, and I hated to see Suleyman getting manhandled. But could we really expect not to arouse suspicion?

A van with an armed guard delivered us to the police headquarters in a small town on the edge of a reservoir fringed by corrugated cliffs. I was upset to be using transport, breaking my rule. Annoyingly, the gliding speed was an enjoyable change.

At the police station, its high concrete walls topped with barbed wire, a grossly fat officer questioned us in a tiny room with a tiny desk, some dumbbells, a safe and nothing else. I was not feeling confident about our prospects. From the fat officer's safe, mugshots of bearded men looked out on the room, several crossed out in biro and marked with the words 'destroyed', 'killed' or 'arrested'.

We were told to wait in a foyer. It wasn't clear to me if we were suspects or merely irritants who had to be dealt with. The old fear of the walk being ruined had returned. A young officer was assigned to us. Gimry, he explained, had been a Zone of Counterterrorist Operations (KTO) until two months earlier, and was now a Zone of Special Complex Prophylactic Operations (SKPO), a more relaxed regime, but one that still required tight control over people entering the village.

Officers milled around. Without warning, the atmosphere changed. A mature man in dark camouflage had entered. He was speaking briskly to subordinates. 'Abdulatip Abdulatipov, deputy minister of internal affairs of Dagestan,' whispered the young officer. 'He's in charge of the operation in Gimry.'

Suleyman stared at the newcomer. I leapt up. I heard myself starting my spiel, stumbling over the words. 'Excuse me, Comrade General. Good day. I am a journalist from Britain, making a journey on foot from the Black Sea to the Caspian. We very much want to see the historic village of Gimry . . .'

Abdulatipov listened calmly without interrupting as I garbled my request. He looked me up and down, and then turned to a man by his side and said, 'Ruslan, help these men make their visit. I give permission. They can stay at the tent camp.' Then, with a curt nod, he was off.

I was stunned, although I should have known that obstacles still lay in our way. Ruslan was the head of Gimry police, and the afternoon passed with him taking a long 'explanatory' from me – a statement that did not imply guilt but recorded an account of a disputed incident, presumably our detention. As he wrote down my answers with a child's care, he seemed to move from suspicion to incredulity and finally a kind of benign support for our ridiculous trek. Eventually, Suleyman suggested taking over interviewing me himself in order to speed things up. Ruslan agreed and stood in the background, mouthing prayers and flicking his prayer counter.

If the head of Gimry was not pleased to see us, he did not show it.

There had been no room in the tent camp, and we were forced to return to the town and stay the night with one of the policemen, eating potato soup with tinned beef in his kitchen, and sleeping the night on his living-room floor – part captives, part guests. Now we had been returned by car to Gimry, with Abdulatipov's imprimatur smoothing our way.

At the centre of the village, piles of severed sheep hooves and entrails lay next to a pool of water used for ritual cleansing: the great celebration of Uraza Bayram (Eid al-Fitr), marking the end of Ramadan, had begun. Across the republic, animals were being slaughtered and feasts prepared.

The village head came down the hill to collect us. He was a well-built man in his mid-forties with a square jaw, white stubble, short hair and, I thought, something of the East End gangster. His name was Alyas and his house had a wide balcony above a steep drop at the end of a spur, and a magnificent view back past slopes strewn with rubbish to the main part of the village where the mosque was situated, its little minaret rising highest in the bowl of air enclosed by the mountains. We shook hands with several groups of men out on the streets to greet the holiday. Two individuals in one gathering had long beards; one of the men was at least six-foot-six and dressed in black. 'Wahhabis,' said Alyas when were out of earshot. 'They killed several people, but got amnestied.'

Gimry had a reputation for looking out for its own. It was split, Alyas said, once we reached his house, between those who supported the Wahhabis – the term used in the Caucasus for Islamic radicals – and those who didn't.

We had taken seats in a large room with plush furniture and heavy velvet curtains. A high ceiling was held up by sturdy timbers painted white, and on one wall hung a Rembrandtesque painting of a little boy with curly hair. It was a likeness of Alyas's son, Daud, who was scooting about the room. His curls had earned him the nickname Pushkin.

To one side, food crammed every inch of a long table – piles of sausages made from sheep offal, stuffed chickens, salads, aubergine rolls, fatty legs of lamb, cakes, sweets, cashews and almonds swimming in honey – and male guests came to sit for a while and celebrate the end of Ramadan.

Alyas had become head of Gimry a day after the federal authorities had blockaded it with troops nine months earlier, in reaction to the assassination of the MP. The crackdown that followed seemed to have united the village in contempt, and the men around the table were angry.

'We couldn't breathe,' said one with hairy hands and a flat cap.

'There were thirty-two checkpoints around the village, on every road, on every path,' said another.

'A child had a kidney condition – they wouldn't let him out or the ambulance in,' said a third.

Under his balcony, Alyas had a vineyard. Gimry, the men round the table explained, was a kind of reproach to the harsh terrain around it, protected from cool winds by the walls of rock, its microclimate conducive to growing fruits and other crops. That afternoon, Suleyman and I took a walk alone, dipping down narrow alleys overhung by balconies where the houses were made from stone blocks fitted perfectly together, without the need for mortar. Liberated from my pack, I felt tipped-forward and strong, and euphoric at having reached this place. Twice we were ushered into homes, and once into a gloomy workshop smelling of oily rags that was said to be Shamil's father's smithy. One of our hosts was an eighty-one-year-old retired shepherd in spectacles with thick scratched lenses who called through a tiny window, and then trotted up a ladder out of his courtyard onto a neighbour's roof to invite us in for tea and cakes.

Towards the end of the afternoon, at the edge of the settlement, a sunlit incline presented a remarkable sight: scores of flat head-stones like the curved handles of Caucasian sabres with their blades sunk in the earth, each pommel rough-hewn, irregular and unique. By the graves, amid clumps of dry grass, women in black sat reading prayers, honouring their ancestors on this special day in the Muslim calendar. By a tomb, a group of them – immobile, or seemingly so in that instant – held up their palms, strings of prayer beads looped under their hands. A warm breeze was at play as Suleyman and I sat at a distance, drinking in the scene, tempted to stretch out and remove our shoes but fearful it would show disrespect. Something about the attitudes of the women, their stillness and their quiet reverence, their drawing of strength, was a salve to my memories of the mothers in Beslan, contorted by grief. If only they too could find this peace.

Later, I learned the tomb was that of the first imam, Ghazi Muhammad, who had died in Gimry in 1832, three years after proclaiming the *gazavat*, or holy war, against Russia's advance in the Caucasus. Ghazi Muhammad and Shamil had known each other since childhood, running these same slopes and alleys. Russian troops killed the first as they fought to take the village. Shamil managed to leap clean over a phalanx of soldiers from a stoop and escape with bayonet wounds. By 1834, he was the third leader of the Caucasus Imamate. He named his second son after his friend.

At Alyas's house, his brother Magomed had joined the company: a cheerful smoker with a generous frame who had worked as a driver but was now unemployed. He spoke with an honesty that seemed to irritate most of the guests.

'We only have ourselves to blame for the blockade,' he declared. 'We protect each other, we don't betray criminals to the police and we don't abide by the law.'

There was a murmur of discontent and a voice said: 'Why should we all be made to suffer because of a few murderers?'

Magomed was standing with one hand in his pocket and the other holding a cigarette. He took a draw and laughed. 'Look, I used to be a pickpocket and racketeer,' he said, addressing me. 'Eighty or ninety per cent of Dagestanis who go to Russia are criminals and chancers. We don't deserve respect.' Smirking, he pointed to one guest, raising his voice to drown out the man's protestations: 'You, for example, should be put in jail – do you pay your taxes? Do you pay for your electricity?'

The man threw up a hand in disgust and stormed out.

'Who was that?' I asked my neighbour at the table.

'Head of the audit chamber.'

Alyas agreed with his brother. 'For example, that's a Wahhabi right there,' he said, pointing at a pale young man in a baseball cap with a beard and shifting eyes, as if to say: 'And we don't shop him to the police.' The young man, who had come in and sat down without a word a short while earlier, smiled nervously and said nothing.

Following his own train of thought, Alyas went on confidently: 'Mankind is doomed but it could be saved, because when every person dies, there is a small part at the end of his spine containing all the vital information, which remains intact even when the rest of the body decomposes. And when you put this piece of spine into water, it regenerates the whole person.'

To a Rebel Village

There was a silence, into which Suleyman felt compelled to say: 'Er, yes, I have, um, heard something about a blueprint for human life.'

Late in the evening, when the guests had gone, Magomed offered us a hundred grams each of vodka before going to bed. We drank it clandestinely in the pantry. 'You can't be too careful,' he said. 'Gimry's very devout. A kiosk selling alcohol got burned down a couple of years ago.' He brightened. 'On the other hand, there are only eight or nine drunks in the village.'

Before we lay down, Magomed and Alyas, tossing back a last shot of vodka, asked Suleyman why he did not perform evening prayers.

'Because I had an atheist education,' Suleyman replied matter-of-factly.

On his mobile, Alyas had shown me a video of a teenage boy from Gimry performing a protest rap about the blockade.

'This is the village of two imams, this is the village where rules Islam!' sang the lad in the fuzzy footage, rolling his body and throwing hip-hop gestures. 'Those two imams set an example – never give up, never step back.'

In Gimry, I thought that night, the people had their differences, but they had found common cause in their mutual hatred for outside interference. Resisting and subverting the demands of the blockade was a kind of sport – and Alyas was less an instrument of the regional authorities than a proud arbiter and champion of his fellow villagers, whatever their persuasion.

A person's bond with a physical environment is sometimes referred to as topophilia. Through decades of absence, I felt a pull to the low country of East Anglia where I grew up: to the flooded turbaries that make up the Broads, and the pollarded willows spraying their wand-like branches into the sky. Such love is not for an unpeopled countryside, but for places where the past feels tangible, where landscape is marked by time and human endeavour.

The story of Shamil and Ghazi Muhammad seemed to permeate everything in Gimry: you could sense them in the stones. A century and a half on, young men were still propelled by their mystique. Some stepped down a path that ended in terror and bloodshed. For others, the imams' struggle was a proud part of their Avar identity.

Yet the overriding loyalty in Gimry was, I sensed, not to religion or nationality. It was to the very place itself: to the sandy soil underfoot, to the scattering of houses at the bottom of a cake tin of rock, to the scents of dry grass and goat droppings and peaches.

13

Mountain of Tongues

OCTOBER

A long afternoon had been spent crossing a ravine and a series of crumbling terraces, until finally, in the first hour of dark, we were climbing a switchbacking track towards a hamlet on top of a cliff, its few lights making silhouettes of roofs and walls.

Our former host from near Khasavyurt, the moustached Shamil enthusiast named Apandi, had called ahead and arranged for a friend to meet us. The friend, a slight, middle-aged man, took us home through black, winding alleys and fed us soup in a house that was being built for his son.

Suleyman and I were ready to collapse into bed, but when we were taken to the next room, where we would sleep, we found it occupied by the son, Akhmed, and his friends. That was only natural, but we could barely keep our eyes open from fatigue.

The room was gloomy and bitter with smoke. Akhmed and his four mates in their early twenties were puffing cigarettes and watching pop videos on a flat-screen TV. Akhmed said his Russian was bad and mostly stayed silent. Another of the lads, with an Inspiral Carpets haircut, was toying with a knife and making roll-ups from homegrown tobacco. A third spoke better

Russian, albeit sprinkled so liberally with the parasite word *koroche* ('in short') that it was hard not to laugh.

There was no menace but, in my enervated state, the lads' brooding manner was unsettling. It was the first time since the encounter with the partisan months earlier in Abkhazia that I had felt nervous inside someone's home. Looking back, I wonder if it was just the studied cool of the young men that rankled. We met such overt hospitality through most of our walk in Dagestan that sulky indifference seemed a greater affront than the occasional bouts of suspicion. In short, we'd been spoiled.

Not unfriendly, the lads said we were the only foreigners to visit this place since 1985, when 'some people came here to study our traditions'. A single Russian lived among them, a teacher in the school who had married a local man. Despite its tiny population, the village had been racked in the past by blood feuds, they said; seven people were killed between 1991 and 1997 alone. (Later, we were told the village had a reputation for *derzost*, the Russian word for rude audacity.)

Changed into his evening gear of a voluminous set of ruby-red fleece trousers and zip-up top, Suleyman was settling into an armchair when the Russian-speaker asked him if he prayed.

'I don't, to be honest.'

'How is that someone your age doesn't pray? That's a sin.'

Suleyman's cheek twitched. 'You smoke, don't you?' he said. 'That's a sin, too. And a worse sin, according to the Koran, is hypocrisy.'

The lad said: 'I used to drink, smoke dope and fool around with girls, but I realized it was wrong. *Inshallah*, I will also quit smoking.'

'Well, while you're summoning up the courage, make sure you don't die with your sins,' Suleyman shot back. 'Allah could take one of us at any moment.'

The lad was humiliated. 'You should still pray,' he mumbled.

'*Inshallah*, I too will find the strength to stop sinning,' said Suleyman acidly.

Akhmed defused the tension a little (his Russian was not so bad, after all). 'I have two or three girls in every village,' he said, flicking his head to remove his fringe from his eyes. 'No one permanent. They probably get around as well. If I have a girl in Makhachkala, how do I know what she's up to?'

Later, once the lads had gone and we were preparing to sleep, Suleyman was furious. 'Cool guys, eh?' he said. 'Smoking in front of their elders – which is forbidden. And they wanted to teach me how to behave.'

Our host had promised to show us around the village, but in the morning he was still asleep at 9 a.m. We slunk away; half-reluctant, half-glad to leave. In the scent of pine trees, a path climbed to a crest above a sprawling reservoir, its green waters hemmed by crinkled mountains.

Suleyman and I got on well, but did our fair share of annoying each other. His habit of cracking his knuckles, as he did now on the path, and then using his hands to twist his head sharply from one side to the other, emitting a similar noise to the knuckles, made me queasy. In turn, he seemed irritated by the fact he had to defer to my decisions in front of other people, despite being older.

Not for the first time, a North Caucasus man seemed to be working hard to fulfil the stereotype of sex-hungry Romeo. As we traversed about the reservoir, Suleyman received a call on his mobile and hung back, speaking in a soft, soothing voice. Catching up, he said: 'Between you and me, that was a geisha. She likes to earn a bit on the side, five hundred roubles per hour.'

Several girlfriends occupied his free time, he said. One was, like him, a retired judge; another was a thirty-year-old teacher;

a third was a Tatar woman in Moscow who sent him poems by text message. There were further exploits. 'One time, I was driving home in my Jeep Cherokee in cold weather and I picked up these two girls, one fat, one small,' he recalled, his minesweeper foot skimming the path. 'I had a service pistol in those days, and I made out I was a gangster and we had this flirty conversation. Then I took them home and fucked them both. I was pounding the big one really hard, standing up, like this.' He paused to demonstrate, his skinny hips pumping back and forward. 'I may be past fifty but I've still got a lot of energy, and she cried out: "Whoa, daddy. Not bad!"'

He grinned and I laughed, feeling a jolt of desire for Masha.

Our plan was to find a route south through the mountains to the village of Gunib, site of Shamil's final surrender to the Russians in 1859.

It was now the beginning of October and, while it was still warm during the day, the evenings were crisp. That night, we were put up by a retired physics teacher in a village at the head of a valley. In his chilly kitchen, the teacher served Avar dumplings and the stewed meat from a cow's head. There was one Russian in this village, too; he had converted to Islam and married a local woman. 'He's a former bich,' the teacher explained. It was a term that I'd heard before: a Russian man effectively kidnapped and made to work as a slave in the Caucasus, often as a livestock herder. 'He was released a while back,' said the teacher. 'He'd worked many years and people said: "Why not let him go now?" You know, in Moscow, Dagestanis are beaten and killed. The Russians don't like us and we don't like them. But a bich is always well treated. He is a slave, but he is well fed and does not suffer.' The bich had decided to stay in the village of his own accord, the teacher claimed. I would have liked to speak to the emancipated Russian but, with the cold weather coming, I knew we had to push on. Derbent, our final destination on the Caspian coast, was still a hundred miles and a couple of weeks' walking away.

Before we departed the next day, the physics teacher pulled something from a chest: a long sheepskin coat that he draped, reeking, over my shoulders. 'Try that for size,' he said. He was a big man who had played basketball in his youth, now stooped by a bad back. Dangling either side of the coat was a sleeve that tapered to an egg-sized hole, so that an arm could no longer be fitted through. Slung on in squalls and showers, over the generations this kind of coat had become more of a cloak, making the arms redundant, and in a mimicry of natural selection the sleeves had shrivelled from design to design, until one day they would disappear. For now, they clung on, vestiges of an earlier time, and I swung the comically tapering sleeves gently from side to side as I stood in the kitchen, the teacher and Suleyman suppressing sniggers at my transformation into a highlander.

Heading to the Caucasus, I had dreamt of a return to my childhood life of the senses. In the journey through Dagestan, the wish was fulfilled. It was not scenery I was after; not viewing points or postcard beauty. I yearned for what I found on days like this, leaving the teacher's house: a slicing wind across a pass, a dog chewing a cow carcass in a hillside ditch to the sound of a muezzin's call, a festival of air filling the gap between rocky peaks, a pair of bullocks straining at a wooden plough in a field below the path, the work-cracked hand of a villager holding out a perfect apple – fragrant at arm's length – as he invited us inside for plates of fatty mutton and boiled sweets.

*

A morning of climbs and drops and zigzags led to a village where two narrow waterfalls plummeted into a canyon and a fortress of dressed stone loomed squat and massive, built at the end of the Caucasian War. Nearby, locals pointed out the 'tsar's road', a petering track making its way across the Khunzakh plateau.

The plateau was an elevated expanse of cropped grass studded with stones that stretched towards the horizon, flanked by distant ridges. A couple of hours had passed when a shepherd stood with his flock of sheep; five hundred of them, he said, once he had called off his dog and approached to say hello. 'The next village is far off,' he said. 'Why don't you stay the night in my kosh?'

The shepherd's name was Dalgat, and he wore rubber boots, a sheepskin hat and fake Calvin Klein jeans with craggy panache, a staff in his right hand. Like all the shepherds I met in the Caucasus, Dalgat oozed competence. His kosh was a little rectangle of cemented stone with a single window, a steel door and a shingled roof topped by rolled-up sheepskins, and everything inside was in neat order: two narrow beds, a gas stove, an old fridge for storage (there was no electricity here) and stacks of pots and pans. From hooks hung bags of pasta, onions and bread. 'I lived in Moscow for three years, but it didn't suit me,' said Dalgat. 'This is my place.'

Below and to the side of the hut, Dalgat had employed a seam of rock as one side of his sheep pen; a dry-stone wall enclosed the other. 'What are these?' asked Suleyman, eyeing a pile of cylindrical metal objects outside the kosh. Some were unmarked, others dented with flaking green paint.

'Grenade-launcher shells,' Dalgat replied. 'The army use the end of the plateau as a firing range. I find them when I'm fetching lost ewes.' Unfazed, he had scooped them up in the hope they might be sold. There were plastic casings with wires attached that he could not identify, but the red dye inside was useful for marking his sheep.

As evening light yellowed the dry grass and the sheep, Dalgat and his dog drove the animals into their pen. Then he walked us out to the edge of the plateau, where an accretion of rock reared steeply before dropping in a cliff. Far below, a village was already cast in shadows of petrol-fume blue, its darkening houses crowding a slope hemmed in by gullies and scarps. In the east, towards our destination of Gunib, rose a saddleback mountain, and to the south, in the direction of the main range, snowy peaks reached to catch a last glow of sun.

That night, Suleyman insisted on sleeping on the earth floor between the two beds – an act of valour slightly deflated by Dalgat conjuring him a mattress and blankets. I put on all my clothes and wrestled into a sleeping bag that Dalgat gave me alongside a felt burka, a shepherd's cloak, to lay on top. The door to the kosh had to be kept open all night in case of trouble with the sheep. 'A lynx came after them recently,' Dalgat explained.

Breathing frigid air but cosy in our bundles, we slumbered like the dead.

The journey was moving slowly towards its conclusion. I was at once desperate for it not to end, and deeply tired. The cartilage in my knee ground alarmingly and the top of my left thigh was now permanently numb. However exciting, the events of the last months – the arrests, the return to Beslan, the war – had left their mark. It was tempting to believe that one could ride any emotion and venture on, touched but nonetheless impregnable. That was not the case.

Early the next day, Dalgat took us to the edge of the plateau again and pointed the way down a ravine. We descended it, climbed out and then descended once more, squeezing between split cliffs and freestanding pillars of rock, to rejoin the tsar's road. The road was still a stony track, but on bends and steeper slopes, it had supporting buttresses, handsomely made from tightly fitting stones. A long, looping route past orchards and cows grazing on terraces led down to the Avar Koysu river, flowing towards Gimry. By a bridge, a cluster of apricot trees, startlingly green, topped a crescent-shaped island of land that separated the old and new courses of the river. Suleyman plucked orange-red berries from a sea buckthorn bush and made a face as he chewed them. 'Still bitter; they'll be sweeter after the first frost,' he said.

Dalgat had spoken of a defile that would shorten our route to Gunib, and here it was, beyond the bridge: an opening in the cliffs that soon narrowed to a horse's length, its warping ochre walls rising hundreds of feet in the air, the sky above glimpsed and then lost again in semi-darkness. A stream ran in the bottom of the defile, and in darker corners, patches of moss covered the foot of the walls. Here and there, rocks had wedged in the aperture overhead; as the canyon widened again, larger boulders, as big as cars, slumped together in the stream. We scrambled over them, reaching for handholds in their pitted surface, our rucksacks swinging.

Eventually, the walls fell back further still and trees appeared by the stream. A faint path on the bank climbed over a lip to a clearing where smoke rose from the chimney of a hut and a cat napped outside. No one answered a call at the door.

Suleyman and I split up to search for the way forward. There were steep slopes rising on all sides. I climbed one, turning to look down on the clearing. Something about the oppressive silence in the defile and the deserted hut had set me on edge. I thought I heard a noise in trees behind me but, swivelling round, saw nothing. In a moment, I was panicking and shouting Suleyman's name. There was no reply. He had left noisily enough, his boots grinding on the shingle by the stream; now there wasn't the slightest sign he had ever been here. The back of my neck had gone cold and prickly; there was another sound in the wood. My head jerked from side to side, seeking the source. I shouted again, louder. Nothing.

It can't have been fifteen minutes before Suleyman arrived back. By then, I was trembling and furious, although I hardly knew why. 'Where the hell have you been?' I said angrily, as he emerged from behind a screen of bushes. 'I've been shouting for ages. Didn't you hear?'

'I was looking for the path,' he said nonchalantly, leaning on his ski pole. 'What happened?'

I gulped. 'Nothing. I just wondered where you were.'

Suleyman shrugged. 'Guess I didn't hear because of the stream,' he said. 'Let's go?'

To add to the humiliation, we found the way with little trouble once we put our minds to it. Beyond a spur covered in fine black scree, a path led through two glens to a terraced saddle where horses grazed. Further down was a high pasture settlement, where a tiny old man was whaling a post held steady by his wife into the ground with a sledgehammer, and, lower still, stone houses.

In the gathering dark, a man pointed the way to the house of the head of the village. The head's name was Magomed, and without hesitation he invited us in to stay.

Sitting down for dinner on the floor, Magomed said to Suleyman: 'Don't I know you?'

Suleyman smiled nervously and replied: 'Yes, I believe we're acquainted.'

Magomed's face was impassive. 'Yes, that's it; you adjudicated my case a few years ago.' It had been a business dispute of some kind, back when Suleyman was an arbitration judge.

Suleyman looked queasy. 'Was — was everything alright?' he asked.

'Oh yes, you did a fine job. Very professional.'

A look of relief came over Suleyman. 'Ah, good,' he said.

When Magomed had left us for the night, Suleyman smiled ruefully and said: 'That could have been awkward. For a moment, I thought he was going to say I asked for a bribe.'

Why had I been so upset in the gorge? It was a nasty moment of adrenaline, fear with no rational cause apparent. Perhaps it was simply a protest from the body, a reaction to the accumulated anxieties of the journey — and to the long shadow of Beslan.

But it also felt like a catharsis. I had begun to think less often of events at the school, to allow them to slip. I'd had the recurring dream about the falling woman only a few days earlier — the first time since a month or so before I'd started the walk in the spring. But the circumstances somehow extinguished its power. A couple had taken us into their home, and I woke with a start in their living room. Suleyman was snoring contentedly, his ruby-red fleece pulled over his head. We were safe, warm and full of food.

The house was a traditional one with a byre on the ground floor, lending animal heat to the family above. Shaken, I descended steps on the outside of the house to go to the loo. It was situated at the back of the byre; a bench with an oval cutout.

The family cow shifted and lowed a few feet away. There was a whiff of manure and an ammonic note of piss, both softened by the sweet smell of the hay in the cow's manger. A chicken had laid two eggs on the low wall that separated the toilet from the stall. These same sights and sensations would have met the Caucasus guest a century earlier, even two, I thought.

Afterwards, I stood outside for a while in the nip of early morning, the stone house behind me, the buttery light of a single bulb spreading from the byre. The moment seemed to say: this too is real, this too goes on, this calmness, this cycle of living.

Magomed's eighteen-year-old nephew, Shamil, showed us the way to Gunib. Climbing through coppices of silver birch, a path reached a band of rocks fixed with iron handholds and short stretches of ladder, the only way up and over a fist of crags.

'A man slipped and died here last year,' said Shamil, ascending like a mountain goat. He pointed down the cliff into thickets. 'He fell down there.' Following Shamil with slow and awkward movements, we eyed the drop. On top, he was sitting in the sun and chewing a piece of grass. His sure-footed nonchalance made me think me of his namesake, Imam Shamil, leaping over the abyss on his escape from Akhulgo.

Caucasus braves were famed for their physicality and exuberance. In the nineteenth century, their custom of daredevil trick-riding became known as *jigitovka*. I had seen the modern-day *jigits* in Grozny: lads who drag-raced souped-up Ladas and Moskvitchs on a straight on the edge of town. In Dagestan, there were tales aplenty of cars pitching over precipices as they hammered down mountain tracks, head to head. Our guide, Shamil, had had a taster of things to come. 'When I was younger, we used to have arranged fights with boys from the next village,' he said. 'And we stole horses for joyriding. Just left them wherever we ended up.'

'Did they steal yours as well?'

'No, we don't have many horses.' He looked downcast, before recalling happily: 'They used to take our donkeys, though.'

Gunib was an extraordinary sight: a massive soufflé of rock, its sides a ring of tiered cliffs, its collapsed top a depression filled with houses and trees. At the back of the village, jagged crusts of stone pitched into the sky. We had a contact who had offered to put us up, a seismologist with a cupboard full of winking lights. Once more, we pulled off our stinking boots and settled in to a stranger's home.

That night, waiting for sleep in the comfort of the seismologist's living room, my thoughts drifted to a figure standing by a river in 1855. Dark-skinned and slim, with a light freckling of smallpox scars on his neck, he wore an immaculate mundir, the uniform of a Russian army officer, and sported a neatly trimmed moustache. A speaker of French and German with a passion for dancing and the novels of Walter Scott, this finely tooled young man was Jamal al-Din, the son of Shamil, who had been taken as an amanat, a surety hostage, by the Russians at the Battle of Akhulgo sixteen years earlier.

Jamal al-Din, I knew from my pre-walk reading, had remained a Muslim but become deeply Russianized during his long sojourn in the north, studying at the imperial cadet corps in Moscow and St Petersburg, an education overseen by Nicholas I himself, before becoming an officer.

What disquiet must have gripped him in this moment, his hands clammy, his stomach turning. At twenty-five, he was facing a personal cataclysm. Within a few minutes, he would be swapped for two Georgian princesses and their children, whom a team of Shamil's horsemen had, with enormous temerity, whisked from a country estate to the south of the Greater Caucasus range the previous year. Kidnapped by Shamil with the express purpose of trading them for his son, the princesses – from Georgia's pro-tsarist aristocracy – had spent months in captivity at the imam's new capital in Chechnya, Vedeno. Polite society demanded their release from this ordeal at the hands of a primitive despot. (Confusingly, the princesses told the author of a book about their kidnap that Shamil was an enlightened and noble man who adored his family.)

Now, rival Russian and highlander delegations were gathered for the prisoner swap on the banks of a river twenty miles from the Dagestani settlement of Khasavyurt, where Jamal al-Din had spent weeks awaiting the handover.

Resigned to his fate, in private he was horrified at leaving behind his sophisticated Russian existence for the stringent life of the mountains. He remembered his father with difficulty: Shamil had not replied to the pleading letters Jamal al-Din had sent under the watchful eye of his superiors. The young officer enjoyed witty conversation and mingling with ladies at balls; he loved reading about physics and mathematics. Piles of books, atlases, pencils, drawing instruments and good paper filled his luggage – testament to his fear of losing the skills he had culti-vated. He had missed his family – his mother had died without seeing him again – but he must have wondered how he could live once more in the smoky rooms of mountain *sakli*.

By the river, the exchange was made. The princesses rushed forward to be embraced by Prince Chavchavadze. Jamal al-Din was surrounded by dozens of Shamil's murids, dressed in black *cherkeskas* braided with silver and gold. At first, he resisted a request to remove his Russian attire and put on a *cherkeska* him-self, but he acquiesced when he heard it was his father's wish.

What was going through the young man's head in these moments? He had been transplanted from his native land to another soil at the age of nine. That soil, he believed, had enriched him, made him an educated man. By comparison, the future looked arid.

Back in the mountains, Jamal al-Din was a curiosity. He was made to sit on top of a house in Vedeno in an armchair so that rubberneckers could come to take a look. He was overcome by melancholy. A painful circumcision made him ill. He tried in vain to persuade his father of the folly of keeping up his fight against the might of the Russian empire. Shamil was not impressed.

There were some moments of levity. Jamal al-Din debated highland and Russian affairs with his father in the evenings, and impressed the locals by predicting a lunar eclipse. He acquired new books by ransoming a slave Shamil had given him. He married a Chechen girl and managed to get her an umbrella delivered from Russia. But he missed his friends and the atmosphere of tsarist St Petersburg. His spirit seemed to wane; soon his body did, too. At the beginning of 1858, he contracted tuberculosis. By August that year, he was dead at the age of twenty-eight.

In Gunib, I climbed the path at the back of the village to the place where Shamil had surrendered in 1859, a year after his son's death.

A little shrine had been built over a rock where Prince Bariatinsky had sat to receive Shamil's capitulation, now in a grove of silver birch, the afternoon light filtering through the branches.

From the late 1840s, the imam's power had begun to fade. Increasingly, Russian troops exposed the highlanders' positions by decimating swaths of woodland, sending beeches 280 feet high and thirty-five feet in girth crashing down the mountain sides – an ecological crime on a par with the napalming of Vietnam.

As villages were put to the sword, Shamil withdrew once more to the barren hills of Dagestan. By the time he reached the natural fortress of Gunib, he had only four hundred loyal murids left. They were soon overwhelmed.

After his capture, Shamil was treated as a fallen head of state and transported in comfort to Moscow and then St Petersburg, where he was given a tour and visited the cadet corps where Jamal al-Din had studied. He watched pupils fencing, dancing and performing acrobatics, noting that Russian soldiers had deployed such skills to scale the cliffs of Gunib.

The imam was then moved to the town of Kaluga near Moscow to live out his days in relative comfort with several of his wives and children. The authorities acquired the house of a major's widow and fitted it out for his use. It had a closed garden for walks and a small mosque in the yard. Shamil was allowed to lobby for the rights of the highlanders and mix with members of the local nobility. Finally, in 1869, Alexander II granted him permission to perform the hajj to Mecca, where he fell sick. The imam died in Medina in February 1871.

Shamil's Russian chaperones claimed he was content in the gilded cage of his later years. I found that hard to believe. Surely, like his son, he pined for the land in which he had flourished. Did his mind drift to the narrow lanes of Gimry, his childhood home? To the eagles circling overhead, to the walls of ochre and pinkish rock and the persimmons hanging plumply from trees? I felt sure that it did.

In the century and a half since his death, Shamil's legacy has been dissected, debated and forced into service. To Soviets, he was a progressive anti-colonial freedom fighter (and later a feudal cleric); to Russians, he was a former enemy who came to appreciate the culture of the conquering power. To Dagestanis, he was a hero, to Chechens a champion, to Avars a revolutionary, to Islamists a radical.

EAST

Standing by the stone at the back of Gunib, I thought rather of the man of flesh and blood. At once wrong-headed and cruel, kind and intelligent. Succoured by loyalty, tormented by remorse. Aching with the wounds of battle. The father of a stolen son who brought him home but saw him wither and die.

It was autumn now, but hot again, and the land was parched from a summer of sun. Partridges whirred from thickets and clumps of dry thistles rustled at the wayside. For a week, we walked on tracks and paths through the villages stacked on hillsides, the stones of their houses packed so tight that, so the saying went, you couldn't get a razor blade between them.

In many of the *auls*, an ugly new mansion had been built among the modest dwellings, like the *kottedzhi* I had seen at the beginning of my journey in Krasnodar. Each was the home of a local bigwig – one was the house of the head of Makhachkala port, another belonged to a famous Soviet test pilot. One head-man drove a black Mercedes G-Class four-by-four with tinted windows and sheepskin seat covers. He had studied at an elite presidential institute in Moscow, but couldn't remember its name (in the capital, rich Caucasians had a reputation for buying their way into such places and disdaining lectures).

A cop and an immigration official appeared at a headman's house, the first friendly, the second suspicious. The policeman took down our 'explanation' with gusto, composing lyrical lines about our lofty aims and passion for Dagestani history; the official wanted to detain me and take me to Makhachkala. On a dirt road, I sweated as an officer inspected a map I had unwisely marked with hot spots of Islamist violence – surely these were drop-off points where I would leave the militants money? I denied it, grateful that the officer's eye had not strayed to the words 'General Head-quarters' at the fringe of the Soviet military map, and he let us go.

Hospitality was king. One headman refused to take us in, saying we could be guerrillas; a man overheard and jumped forward to save the village's honour. Two tiny men, brothers in their fifties named Zubair and Azdar, made us fried liver and phoned one of their wives to find out where the teaspoons were kept. When I got up to go to the loo in the night, Azdar leapt from under a pile of dirty sheepskins on the porch, where he had been guarding his guests from intruders. His face contorted in accommodating expressions as he ushered me to the outdoor closet.

Dagestan seemed charged with magic. Young men spoke of donning masks made from skins and animal teeth, and a pensioner, marching back and forth on the flat roof of his house, struck theatrical gestures as he told of an attack by janissaries in some distant century. Rain and its absence were constant topics. How could you break a drought? Take a frog from the village well, dress it up in fine clothes – a little outfit covering its torso and legs – and take it to the well of a village with rain. Bring home a frog from there in similar togs, and the rain would come with it. Suleyman said the absence of water or light could shape a village's residents; an ill-situated ridge cast a shadow on both ground and character.

The heat began to diminish, and one morning a sprinkling of snow coated the hills. I startled an eagle on a rock in a gully: a great cantilevered gluing of feathers and limbs, so close I could almost touch it.

The villages here felt more and more remote. Briquettes of dried dung for fuel rose in stacks next to the houses, and cow-dung patties like great buttons were pasted to dry on the sides of buildings. At windows, there were prised-open sheep carcasses drying in the last of the sun. A man jogged next to us, asking: 'Who are you? Who are you?'

I was beginning to fall apart. My clothes smelled, my knee was protesting ever louder, and I was tortured by the lack of opportunity to wash. Most homes we stayed at had no running water, and it felt an imposition to ask for a tub that was heated. I sluiced my face and neck at standpipes, but the rest of my body became increasingly itchy. One night, I found myself inspecting my groin with a torch under the blanket in a guestroom. What was that terrible itch? Fleas, a rash? I could barely sleep. I developed a hacking cough and snivelled through conversations with our hosts. At night, I dreamt of deep baths and saunas.

Most of our journey had been in Avar country, but ethnic faultlines appeared. By a stream just short of Kumukh, a cowherd unleashed a torrent of obscenities on a group of bullocks. Suleyman cocked his ear as if appreciating a musical refrain and smiled. 'Now we are in the territory of the Laks,' he said.

Suleyman's hungers were growing after weeks in the hills.

At a standpipe in the village, a voluptuous woman in her thirties was filling a plastic ewer. Her name was Raya. Often, women in public places had stayed silent or even turned away when we greeted them. Raya was talkative. She invited us for a cup of tea. 'A beautiful lady, I want to get to know her better,' said Suleyman, his eyes boggling. We went to Raya's home, a rented house with a three-hundred-year-old balcony. She spent part of her time in Makhachkala and was an outsider here, despite being half-Lak, she said. Her two daughters were at home learning English; her husband, a builder of elite housing, was away. She was starved of intelligent company, she said, and was glad to talk. She poured tea made from herbs and grasses she had collected in the mountains, dead bees floating in it, their wings crisp, above the surface. 'That makes it authentic,' Raya said, laughing.

We chatted, and Suleyman made embarrassing remarks about Raya's beauty while the girls sat up on their knees and leaned over their homework. Raya's landlady arrived, seeming to have detected our arrival with snooper's ears; she lived a couple of doors away.

'I heard the sound of two men's voices admiring the balcony, and I recognized one of them as my old friend Suleyman,' Raya lied to the landlady. It was the only way of excusing male strangers in her home while her husband was out.

As we left, one of the girls turned her face to me and said, in perfect English: 'What does the word "zany" mean?'

Raya walked us to the edge of the village, and Suleyman kissed her hand in farewell.

On a track across flat, open fields, I said: 'Interesting. Why haven't they planted any crops here?'

Exasperated, Suleyman said: 'BECAUSE – THERE IS – NO WATER.'

A milky fog hung over the track to Kubachi. Only a boisterous volleyball game loomed out of the whiteness by a school, and then a group of curled-up dogs at the wayside. Suleyman had already fended off one cur's attack by poking his ski pole down its throat; a pack like this posed more danger. But the dogs stayed tightly coiled in the chill of the morning.

Kubachi, a large hill village in southeast Dagestan, was famous for its silversmiths. There was a lushness here, close to the coast: Derbent was now only thirty-five miles away. Rhododendron sprouted. In the centre of the village, we found the head of the

administration, Gadzhi-Isa, forty-five years old with – appropri-
ately – spiky silver hair and a moustache that crept down over his
top lip in a silver portcullis. He was thrilled to have guests. Look
at our Islamic inscriptions! Look at our silver-making *kombinat*! At
the *kombinat*, slabs of silver were being flattened through an electric mangle similar to one I'd used as a teenager to thin pastry at
a village bakery in Suffolk, and a silversmith battered out a goblet.
Gadzhi-Isa had something even more interesting at home: a real
bathroom with running hot water. I spent an hour of delirious
pleasure, sploshing and scrubbing.

The end of the journey was approaching. We had walked for
almost three weeks through highland Dagestan without tents or
bedding. Every night, without fail, a stranger had taken us in. It
was hard to comprehend how these people had ever been accused
of lacking 'civilization'. Himself, Gadzhi-Isa had done something
exceptional, something with the grandeur of poetry or saga. That
night, he poured some vodka and told us the story. The road to
the local market town, he said, was about fifteen miles long. 'Too
far for our traders,' he said, but there was no government plan to
solve the problem. So Gadzhi-Isa and five friends had got together
to build a new road that would cut the journey to five and a half
miles by hugging a wooded mountain valley. They would do it all
by themselves, out of charity. They started work with a tractor
and a bulldozer provided by Gamid Gamidov, a popular politician
later killed in a car bombing. 'We began well, but little by little,
my friends lost interest,' said Gadzhi-Isa. 'I was left on my own.'
One man to build a road. He became obsessed. He planted sticks
of dynamite to blast the way from the rock, creeping away to a
safe distance with a detonator. He slept outside, under overhangs,
on beds of leaves. Rain dripped down his collar and he shivered
through the night. The funding ran out, but he carried on with

his own money. The digger toppled over a cliff. Relations with his wife became strained as the family budget was squeezed. 'It was an *idée fixe*,' said Gadzhi-Isa. It took him two years to complete the final three miles of the road. It was a dirt track where plants sprouted through the surface here and there, but it was a road nonetheless, passable by cars.

'Incredible,' I said.

'And tomorrow, I will show you,' said Gadzhi-Isa. 'It will shorten your route as well.'

He was right: next morning, the track pulled us into a wooded glen where the sun passed through leaves turning red, yellow and gold. Gadzhi-Isa caught up in his Lada Niva; I had forgotten a fleece at his house. He walked on beside us, pointing out trees: delicate aspen with whitish trunks, some on tops of cliffs; beech with rich, claret leaves; oak, ash – still green, they would turn later; hornbeam, maple, wild pear, apple and cherry.

'Look, these blackberries grew in these places where I blasted rock and cleared timber,' he said. There were guelder-rose, buckthorn, wild raspberries and red and blackcurrants. We stopped to pick them, the juice staining our fingers. There were plums, too, little bombs of sweetness.

'Wait!' Gadzhi-Isa had stopped. 'This is where we used to *otdykhat*,' he said. A shack had appeared in a clearing by the roadside. 'I came here every night to strip to the waist and wash.' He walked to one side and began overturning rocks in the undergrowth. 'It's got be here somewhere. Yes!' His fist held an earth-stained bottle of vodka and some plastic cups. 'I secreted it here in case of emergencies,' said Gadzhi-Isa.

We drank a toast to his achievement and said our goodbyes. The road continued, clinging to steep wooded slopes above the river, some almost sheer, marked with the shattered drill holes where Gadzhi-Isa had placed his explosives. It ended by a stream and a footbridge that led towards the market town.

That was the thing: Gadzhi-Isa had not yet managed to replace the footbridge with one that would take traffic. I never found out if he managed that final step. I'm not sure I want to. In my mind, his road burns to this day like a comet of human enterprise.

So much of my walk had circled back to familiar themes: home, grief, deracination. To be torn from one's native place and culture was a trauma that could be overcome – even harnessed to advantage. Yet for many, the pain of removal seeped through the years. If you managed to get back, were you ever the same again? Could you restore what was lost?

Beyond the stream at the end of Gadzhi-Isa's road, a scrap of cloth fluttered from a pole and a narrow path climbed through undergrowth into forest, switchbacking over the roots of trees, a ribbon of muddy ground slick with fallen leaves.

There was one last place to see before reaching the coast, and this was the way. I got ahead a little – Suleyman's limp often slowed him down – and met a Dagestani soldier in uniform descending the path. He had a pistol at his hip and was carrying two bulging plastic bags full of walnuts. 'Wow,' he said, on meeting an Englishman. 'Aren't you afraid? I go everywhere with my gun, even when I'm off duty, like now. The boyeviki could be anywhere in these woods.'

My aches seemed to have faded for a day, and I sped up the hill through the trees, feeling fit and unmoved by the soldier's warning. At the top was a grassy knoll with a mosque and a mausoleum on it. To every side spread a vista of thickly wooded slopes and rocky scarps. The mausoleum, protected by the spreading branches of a beech tree and startling in its simple grace, was a hunkered building of stone blocks and rough brickwork with a blunt, tapering tower no more than ten feet high. There was an archway over the door and a single slit for a window. Before the mausoleum stood a cluster of carved gravestones.

This was the location of Kala-Koreysh, literally, 'the fortress of the Quraysh', a place of pilgrimage and veneration with no equal in southern Dagestan. No one can be sure, but it is believed that Kala-Koreysh was founded by Arab members of the Quraysh tribe, to which the Prophet himself belonged, and played an important role in the spread of Islam in Dagestan in the Middle Ages, becoming the centre of the Kaytag Utsmiystvo feudal state.

On slopes beneath the mosque and the mausoleum were the remains of a village: stone walls split by shrubs and trees, the shells of houses and a caravanserai. The sun shone warm and a breeze moved the grass around the ruins. Besides Suleyman and me, there was no one around. Only after a while did a man in his sixties appear from an intact house behind the mosque. His name was Bagomet and he was the guardian of the place, he said: its single resident. The soldier I had met was a relative who had been making a visit.

Bagomet showed us the four tombs inside the mausoleum, draped with green and white satin, and the interior of the mosque with its solid pillars of scarified stone. He was an even-tempered man in a purple skullcap and a tweedy jacket with long cuffs.

Bagomet had grown up in the village of Kala-Koreysh; the ruins we had just explored. 'This is one of the top three Muslim shrines in the world,' he declared as we drank tea and sucked sweets in his cottage. Foreign visitors were rare, he admitted. A Moroccan had come recently. He had complained about the rags that pilgrims had tied to trees and bushes: they were pagan and undesirable.

The last Kaytag ruler had sworn allegiance to Russia in the early nineteenth century. When the Chechens were deported from their homeland in 1944, the residents of Kala-Koreysh were forcibly moved to Chechnya to take over their homes.

'I was six years old, so I don't remember a great deal,' said Bagomet. The villagers were allowed back to Dagestan in the 1950s, but the remote hilltop settlement at Kala-Koreysh, built up with such fearful effort over the centuries, was no longer a fit place to live. They found new homes down on the plain. Bagomet had worked for three decades in a city as a machine operator, only returning to Kala-Koreysh four years before our visit, after the previous watchman, his cousin, had died in an accident. 'I renovated this one room – this is my parents' former house,' he said. There were a few sticks of furniture and a cooker. 'I'm completely alone. Every morning, I get up early and walk around the village. I go down the central street, see if any walls have fallen, and then come back up. Sometimes I cut the nettles with a scythe. When I'm passing the houses, I recall the names of the families who lived there and say their names to myself, not to forget.'

'That's sad,' I said.

Bagomet paused. 'I remember people here working, laughing, arguing. Some days, I go to sleep after lunch because there's nothing to do, no one to talk to.'

Now and then, he would go into town to buy provisions and collect his pension, but in winter, he could go days without seeing a soul. In the warmer months, he spoke to any visitors who made the climb to the hilltop, and in autumn he collected nuts from the trees. 'It's a strange feeling,' he said, pouring some more tea, 'when the place where you once lived becomes a museum.'

*

Mountain of Tongues

In the final days, we came out of the mountains into rolling country where spurs spread like fingers from the hills.

There were more acts of kindness, and moments of stress. As we walked down an asphalt road, a car slewed to a halt, and in a second we were surrounded by commandos with automatics. One took up position in front, legs akimbo, and clicked off his safety catch. I held up my hands and said: 'I'm an English journalist completing a journey on foot, and this is Suleyman, my friend and guide.'

'You're entering Tabasaran district,' said the leader of the squad once he had examined our documents – Suleyman always proffered his mountaineer's bilet – and accepted our story. 'The security situation here is not good. I advise you not to go further.'

It was nerve-racking to get stopped like this, and the warning was clearly serious. But there was no choice but to push on. Derbent was a few miles away.

A last patch of forest blocked the way to the coast. A local man helped us search for a path in thinning trees. Above the foliage, a military helicopter was beating back and forth. Searching for militant fighters, the boyeviki?

All through the journey, I had anticipated a meeting with the militants, turning over the scenarios in my mind. I pictured how they would emerge from the trees, stringy-armed with black beards and motley camouflage, grenade launchers and Kalashnikovs resting on shoulders or strapped to knapsacks. It never happened.

We abandoned the idea of walking through the forest. There was too much of a risk of getting caught in crossfire. Instead, we would walk a dogleg on asphalt roads to double back to Derbent.

Back out of the trees, a shepherd boy stood on a grassy ridge, tending his flock. He was no more than twelve, wearing a hand-knitted jumper, a pair of trousers shiny with use and short rubber boots.

I had started my journey by the Black Sea milky-skinned and clean-shaven, dressed in new hiking trousers and a pristine raincoat: a Norfolk birdwatcher lost in the Caucasus. Now, five months later, my clothes smelled of sweat and smoke, my face was burned and stubbled, and my rucksack had faded to grubby pinks and greys.

I approached the shepherd boy with a smile and asked directions to the next village. Only when I drew close did I see he was shaking uncontrollably, his handsome little face rigid with fear. He tried to open his mouth but could not speak.

'No problem, it's fine,' I said, backing away. 'Really, I'm sorry I bothered you.'

Later, as we walked on, I said to Suleyman: 'Poor lad. What do you think happened?'

'He thought you were a boyevik,' said Suleyman.

Our route turned along the coast and traversed a washboard of spurs, up-down, up-down, the Caspian glittering in autumn sunshine to our left. On the edge of Derbent was a tunnel and then the ancient citadel rising at the back of the city. From its fortifications, two massive parallel walls descended through the middle of the town, to the sea. They had once contained the city, a chokepoint protecting the borders of the Sassanian Persian empire from nomad incursion. Now they were an integral part, encrusted with shops and lean-tos and satellite dishes.

The southern wall guided us down, its blocks of honey-coloured stone interrupted by delightful arched gateways. Ladas sped between medieval pillars fixed with road signs.

At the bottom, the sea was lapping calmly on a deserted beach. Suleyman's right foot made a last sweep over the sand, and he sank to the ground. I cast off my boots and socks and advanced into the water.

'We did it, Tom,' came Suleyman's voice from behind me as a wave caressed my ankles. 'You did it.'

Epilogue

It's almost fifteen years since I walked across the Caucasus.

Afterwards, I went back to my life in Moscow: to my old job, to Masha and to our flat overlooking the river. It was good to be home and see friends, but for a long time I felt adrift. At work again in my grubby office near the Belorusskaya train station, I sometimes longed for the mountains.

Natasha Estemirova was murdered in July 2009, less than a year after I got home. It's still hard to write these words. She was kidnapped outside her home in Grozny, pushed into a car, driven to Ingushetia, shot in the head and chest, and dumped in a wood a few miles from the road down which I had walked with Misha. I was at home working when I heard the news. I remember a chill coming over my back and chest, and a shout of rage bursting into the empty room. Although I had seen Natasha on many occasions, I was closer to the Memorial staff in Nazran than those who worked in Chechnya. But I had always admired her tenacity and the freshness of her outrage at each new act of callousness – a human being just trying to mend the lives of people around her, not some embittered seen-it-all.

The day after Natasha was murdered, I wrote in a comment article:

EAST

A single mother of mixed Russian and Chechen parentage, Estemirova worked at Memorial's poky office in central Grozny, near the monument to a trio of heroic Caucasian figures affectionately known as 'the three idiots' . . .

The friendly atmosphere at the office was deceptive. Because the sweet-looking old ladies who queued in the hallway came not for idle chat, but to tell tales of depravity: a son shot dead at home by masked men in uniform, a nephew detained and tortured, a family made homeless after security forces burned their house to the ground.

'This is how things are in our new, peaceful Chechnya,' Estemirova once told me with a grim smile, after describing the disappearance of a young woman who was kidnapped by camouflaged men in central Grozny. It was such horrors which Estemirova painstakingly recorded and publicised, to the chagrin of Chechnya's Kremlin-backed government.

Natasha had been a symbol that dignity and virtue were alive in the midst of unbridled evil. And now she was gone.

I wanted to step aside from journalism and write about my walk and all I felt about the Caucasus. I couldn't find the right way to do it. So I continued to work as a correspondent, never quite satisfied. Occasionally, I would travel to the region to report. With time, London's interest tailed off as the jihadis lost momentum. I'm only glad, of course, that extremist violence has decreased compared to the time of my walk. What I don't believe is that Chechnya had to be turned into a dictatorship in order to achieve it, for that is what happened: with Kremlin encouragement, a cruel and capricious tyrant made himself emperor of a people whose traditions spoke of just the opposite qualities – of modesty and egalitarianism.

Life went on. I wasn't unhappy but I retreated a little, spending a lot of time in our neighbourhood by the Moscow river. Masha was my lodestar. Every summer, we travelled to the family dacha in the hot, sandy country by the Volga-Don canal; a proper, rustic dacha where our hair thickened in the sun and spring water turned your feet deliciously cold in the swimming pond, and we went fishing for rudd with rods made from branches, and Masha's grandfather collected dried cowpats in a little cart to fertilize his vegetable patch, scooping them up with a specially fashioned implement like a pizza peel.

In 2012, Masha and I got married, and in 2019 we had a son, Leo. We call him Lyovushka, the same diminutive that Tolstoy's family used for him as a child. Leo's first language is Russian, but he understands everything I say in English. We resolved that he should grow up knowing both cultures, and being equally proud of each.

Then, in early 2022, Russia troops poured into Ukraine. Within a few short months, before we could fully take on board what was happening, Masha and Leo and I had to leave Moscow. The Kremlin had pushed through legislation that meant you could be sent to a penal colony for 'discrediting' the Russian army – something that could include factual reporting about atrocities against civilians.

We packed up our apartment in a state of distress, pulling memories from the cupboards – my mouldering tent from one, files of Masha's yellowing cuttings from Yekaterinburg from another. It was a difficult moment for us – insignificant compared to what was happening to people in Ukraine, but difficult none-theless. Masha agreed to leave but did not want to go, to abandon her country, not knowing when she might next be with her parents, or whether she would see her beloved grandmother ever again.

I too felt deeply ambivalent. I still do. My head tells me that in any case, we had to move to Britain one day my parents were getting elderly and I needed to take a fresh step in my career. Yet I feel awful for Masha. So many things in Russia are dear to us, whatever iniquity has been committed in its name. I can't get used to the idea that our life there is over, that we'll no longer look out over the limes in winter, their branches coated in rime, that I won't hear the sough of the draught in the keyhole when Masha comes home and opens the outer door to the stairwell, that we won't smell the lilac by our son's nursery in the spring, or go out to sit in the yard on an autumn evening when the field-fares are chattering softly overhead. My Moscow was never the city of Maybachs and oligarchs. It was our little kingdom of green opposite the Not-Boring Garden, with Sparrow Hills just round the bend in the river.

It is summer 2022, and I am walking down a quiet residential street in East London. I have finally agreed a publishing contract to write this book, and I've arranged to see someone I've thought of often over the years but never met: Natasha Estemirova's daughter, Lana.

Lana was fifteen when her mother was murdered. She had spent most of the previous year living with her aunt in the Urals because Natasha was being threatened and considered it too dangerous to keep her daughter in Chechnya. Lana had already become an activist in her own right, the only girl in her Grozny

Epilogue

school who refused to obey the rule that girls should wear headscarves. After Natasha's death, Lana moved to Britain, going to school in Oxford with the help of sponsors and then studying at the London School of Economics. Now, at twenty-eight, she is an experienced campaigner, working for a UK-based group that advocates for media freedoms.

She knows I'm coming and leads me to her dining room, where she serves grilled halloumi, delicious Turkish olives and hummus with flatbread. French doors open onto a small garden with a hammock and unkempt grass, for which she apologizes.

Lana has the same soft features as her mother. We talk about Natasha's childhood. She was, Lana says, a product of the Soviet repressions. At the age of twelve, Natasha's father, a Chechen named Hussein, had been sent to Kazakhstan during the deportation of 1944. On the way, he became separated from his sisters. Alone in Kazakhstan, he picked up odd jobs, and fell into crime. It was the time of desperate hunger, when dozens of Caucasus exiles were dying every day. Eventually, Hussein was convicted after a brawl and sent to prison in the small town of Kamyshlov in Russia's Urals. There, he began to correspond with a local Russian girl, Klavdiya, who had signed up to be a convict's pen pal. When Hussein was released, they married, and Natasha was born in 1958. She was the first of four children.

'My grandparents, my mum, her three siblings and my great-grandmother lived in a tiny, two-room apartment in a wooden building,' says Lana, pouring tea. 'It was a typical toxic Soviet family, not intelligentsia. Granny worked in a flour mill. My grandfather had had a tough life. He worked at a series of different places while drinking his own weight in vodka. But he was a very smart guy, he loved to learn. He kept books and my mother's retreat from everything was to read.'

As a young woman in the early 1980s, Natasha went to Grozny to study history and became a teacher. The First Chechen War broke out in 1994, the year Lana was born. Natasha went back to the Urals for the birth and then returned to Grozny. The infant Lana stayed behind for a while with her relatives before being taken to Chechnya.

Lana remembers the war years in patches. She barely knew her father. A Chechen, he was killed during the Second Chechen War, in 1999, when she was five. Around the same time, Natasha began working for Memorial.

'My mum and I were incredibly close, we were like two halves of one whole,' says Lana. 'Sometimes she had to send me away to relatives in the villages while she was on a trip, but we spent a lot of time together. I used to go with her to work and see the crying women. People called me "Natasha's little tail" because I was always following her around. The connection that I had with her – I don't think I'll have a connection like that ever again. It was as if our bond was made of stuff that was unbreakable.

'She didn't teach morals, she showed by example. I received her values like mother's milk. I remember how she used to walk me to school in the mornings, along Pervomayskaya Street. It was the most beautiful street in Grozny – there were trees either side of it. As we were walking along, my mother would lift up the handle of my backpack to make it lighter for me on my back. And either side of us, there would be sappers checking the verges for mines. I was convinced that their idea was to step on a mine and blow it up; that it was a suicide mission. And all the while, I would be chattering away, telling my mum about Harry Potter, or the latest book I was reading.'

When Natasha dispatched her to the Urals in 2008, Lana felt resentful. She was fourteen and spirited. She emailed her mother,

Epilogue

saying: 'I hate it here. Why won't you take me back? You care more about your work than me.'

Natasha was devastated. 'She wouldn't apologize, she believed a parent did not need to apologize when they made decisions, but she was really emotional,' Lana recalls. 'It really broke her that I sent that message.'

Lana knew, though, that her mother had good reason to send her away. 'When she was frightened, she became snappy and frantic. My biggest dream was to protect her,' she says. Lana had overheard conversations at home about Kadyrov openly threatening her mother after she publicly criticized the headscarf policy. Kadyrov called Natasha to a meeting, where he flew into a rage, and told her he knew where she lived. 'He also said he knew where I went to school and that he'd heard I was a troublemaker,' says Lana. This chimes with an account of the meeting I had heard, at which Kadyrov insulted Natasha and clawed himself, crying: 'What can I do to stop you people writing these things about me?'

At the meeting, Natasha – the former schoolteacher – saw before her an impudent child. 'Why are you talking to me in this way?' she said to Kadyrov, coolly. 'I could be your mother.'

Lana can't talk about the day when Natasha was killed. The memory is triggered easily enough as it is, without approaching it directly. As we sit and talk at the dining table, she thinks she hears a rustle in the grass outside and is suddenly anxious. She and her husband recently suffered the death of their cat and every time there's a sound in the garden she thinks it's come back, before she remembers. Moments later, she notices some missed calls on her mobile: the same thing that happened the morning the cat was knocked down on the road – and the same thing that happened when her mother was shot.

'Some tragedies seem almost cinematic,' she says of Natasha's assassination. 'They're so overwhelming that it's hard to believe you could really live through that. It's almost like they're too fictional to be true; all the coincidences, some song that was playing, the phone call…I couldn't get rid of this feeling of unreality. You know, when I read *The Myth of Sisyphus* by Camus as a student, that really helped me; this idea of living in a state of the absurd. Finally, I found something that matched the state that I was in for years after my mother was killed. Because sometimes I couldn't even get angry properly; I felt like I wasn't even living my life. I was desensitized to everything happening around me. Part of me died that day, and I'll never be able to retrieve it. They didn't just kill her, they killed me as well.'

We pause for a moment, and I breathe out and say: 'Although the other things we've talked about actually suggest that isn't completely the case. I don't think you *were* killed, were you?'

'Yes, that's right, there is some kind of stubborn, living force,' Lana replies. 'You're like an animal with a broken leg, but still dragging yourself on with three paws, with this atrophied part of your body. That's what it's like, living with grief every day. But at the same time, the desire to live is very strong. To live against all odds, and not just to be a ghost, but to be a fully formed individual. That's what my mum would have wanted. I have this distinct feeling that I'm living for both of us, not just for myself. I said that a part of me died that day, but a part of her lives on inside of me, and sometimes I can almost feel that she's watching the world through me. This is getting a bit esoteric, perhaps, but it's true.'

I say: 'When I think of your mum, I think of Tom Joad's speech when he's saying goodbye to his mother in the film of *The Grapes of Wrath* by John Steinbeck. Do you know it? He's telling her that he'll be a kind of silent presence wherever injustice is done, even if he's not there in person. And he says this beautiful thing: "I'll be all around in the dark. I'll be everywhere."'

Lana nods and says: 'I like that thought. Well, I can't be as eloquent as Steinbeck. But maybe I am being a bit too pessimistic. Because so many people write to me and tell me that my mum inspired them. I guess it just really upsets me that people in Chechnya can't express their respect for her – that she is not the kind of individual who is put on a pedestal there now. Instead of someone who shaped the place through kind acts and courage, we have these macho guys persuading us that they are heroes while they are literally erasing our history and our trauma, and creating a new kind of history where Russian colonialism is barely mentioned and you're not even allowed to mourn on the day of the deportation.'

The afternoon is drawing on, the little walled garden still flooded with summer light. I ask Lana what is Natasha's legacy. She says it's hard to gauge, because her mother cannot be publicly acknowledged in Chechnya, in a dictatorship. 'She's a whisper there,' she adds. 'People are terrified to even think.' Yet Lana has hope. She believes that the Chechen leadership today is a strange chimera that is fated to perish.

She is remarkably sanguine about the future. 'You have to work for every small victory. As I've got older, I've realized the value of waiting. I'm hoping to live a long life. I'll outlive Putin and Kadyrov. I'll see the end of this regime; I'll go back to Chechnya. I know it.' (For now, it's too dangerous. She hasn't been to her mother's grave since 2012.)

Lana seems to have developed a wisdom beyond her years. 'Be stubborn and live, that's my philosophy,' she says, as we prepare to say goodbye. 'And don't feel guilty about enjoying yourself. Living and thriving is a form of resistance.'

It a truism that those who do not remember the past are condemned to repeat it. The very mission of the group that Natasha worked for, Memorial (now banned in Russia), was to preserve the stories of victims of repression. But is it always right to nurture memories of personal or national suffering?

There is no place without history. There are, however, places where history seems to cast a greater shadow. The Caucasus is one of those. Many times there, I wished people could be set free from the torment of their memories, or from the recall of national hurt. To the south of the mountain range, Armenia is locked in one such deathly embrace. As Sebouh Aslanian put it in a 2015 article in the *Jadaliyya* ezine: 'the continued denial of the Armenian genocide has created a hypertrophied or bloated historical memory coiled around pain that has, for many Armenians, shaped what it means to be Armenian and has held them captive to a past full of unspeakable pathos and trauma'. To the north, on my walking route, the Circassians, the Balkars, the Karachays, the Ingush and the Chechens face similar agonies.

Psychiatrists treating PTSD have been known to use techniques such as 'imagery rescripting', in which sufferers take charge of their nightmares, assigning them new, less upsetting meanings. Could such a thing be possible on a national level?

Friedrich Nietzsche opened his essay 'On the Uses and Disadvantages of History for Life' with an engaging image of a group of cows frolicking in a field. 'They do not know what is meant by yesterday or today, they leap about, eat, rest, digest, leap about again, and so from morn till night and from day to day, fettered to the moment and its pleasure or displeasure, and thus neither

melancholy nor bored,' he wrote. By contrast, Nietzsche suggested, the human animal was a being chained to the past, unable
to escape the pain of yesteryear. 'There is,' he concluded, 'a degree
of sleeplessness, of rumination, of the historical sense, which is
harmful and ultimately fatal to the living thing, whether this
living thing be a man or a people or a culture.'

The answer, Nietzsche wrote, was 'selective forgetting', a
means to unburden oneself from past and future, to 'close the
doors and windows of consciousness for a time; to remain undis-
turbed by the noise and struggle of our underworld of utility
organs working with and against one another . . . to make room
for new things'. By striking the right balance between knowledge
retention and forgetting, Nietzsche argued, one could reinterpret
a traumatic past, healing wounds and recreating 'broken moulds'.

It's a delicate question, of course. A call for selective forgetting
can sound like a call for compromise – with evil. Who will be the
first to tell a Beslan mother that a descent into bovine ignorance
could help her more than the candles she places in the church
every year, in memory of her dead daughter? Should I advise Lana
Estemirova to reimagine her mother's fate in a milder version?

Maybe the solution is for violent, traumatic events like the
Caucasus deportations and the slaughter at Beslan to be simultaneously remembered and forgotten, scorched in a nation's soul,
yet – vitally – afforded such widespread recognition by others that
they are shorn of the daily tussle to prevent them from slipping
from view; a kind of reprieve from the relentless demands of
memory. In Russia, sadly, the authorities often ignore or muffle
the history of such atrocities. Sacrifices of the glorious war against
Nazism are endlessly celebrated and exploited for political gain;
the messy, contradictory tragedies of smaller nations are less
convenient. The Kremlin recognized the wickedness that took

place in Beslan, but once the mothers of the dead began accusing Putin of bungling the rescue, interest quickly waned.

This is a book about resilience as much as the hauntings of history. So many times on my walk, I met people who were surviving, even thriving, on the stoniest of ground. To see a shepherd crouched in his kosh on a wild Caucasus slope, his face lit by a fire like a medieval anchorite, is to feel a sense of permanence on Earth.

In Chechnya, Musa still dreams of flying around the world. He bought a motorized hang-glider and keeps it in a hangar by a lake, where he plans to build a house once he retires. Before I left Russia, we took a flight above the Terek, swooping high over the water, the reeds swaying on either bank.

I don't wake at night anymore to the sound of the woman's scream at Beslan. Sometimes, I think about Natasha Estemirova being taken on that final ride in the car before she was shot, and I wonder what was going through her head. As she faced the dreadful realization of what was about to happen, I hope she had a moment, however brief, to reflect on the good she had done in the world. If only she knew how it lives on in others. The Russians I admire the most today are those who continue Natasha's work, who carry her flame.

Back home in England, I have come to realize that the ghosts of Beslan will never disappear. Nor should they. Remembrance is, in itself, a kind of restitution. Letting go is not an option. Every year, friends and colleagues write messages on social media on the anniversary of Natasha's murder. One of the most common phrases we use is 'Ne zabyta'. Not forgotten.

Occasionally, a scene of horror from School Number One slides into my mind. What helps is that such images are laved by

Epilogue

a pool of fresher recollections. When I think of the Caucasus now, I think of a curtain of cloud rising like smoke over a ridge, or a shepherd riding his horse by a river. Misha in Ingushetia is resting his hand tenderly on his daughter's neck; a bowl of mulberries sits on a sunlit windowsill. Above it all, filling the horizon from west to east in a chain of wonder, rises the frosty palisade of the mountains: vast, sparkling, immutable.

Acknowledgements

Any reader of this book will recognise my debt to the numerous people of the Caucasus who offered food and shelter during my journey, with no thought of reward. It may seem futile to thank them in a book that most will never read, but, nonetheless, I would like to record my enormous gratitude here.

In Moscow, I was helped and encouraged by the irrepressible Ruben Sergeyev, our consultant at the *Guardian* bureau. Colleagues Mike Mainville, Julius Strauss, Yulia Ochetova, Nick Paton Walsh, Luke Tchalenko, Olga Gusarova, Carolynne Wheeler, Mark MacKinnon, Douglas Birch, Oliver Bullough, Irina Sandul, Howard Gethin, Miriam Elder, Andrew Osborn, Justin Jin, Shaun Walker, Luke Harding, Phoebe Taplin, Roland Oliphant, Christian Esch, Simon Kruse and Marc Bennetts provided companionship and wisdom. Elena Milashina led by example in her brave reporting. Tanya Lokshina was a rock. Nabi Abdullaev shared his thoughts on Dagestan and Yury Kolomiets furnished me with climbers' tips about paths and passes. Love and respect to my friends at Memorial. I am particularly in debt to Katya Sokirianskaia. In Vladikavkaz, the journalist Alan Tskhurbayev was always a welcoming face.

Over his delicious lentil soup in London, Nicholas Crane gave advice on long distance walking and made me realise I had

Acknowledgements

no idea of the height of the Caucasus snowline. Zeynel Besleney was an essential source on the Circassians. Without the Royal Geographical Society, and Neville Shulman, who sponsors the award in his name, I would never have been able to embark on my walk. Special thanks to the society's Catherine Souch.

Tom de Waal and Charles King have been my Caucasus oracles. In Washington, I'm very grateful to the staff of The Wilson Centre, in particular Maggie Paxson, William Pomeranz and librarians Janet Spikes, Michelle Kamalich and Dagne Gizaw. It was there that the first drafts of this book were written. Profuse thanks to the staff of the Library of Congress. Andrew Meier in New York imparted much experience. At the University of Michigan, where I was a Knight Wallace Fellow, I salute Charles Eisendrath, Birgit Rieck, Gerard Libaridian, Ron Suny, and my fellow fellows. Albest to everyone.

Peter Duncan, my lovely tutor at the School of Slavonic and East European Studies before I left for Russia, suggested empathy should be the core of the writing. He was right. At Bath Spa University, I thank Richard Kerridge, Philip Hensher and my classmates. Without you, this book would not have come to fruition. In Norwich, the writer Paul Willetts went far, far beyond the call of duty to push me forward. I was immensely lucky to discover my agent, Patrick Walsh, a man of outstanding diligence and dedication and a thoroughly decent person to boot. At Headline, Iain MacGregor set the ball rolling and my editors Bianca Bexton and Holly Purdham were tireless and always enthusiastic. Likewise, publicist Rosie Margesson.

It remains to thank my friends and family. The adventure all began with Rob, Mike and Joe. Thanks, bors, you're the best. My mum Chrissie, my dad Rob and his wife Christine, and my brother Matt and his family have been constant cheerleaders. I owe

Acknowledgements

them so much. Last and most important of all, Masha and Leo. Masha, you believed in me all the years when I doubted this book would see the page. Спасибо тебе за все. Leo, now daddy will have more time to play. Don't forget: one day we'll walk together in the high Caucasus.

Glossary

amanat – a hostage given to an enemy as part of a pledge to fulfil
  an agreement

aul – a village in the Caucasus

araka – an Ossetian drink distilled from maize or barley

ataman – a Cossack leader

bilet – a ticket or pass

boyevik – a militant fighter

cherkeska – a traditional collarless caftan of woven felt worn by
  Caucasus peoples

FSB – Russia's Federal Security Service, a successor agency to
  the KGB

jamaat – an Islamic council or assembly; sometimes, a militant
  group

kaban – a wild boar

kombinat – an industrial plant or enterprise

kosh – a shepherd's hut, usually beside an enclosure for livestock

kottedzh – a house or villa, often modern and bigger than a
  cottage, from which the word comes

lezginka – a dance popular across the Caucasus, said to have
  originated with the Lezgin people of Dagestan. Often
  performed by a strutting male solo

marshrutka – a shared minibus taxi following a set route

Glossary

murid – a Sufi disciple

MVD – Ministry of Internal Affairs

naib – a deputy of Imam Shamil

namaz – daily prayers performed by Muslims

NKVD – the People's Commissariat of Internal Affairs of the
Soviet Union, operating in the 1930s and 1940s

otdykhat – the verb 'to relax', ranging from a nap to a boozy
picnic

papakha – a sheepskin hat

pelmeni – meat dumplings

sakli – highland dwellings, often with flat roofs

SGB – Abkhazia's State Security Service

shakhidka – a female suicide bomber

shashlyk – grilled meat on skewers

siloviki – the police, military and security services

tyubeteyka – a close-fitting cap without a peak

UAZik – a four-wheel-drive Soviet-era vehicle. One version is
popularly known as the bukhanka (bread-loaf), because of
its shape

zona – a prison or penal colony

Image Credits

337

Image Credits

Second Plate Section